USE THE RIGHT SALT

(PLEASE!)

COARSE SALT, ALWAYS.

t table salt (too fine!)

salt flakes (too expensive!)

ry for rankings (and actual explanations
hat to do if you don't have coarse salt.

RECIPETIN EATS

TONIGHT

NAGI MAEHASHI

Dedicated to Dozer, Chief Taste Tester of RecipeTin Eats, for his unwavering loyalty and unconditional love. I love you with all my heart, Dozer!

In the middle of making this cookbook, Dozer was diagnosed with a medical condition called bilateral laryngeal paralysis, a nerve deterioration problem where both his larynxes were paralysed, inhibiting his ability to breathe. He underwent surgery to help treat the condition but, combined with related health issues and the fact that he is an older dog (he's 12), he will never be the same boisterous, energetic boy he was just a few months ago.

But, he is happy, comfortable and making the most of his new life. And through it all he has never lost his desire for food!

It is my greatest hope that he will still be with me to celebrate the launch of this cookbook when it hits stores around the world. No matter how long I have left with Dozer, this book is dedicated to him – a book filled with recipes created, photographed, filmed and written by me, with Dozer by my side every step of the way.

RECIPETIN EATS

TONIGHT

NAGI MAEHASHI

BLUEBIRD

CONTENTS

Cayenne
Curry powder
Cumin (Ground)
Garlic Powder
Thyme
Coriander (Ground)
Paprika (Sweet)
Oregano

Before we get going ...

MY MUST-HAVE SPICES

Truthfully, I have many more in my pantry.
But these are the ones I can't live without!

ONCE UPON A TIME ...

... there was a girl who was a chartered accountant working in the real estate corporate finance industry in Sydney, Australia. She was very dedicated to her job, working long hours and climbing the corporate ladder.

One day, she woke up and realised she was putting all her blood, sweat and tears into a job for a faceless company owned by men in suits in a faraway land. And she made the crazy decision to walk away from the security of a job and put all that energy and passion she was giving to a soulless company into starting something of her own.

And with that, her recipe website, RecipeTin Eats, was born ...

A FEW THINGS HAVE CHANGED. BUT ACTUALLY, NOTHING HAS.

My website is viewed half a billion times annually.

Ten years ago to this exact day that I am writing this introduction to my second cookbook, I published the first recipe on my website, RecipeTin Eats.

Many people would say that much has changed for me over the years. But to me, everything is still fundamentally the same.

I am still just that girl who cooks food she likes to eat, snaps a photo of it, then bashes away on her keyboard to publish it on her website with a large mass of golden fur at her feet.

I am still that girl with an irrational obsession with making sure her recipes work.

I am still that girl who feels a warm glow of happiness when she reads a message from someone who made and enjoyed her lasagne.

And I am still that girl who lies awake at night, irritated that she hasn't cracked the code for 'My Perfect Orange Poppy Seed Loaf Cake' (it's on page 300, by the way).

That is me. I think my official job description is *recipe writer*. (Oh, and the official name of the large mass of golden fur is *Dozer*.)

However, if you are one of those detail-oriented people, you might consider that a few things *have* changed for me over the years.

THE FEW THINGS

I guess one example of something that has changed is my online community. On the day I published my first recipe, a grand total of two people visited my website. One was me. The other was my mother.

My website is now viewed half a billion times annually.

I feel a little fidgety with discomfort with what I am about to tell you.

Being a homebound tester and writer of everyday recipes has brought me into the public eye at a level that I just never imagined nor ever sought.

I have a social media following of more than 5 million people. I have a team of 10 employees, and a foodbank – RecipeTin Meals – where we make and donate more than 130,000 meals each year to the vulnerable in our community.

My first cookbook, *Dinner*, was awarded Australian Book of the Year in 2023 – the first time a cookbook has been bestowed with that honour. It also made the *New York Times* Best Sellers list.

The press have called me 'the biggest name in Australian food'. Production companies have pursued me to make TV shows. Big brands have asked me to endorse them for big bucks. I should have been thrilled, jumping at these opportunities. To have my own TV show! Be on magazine covers! Get free travel, eat at fancy restaurants!

But I wasn't thrilled, and I didn't jump. And when I turned down yet another fabulous opportunity that recently came my way, I took a moment to pause and wonder, *What is wrong with me?*

I realised that the answer is actually very simple ...

... I JUST WANT TO COOK AND WRITE RECIPES, WITH DOZER BY MY SIDE

Cooking, eating, photographing and sharing recipes of damn tasty food with people all around the world, with Dozer by my side, is what makes me happy. Full stop, end of story.

I have no interest in fame, whatever that means these days. I have no desire to be on TV, to attend glamorous events, or of raising my profile to become 'a household name' (PR lingo).

It's just not what interests me.

I have a deep, genuine love for what I do. It's why I work so hard at it, why I work such long hours, why being faced with piles and piles of dirty dishes does not deter me in the slightest. It is why I stay up late into the night answering questions that readers ask about recipes on my website.

It's why I am so driven to make recipes over and over again until I am confident they are foolproof and as good as they can be (my record stands at 89 times for my vanilla cake recipe – find it on my website!).

This brings me to the point that seems to fascinate so many people ...

MY OBSESSION WITH MAKING SURE MY RECIPES WORK

I have what the press have described as an obsession with ensuring my recipes are rigorously tested so they always work. It actually amuses me to see this as a topic of focus in articles because, honestly, there's nothing deep and meaningful behind why I do it.

It's simply because I want to make sure that I don't waste anybody's time or money, **and that includes my own**. Because at the core of it, the reason I make all this effort to create these recipes is because I myself want to eat good food!

So yeah, actually, the reason I work so hard on making sure my recipes always work is not for you. It's for me! It's for completely selfish reasons!!

FOOD FOR BUSY PEOPLE

Maybe one day I will have my own TV show.

But for now, and for the foreseeable future, all I want is to keep doing what I love: creating recipes for people who want to eat good food, with a focus on dinners for busy people and a sprinkle of fancy for leisurely weekends. And this cookbook is filled with recipes that are exactly that!

BECAUSE OF YOU

This second cookbook is here because of *you*. I am so grateful for all your feedback on my first cookbook, *Dinner*. I listened, absorbed, thought, went into the kitchen and cooked.

Then I wrote *TONIGHT*.

My new book is designed to be your go-to answer whenever your family, partner, flatmates or friends ask, 'What should we have for dinner?' It's a book filled with recipes with maximum flavour that you can cook *tonight* – recipes that make clever use of pantry staples, are easy to put together and are highly versatile, so you can make something delicious for dinner using whatever you've got in the fridge.

There's a whole suite of recipes that use my beloved master stir-fry sauce, Charlie; an entire chapter dedicated to recipes made in just one pot, pan or tray; and a handy matrix that tells you how to roast almost any vegetable – a copy of which is now permanently stuck on my fridge!

If your cupboard is looking a little bare but you don't want to go out to the shops, head straight to What You've Got on Hand to find something delicious to make. And for weekends when you have more time, flip to the Sunday Suppers section. Got your extended family coming over? Look no further than my sparkling new signature food-for-a-group: Vietnamese Coconut Lemongrass Pulled Pork, which includes more than four different ways to serve it.

Oh, wait ... have a look at the Slow-roasted Middle Eastern Lamb Shoulder while you're there, as that's a great one for sharing too ... and the Duck Ragu Pappardelle, the Seafood Pie ... and my Roast Chicken for Company! (You can find all these recipes in the Sunday Suppers chapter.)

Gosh, I love food. I love every single recipe in this book and would happily make any of them, right now, for dinner tonight.

I hope you enjoy them too!

Nagi xx

(PS: In case you are wondering, the very first recipe I published was Sticky Pantry Chicken and it's the only recipe on my website that I've included in this cookbook. Find it on page 122!)

MEET DOZER

This is Dozer, my abnormally large, 12-year-old golden retriever.

His official title is Chief Taste Tester of RecipeTin Eats and he takes his job very seriously.

Every morning, he trots into the office with his tail wagging, ready to tackle his duties with the utmost dedication. He's an incredibly fast worker – the speed at which he can eat meatballs is impressive – and a great team player, always willing to help out anybody with food on hand.

He was the pioneer of a highly effective yet simple taste-testing reporting tool we are currently in the process of patenting: if he eats it, he approves. If he spits it out, he does not.

Genius.

Mind you, there are very few things he rejects. Pretty much only kale!

Outside the office, Dozer enjoys eating for pleasure (I know, shocking) and playing. His second-favourite place in the world is the beach where he splashes and swims with his golden retriever friends.

His first favourite place is wherever I am.

I love this dog so damn much!

recipetin meals
recipetineats

RECIPETIN MEALS

> RTM is the proudest achievement of my professional career.

RecipeTin Meals (RTM) is my foodbank, which I started during the pandemic in 2021. We make and donate over 130,000 homemade meals annually (plus desserts!) for the vulnerable in our community.

I have a full-time team of three professionally qualified chefs who work in a commercial kitchen in Sydney to make these meals, many of which are recipes from my website. We deliver them to a wonderful organisation called One Meal, who then arrange for the distribution of the food to people in need across the Greater Sydney area.

Some of the meals go directly to individuals and families, while others are handed out at meal service centres that are open to the public.

RTM is a registered charity and, at the time of writing, it is fully privately funded by our benefactor, Dozer*. That's a cute way of saying that revenue from RecipeTin Eats – such as royalties from the sale of my cookbooks – is how I fund RTM!

I have ambitions to grow RTM. It is my hope that by the time this cookbook hits stores around the world, we will have opened our doors to volunteers, be able to accept donations from the public and have found a corporate partner with whom we can expand our operations so that we can make more meals and fill more hungry tummies.

Many have asked why I do RTM. The reason is simple: it makes me happy. RTM is the proudest achievement of my professional career and it is what motivates me to keep working so I can continue to support RTM.

Because no one should go hungry.

Nagi and Dozer x

Saturday night city meal service.

Chef Jean-Baptiste 'JB' Alexandre and me loading up the car.

RATIONAL
recipetin meals
recipetin meals

RecipeTin Head Honcho Chef Jean-Baptiste 'JB' Alexandre (left) and RTM Boss Chef Stephen Fixter (right).

Daniel Smith, RTM kitchenhand.

At One Meal, who distribute our meals.

RTM Chef Xiao (Hannah) Huang.

The RTM team! Left to right: Daniel Smith, JB, Stephen Fixter, Xiao (Hannah) Huang, a girl and a dog.

HOW TO USE THIS BOOK

I know you know how to read a recipe! But here's a little map featuring some pointers for how to read the recipes in this cookbook, highlighting the different elements on the page. Consider this a bonus recipe – it's real, it works and it's delicious!

INTRODUCTION This is the part where I tell you why your life is not complete until you've made this!

chicken thighs[1]

[1] **NOTES** Small superscript numbers in the recipe direct you to the Notes.

salt*

***GLOSSARY** At the back of the book (pages 337–43) there is a Glossary with information on ingredients that may be unfamiliar to you, or where I have something extra to say (and let's face it, I often do!). See the Glossary if text is marked with an asterisk.

QR CODE Hover your phone's camera over the code to go to a section of my website where you can watch a how-to video for each recipe (along with extra helpful notes!).

ONE-TRAY CHICKEN FAJITAS

A big Mexican dinner cooked on a tray – no stove splatter!

SERVES: 4–5 | PREP: 12 MINUTES | COOK: 22 MINUTES

This recipe works phenomenally well and has such a great flow to it! Chicken tossed in my homemade fajita seasoning gets great colour on it by popping it under the oven grill (so much more effective than using the oven). As it rests, we cook the vegetables, which get a great char on them under the grill. The tortillas, meanwhile, are wrapped in foil and warmed through at the same time. Then all that's left to do is slice the chicken and toss it with the vegetables. Serve it alongside the tortillas with sour cream and avocado slices and let everybody make their own fajitas. Dinner, done – with such little effort!

600 g boneless, skinless chicken thighs[1]

olive oil spray

FAJITA SEASONING

1/2 tsp dried oregano

1 tsp onion powder

1 1/4 tsp garlic powder

1 1/2 tsp ground cumin

2 1/2 tsp smoked paprika*[2]

1/4 tsp cayenne pepper (optional)

1/4 tsp white sugar[3]

1 tsp salt*

2 tbsp olive oil

2 tbsp lime juice

VEGETABLES

3 bell peppers (one each red, green, yellow), deseeded and cut into 7 mm thick slices

1 red onion, peeled and cut into 1 cm thick wedges

2 tbsp olive oil

3/4 tsp salt*

FAJITAS

16 small corn tortillas* (13 cm wide)

Sour cream, to serve

1 avocado, halved, seed removed, cut into thin slices

6 g (1/2 lightly packed cup) coriander leaves

Preheat the oven grill to 250°C or as high as it will go, with the oven shelf 10 cm from the heat source.

Wrap tortillas – Wrap the tortillas in foil (8 per foil packet).

Season chicken – Put the fajita seasoning ingredients in a bowl and mix to combine. Add the chicken and toss to coat. Place the chicken on a large baking tray (do not use paper – it will burn).

Cook chicken – Place the tray under the oven grill. Put the tortillas on the shelf underneath. Cook the chicken for 4 minutes. Turn, spray generously with oil, then cook the other side for 8 minutes. Remove the chicken but leave the tortillas in the oven.

Squidge and rest – Squidge the chicken around the tray to coat them in the tasty red juices. Transfer the chicken to a plate and loosely cover with foil to rest for 5 minutes, then cut into 8 mm thick slices.

Char vegetables – Toss the peppers and onion with the oil and salt using the same bowl used for the chicken. Spread the vegetables on the same tray used to cook the chicken. Place under the oven grill for 10 minutes or until they are lightly charred and just cooked (they will soften a bit as you serve).

Serve – Remove the tortillas from the oven and unwrap. Add the chicken to the vegetables on the tray and toss together. Place the tray on the table with the tortillas, sour cream, avocado slices and a bowl of coriander leaves on the side. Then let everybody make their own fajitas!

NOTES

1. Chicken breast will also work but is not as juicy as thigh.
2. Substitute with regular paprika*.
3. Just a touch of sugar gives a little helping hand to make the chicken caramelise a bit faster. It doesn't make it sweet!
4. This is how I build my fajitas: Stuff a warm tortilla with the fajita chicken and vegetables. Tuck in a couple of avocado slices, add a dollop of sour cream and a pinch of coriander leaves. Fold and devour!

LEFTOVERS Fridge 3 days, freezer 3 months.

22

RECIPE SYMBOLS
Great for those with these dietary preferences:

VEGETARIAN

GLUTEN-FREE

BONUS RECIPE!

ONE

NOTES You'd hardly expect me not to have notes! Look here to get extra info on techniques and ingredient swaps.

LEFTOVERS I can't bear food waste. Whenever a dish can be stored, I will tell you how and for how long.

WHAT I CRAVE

Outrageously delicious dinners
that you'll crave, night after night ...

CRISPY LEMON GARLIC BUTTER CHICKEN

Lemon takes the spotlight in this easy but classic baked chicken.

SERVES: 5 | PREP: 10 MINUTES | COOK: 45–50 MINUTES

Most of the time, lemon is used in food to flatter the other ingredients and gently lift the dish with just a 'finishing squeeze'. Not here! Lemon is the superstar of this dish. I love the cheery brightness that the layers of citrus bring to these crispy-skinned chicken thighs swimming in a buttery, garlicky sauce. It's a simple yet elegant dish – easy enough for a weeknight, yet chic enough for guests!

---

5 x 250 g bone-in, skin-on chicken thighs[1]

1 tbsp olive oil

½ tsp salt*

¼ tsp black pepper

60 ml (¼ cup) chardonnay wine*[2]

1 lemon, cut into 8 wedges

3 tbsp lemon juice

LEMON GARLIC BUTTER

75 g unsalted butter, softened

2 tsp finely grated garlic*

2 tsp finely minced parsley

½ tsp salt*

¼ tsp black pepper

1 tbsp lemon zest (1 large or 2 medium lemons)

Preheat the oven to 200°C (180°C fan).

Smear chicken – Mix all the lemon garlic butter ingredients together in a bowl. Loosen the chicken skin to create pockets. Smear about three-quarters of the butter under the skin, then smear the rest of the butter on the flesh (underside).

Prepare for baking – Place the chicken in a 23 x 33 cm roasting pan, skin-side up. Rub the skin with olive oil and sprinkle evenly with salt and pepper. Pour the wine around the chicken, then scatter the lemon wedges around too.

Bake – Bake for 45–50 minutes or until the skin is golden and crispy.

Rest and serve – Transfer the chicken to a serving platter and let it rest for 5 minutes. Meanwhile, stir the lemon juice into the pan juices, then either pour the sauce into a jug for serving, or around the chicken on the platter. Serve!

NOTES

1 Drumsticks will work too, though it's a bit trickier to smear the butter under the skin. You could also use a whole chicken. Prepare it using this recipe, then follow the roasting temperature and times in Roast Chicken for Company on page 249.

2 Or any dry white wine or non-alcoholic white wine.

LEFTOVERS Fridge 3 days, freezer 3 months.

CREAMY SAUSAGE PASTA

Pre-seasoned meat inside a sausage is a highway to flavour that bypasses all the work.

SERVES: 4 | PREP: 10 MINUTES | COOK: 25 MINUTES

Sausage meat is one of the best shortcuts to keep handy in your cooking toolbox. The butcher has already done the hard work of flavouring and perfectly seasoning the fatty mince inside a sausage. All we need to do is squeeze the meat from its casing and use it! I chose pork sausages for this decadently creamy pasta with white wine. Chicken sausages would also be excellent. Wide-ringed calamarata pasta is the ideal shape for hugging the nuggets of broken-up sausage, but it will still be amazing with any short pasta. Obviously!

---

2 tsp salt*, for cooking the pasta

400 g calamarata pasta[1], rigatoni or other largish short pasta

CREAMY SAUSAGE SAUCE

1 tbsp extra-virgin olive oil

1/2 brown onion, finely chopped

3 garlic cloves*, finely minced

500 g pork sausages[2], removed from casings

125 ml (1/2 cup) chardonnay wine*[3]

185 ml (3/4 cup) low-salt chicken stock*

250 ml (1 cup) double cream*

1/2 tsp salt*

1/4 tsp black pepper

90 g (2 tightly packed cups) kale*, torn into bite-sized pieces

TO SERVE

Finely grated parmesan*

Pinch of dried chilli flakes* (optional)

Cook pasta – Bring a large pot* of water to the boil. Add the salt and cook the pasta according to the packet directions. Just before draining, scoop out a mugful of the pasta cooking water. Drain the pasta in a colander. *Time the pasta cooking so it's ready at the same time as the sauce.*

Cook sausage – Meanwhile, heat the oil in a large non-stick frying pan* over high heat. Add the onion and garlic and cook for 1 minute. Add the sausage meat and cook, breaking it up as you go as you would mince. Get some colour on the pork by leaving it undisturbed for 30 seconds. Toss briefly, then leave it for another 30 seconds.

Creamy sauce – Add the wine and let it simmer rapidly for 2 minutes, scraping the base of the saucepan to loosen any golden bits stuck there (free flavour!). Reduce the heat to medium–high. Add the stock, cream, salt and pepper and simmer for 5 minutes. The sauce will still be quite thin, but it will thicken more in the next step.

Toss with pasta – Add the cooked pasta, kale and 60 ml (1/4 cup) of the reserved pasta cooking water to the sauce. Use two spatulas to toss well for 1 minute or until the sauce is coating the pasta instead of being a watery pool in the pan.

Serve – Immediately divide among bowls and serve sprinkled with parmesan and a pinch of chilli flakes, if desired.

NOTES

1. Calamarata pasta is a big, ring-shaped pasta that gets its name from calamari rings. I live in a neighbourhood with some good Italian delis, so I get to have fun trying new pasta shapes! But you can make this with whatever pasta you want. I feel that sausage-catching shapes like large shells and rigatoni work best with the sauce, though I wouldn't hesitate to use spaghetti if that's all I had.
2. I like to use pork sausages in this recipe, but beef and chicken would work nicely, too. Skip the really economical sausages that are a uniform pink colour. Look for good-quality ones made with more meat and less fillers, with specks of fat. Read the ingredients label or ask your butcher – aim for 90%+ meat.
3. Substitute with any other dry white wine that's not too sweet or woody. For non-alcoholic, it is best to use non-alcoholic white wine, otherwise, substitute with more low-salt chicken stock.

LEFTOVERS As with all pastas, this is best eaten freshly made. However, it will keep in the fridge for 3 days. Not suitable for freezing.

HONEY SESAME GINGER BEEF

Got mince? Got dinner!

SERVES: 4 | PREP: 15 MINUTES | COOK: 10 MINUTES

Frying up beef mince seasoned with Asian flavourings isn't something that's especially common, but it's become a bit of a signature of mine. I like it because beef mince is super convenient – no chopping! – and it's a sponge for flavour. This latest variation I'm sharing leans on honey and ginger, so it's fragrant, sticky and savoury. Serve over fluffy rice to jumble the beef through, and eat with a spoon.

---

1 tbsp vegetable oil

1 brown onion, finely chopped

1 tbsp finely minced ginger*

2 garlic cloves*, finely minced

500 g beef mince[1]

3 tbsp white sesame seeds, plus extra for sprinkling

2 tbsp water

SAUCE

1½ tbsp dark soy sauce*[2]

1½ tbsp Chinese cooking wine*

1 tbsp sesame oil*

3 tbsp honey

2 tbsp oyster sauce

TO SERVE

White rice of choice (see pages 318–21)

1 spring onion*, very finely sliced diagonally

Cucumber Ribbons (page 316)

Sauce – Measure out and add the sauce ingredients to a bowl in the order listed. (The honey will slide right out of the spoon coated with sesame oil!) Mix until combined.

Cook – Heat the vegetable oil in a large non-stick frying pan* over high heat. Add the onion, ginger and garlic and stir for 1½ minutes. Add the beef and cook, breaking it up as you go, until the beef is no longer red. Add the sauce and continue to cook for 1 minute or until the sauce is mostly evaporated. Add the sesame seeds, stir, then leave the beef undisturbed for 30 seconds to give it a chance to caramelise. Stir, then leave it again for 30 seconds. Repeat twice more or until the beef is nicely caramelised, as pictured.

Finish and serve – Add the water and stir for 30 seconds – this will juice up the beef a bit. Serve over rice, garnished with extra sesame seeds and spring onion, with the Cucumber Ribbons on the side.

NOTES

1 While this sauce has been made specially to complement the flavour of beef, this recipe can also be made with pork, chicken or turkey mince.

2 Dark soy sauce stains the beef a rich mahogany colour and adds soy flavour. Using light soy sauce* or all-purpose soy sauce* won't achieve the same flavour or colour, but they will make an adequate substitute in the event of an emergency!

LEFTOVERS Fridge 3 days, freezer 3 months.

DOUBLE CRUNCH HOT HONEY SALMON

Baked with a double crumbing for extra crunch!

SERVES: 4 | PREP: 15 MINUTES | COOK: 20 MINUTES

This easy salmon has an extra-thick coating of seasoned panko crumbs for ultimate crunchiness! The honey sauce drizzled over the fish packs a mild chilli hum to keep things interesting. And the best part? It's baked and all done and dusted in just 35 minutes. Serve with steamed rice (see pages 318–21) and roasted green beans or asparagus (see page 218). The vegetables can roast at the same time as the salmon – could a weeknight fish dinner be any easier?

---

4 x 180 g salmon fillets[1], skin on or off

DREDGE

1 egg

2 tsp dijon mustard

DOUBLE CRUNCH CRUMB

30 g (1/2 cup) panko breadcrumbs*

3 tbsp finely grated parmesan*[2]

4 tbsp extra-virgin olive oil

1 tsp paprika*

1/2 tsp garlic powder

1/2 tsp onion powder

1/2 tsp dried thyme, crushed with fingers to make it finer

1/2 tsp salt*

1/4 tsp black pepper

HOT HONEY

175 g (1/2 cup) honey

2 tbsp sriracha*

1/4 tsp dried chilli flakes*

1 garlic clove*, finely grated or crushed using a garlic crusher

TO GARNISH (OPTIONAL)

Pinch of fresh thyme leaves

Preheat the oven to 200°C (180°C fan).

Preparation – Whisk the dredge ingredients together in a bowl. Mix the crumb ingredients together in a separate bowl.

Double crunch – Dip the salmon into the dredge to coat the top and sides of the fish – not the underside. Place the salmon on a baking tray lined with baking paper. Sprinkle/press the crumb onto the surface and sides of the salmon (most on the top). Use it all so you get a nice thick layer of double crunch!

Bake – Bake for 15 minutes or until the internal temperature reaches 50°C using a cooking thermometer*[3].

Hot honey – While the salmon is baking, put the hot honey ingredients in a small saucepan* over medium–low heat. Once it comes to a simmer, cook for 1 minute, then remove the pan from the heat and let the flavours infuse while the salmon finishes cooking.[4]

Serve – Once the salmon is done, remove it from the oven and immediately transfer to serving plates. Rest for 3 minutes. Drizzle with the hot honey just before eating, garnished with thyme, if desired!

NOTES

1 If you have skin-on salmon, you can just eat the flesh off the salmon skin if you prefer not to eat the skin. The skin won't become crispy using this cooking method.

2 Grate your own or use the store-bought sandy type.

3 See the Internal Cooked Temperatures chart on page 335.

4 If you want to reduce the spiciness, you can strain out the chilli flakes.

LEFTOVERS Fridge 3 days. Not suitable for freezing.

KOREAN BBQ CHICKEN

Everybody goes crazy over flavoursome Korean marinades!

SERVES: 5 | PREP: 10 MINUTES + 3 HOURS MARINATING | COOK: 15 MINUTES

Sweet and savoury with a subtle warm hum and a good hit of garlic, the marinades used for Korean barbecued meat are lip-smackingly delicious. But few people know how easy they are to make at home! It's all about getting the marinade ingredient ratios right. For a midweek meal, I like to use the oven grill using boneless chicken, or bake it using bone-in chicken. No stove splatter, no stressing about burning the sugars. On weekends though, it's all about the outdoor grill for that crisp and charry barbecued taste!

CHICKEN – CHOOSE ONE METHOD

1 kg boneless, skinless chicken thighs – oven grill method

1.5 kg bone-in, skin-on chicken thighs (about 6 pieces) – baked method

KOREAN BBQ MARINADE

3 tbsp gochujang*[1]

2 tbsp brown sugar

1 tbsp light soy sauce*[2]

1 tbsp mirin*

1 tbsp finely grated garlic*

1 tsp finely grated ginger*

1 tbsp sesame oil*

½ tsp white pepper

TO COOK

Vegetable oil spray (or other neutral-flavoured oil)

TO SERVE

Cucumber Ribbons (page 316)

White Rice (page 318)

Spring onion*, finely sliced diagonally

Marinate chicken – Mix the marinade ingredients in a large bowl. Add the chicken and toss to coat well. Marinate for at least 3 hours, preferably overnight. (Reserve the bowl with any left-over marinade.)

FOR BONELESS, SKINLESS CHICKEN THIGHS (OVEN GRILL METHOD)

Preheat the oven grill to high with the oven shelf 20 cm from the heat source. Line a baking tray with foil (not paper, it will burn). Place a wire rack on the tray and spray it with oil.

Oven grill – Place the chicken, smooth-side down, on the rack. Grill for 4 minutes or until the chicken is lightly browned. Turn the chicken over. Use a brush or rubber spatula to scrape out half the residual marinade from the bowl and dab it onto the surface of the chicken. Spray generously with oil, then grill for 2 minutes. Remove from the oven, dab with the remaining marinade and spray with oil again. Grill for 5–6 minutes until the surface is caramelised.

FOR BONE-IN, SKIN-ON CHICKEN THIGHS (BAKED METHOD)

Preheat the oven to 200°C (180°C fan). Line a baking tray with foil, then baking paper (you'll thank me later!).

Bake – Place the chicken on the tray, skin-side up. Use a brush to dab half the remaining marinade in the bowl onto the skin. Bake for 30 minutes. Dab the remaining marinade onto the skin. Bake for 10 minutes. Dab the skin with the tray juices, then spray with oil. Bake for a further 10–15 minutes or until the skin is caramelised. Remove from the oven.

Serve – Transfer the chicken to a serving platter and leave to rest for 5 minutes. Baste the skin one last time using the tray juices (or pour over the chicken). Pile the Cucumber Ribbons on the side and serve with rice, garnished with spring onion.

NOTES

1. A sweet-spicy Korean rice and soybean-based paste that is packed with a ton of savoury flavour! I used mild (spice level 3). Readily available at large grocery stores these days, otherwise find it in Asian and Korean grocery stores. If you want to reduce the gochujang in the marinade, substitute it with red miso plus ½ teaspoon of white sugar for every 1 tablespoon of miso.
2. Or all-purpose soy sauce*. Do not substitute with dark soy sauce*! It's too intense.
3. The chicken can also be cooked on the stove or barbecue, but take care and use medium or medium–high heat or the sugar in the marinade has a tendency to burn.

LEFTOVERS Fridge 3 days, freezer 3 months.

CREAMY MUSHROOM WILD RICE SOUP

A down-home bowl of comfort, full of texture and character.

SERVES: 4 | PREP: 15 MINUTES | COOK: 45 MINUTES

Wild rice instantly makes any dish more rustic and interesting, with its striking black grains and firm, nutty bite. I just love how the dark grains visually pop against the smooth, white surface of this soup. Meanwhile, deeply browned mushrooms, thyme and sage build woody flavours that are a perfect match for the rice. This is just the soup for a brisk winter's night – all that's maybe missing is a log cabin in the woods with a flickering open fireplace!

- 50 g unsalted butter
- 2 tbsp olive oil
- 500 g button mushrooms[1], sliced 5 mm thick
- ¾ tsp salt*
- ¾ tsp black pepper
- 2 tsp finely minced garlic*
- 1 brown onion, finely chopped
- 1 carrot, peeled and chopped into 5 mm thick pieces
- 1 celery stalk, chopped into 5 mm thick pieces
- 2 tsp finely minced fresh thyme leaves
- 1 tsp ground sage (optional)
- 150 g (¾ cup) wild rice[2], uncooked
- 1 litre (4 cups) low-salt chicken stock* (substitute veg stock)
- 2 bay leaves*
- 2 tbsp plain flour
- 250 ml (1 cup) double cream* (substitute milk)
- 100 g (1 tightly packed cup) finely grated parmesan*

TO GARNISH

- ½ tsp fresh thyme leaves

Mushroom topping – Melt half the butter and heat half the oil in a large heavy-based pot* over high heat. Add half the mushrooms with ¼ teaspoon of the salt and a ¼ teaspoon of the black pepper. Cook for 4 minutes until the mushrooms turn light golden – initially they will dry out, then go wet and floppy, then start to become golden. When the mushrooms are light golden, add ½ teaspoon of the minced garlic and cook for another 1 minute until the mushrooms and garlic are golden. Transfer the mushrooms to a bowl and set aside – these are to top the finished soup.

Sauté – Melt the remaining butter and heat the remaining oil in the same pan, still on high. Add the onion, remaining garlic and the carrot and celery and cook for 2 minutes. Add the remaining mushrooms and the thyme and sage (if using) and cook for 4–5 minutes or until the mushrooms are softened (they won't turn golden) and the onion is translucent.

Broth and rice – Add the wild rice and stir for 30 seconds to coat it in the tasty flavours. Add the stock, bay leaves, the remaining ½ teaspoon of salt and ½ teaspoon of pepper. Bring to a simmer, then put the lid on and reduce the heat to low so the broth is simmering gently.

Simmer – Simmer for 30–35 minutes until the rice is just about done – mostly soft but still with a bit of a firm bite in the centre (it will cook more in the next steps).

Thicken – While the rice is cooking, whisk the flour with 80 ml (⅓ cup) of the cream in a bowl until lump-free. Whisk in the remaining cream, then slowly pour the mixture into the soup while stirring.

Finish – Cook the soup for a further 5 minutes until it thickens enough to coat the back of a spoon and the rice is done (it shouldn't be super soft and mushy). Add the parmesan and stir it through until melted.

Serve – Reheat the mushroom topping (I just use the microwave). Ladle soup into bowls, top with the warmed mushrooms and a pinch of fresh thyme for garnish. Crusty bread for dunking goes down a treat. Devour!

NOTES

1. I just use regular button mushrooms. Swiss brown mushrooms would also be great.
2. Wild rice is a type of rice with black grains that have a firmer texture and nuttier flavour, which sets it apart from regular rice. It's a little bit gourmet! The best substitute is brown rice, though it doesn't have as much flavour as wild rice.

LEFTOVERS Fridge 3 days, freezer 3 months. Store the rice and vegetables separately from the soup or the rice will bloat overnight. To do this, drain in a colander set over a bowl.

STICKY ASIAN MEATBALLS

Five spice–infused pork meatballs in a glossy, sweet glaze.

SERVES: 4 | PREP: 20 MINUTES | COOK: 10 MINUTES

I've been rolling canapé-sized versions of these meatballs for years. Why it took me this long to make them dinner-sized is beyond me! I find pork makes the most tender meatballs and is perfect with the aniseed notes of Chinese five spice and hoisin. As for that shiny glaze? It's sweet, savoury and a little bit spicy – perfect for smothering and soaking into warm steamed rice!

1½ tbsp vegetable oil

250 ml (1 cup) water

MEATBALLS

500 g pork mince[1]

1 egg

60 g (1 cup) panko breadcrumbs*

1 tsp finely grated garlic*

1 tsp finely grated ginger*

½ tsp salt*

1 tsp Chinese five spice*

½ tsp white pepper (substitute black pepper)

SAUCE

3 tsp cornflour

2 tbsp Chinese cooking wine*[2]

2 tsp dark soy sauce*[3]

1 tsp light soy sauce*[3]

1½ tsp sambal oelek* (or other chilli paste or sriracha*)

1 tbsp rice vinegar[4]

2 tbsp hoisin sauce[5]

¼ tsp Chinese five spice*

1 tsp sesame oil*

TO SERVE

Rice of your choice (see pages 318–21)

1 tsp white sesame seeds

1 spring onion*, finely sliced

Steamed broccoli

Asian Sesame Dressing (page 313)

Meatballs – Mix all the meatball ingredients in a bowl with your hands until well combined. Roll into 24 balls, about 3 cm wide, using slightly wet hands if needed to prevent the mixture from sticking. Refrigerate to firm slightly while you make the sauce.

Sauce – In a large jug, mix the cornflour with the Chinese cooking wine until lump-free. Add the remaining sauce ingredients and mix to combine.

Cooking – Heat the vegetable oil in a large non-stick frying pan* over medium–high heat. Cook the meatballs until they are browned all over, but still raw inside – about 4 minutes. Add the sauce and water. Bring to a simmer, then reduce the heat to medium and cook the meatballs for a further 5 minutes, rolling them in the sauce, until the sauce reduces and thickens to a syrupy consistency.

Serve – Serve the meatballs and sauce over rice, sprinkled with sesame seeds and spring onion with steamed broccoli drizzled with Asian Sesame Dressing on the side.

NOTES

1 Chicken and beef mince will also work, though the meatballs will not be as soft.

2 This adds depth of flavour to the sauce. Substitute with dry sherry, cooking sake* or mirin*. For non-alcoholic, substitute with low-salt chicken stock*.

3 The dark soy sauce can be substituted with more light soy sauce, but the sauce will not be as dark. The light soy sauce can be substituted with an all-purpose soy sauce*, but not dark soy sauce (the flavour is too intense).

4 Substitute with apple cider vinegar.

5 Substitute with oyster sauce plus ¼ teaspoon of extra Chinese five spice.

LEFTOVERS Fridge 3 days, freezer 3 months.

SHAKSHUKA FISH

Classic shakshuka gets a seafood makeover, with eggs swapped for fish in this one-pan braise.

SERVES: 4 | PREP: 10 MINUTES | COOK: 20 MINUTES

I'm always trying to think up tasty but fuss-free new ways to cook fish. Here I've taken a cue from the traditional North African breakfast dish, shakshuka, where eggs are poached in a rich, spiced tomato sauce and served bubbling hot with flatbread. I've swapped out the eggs for monkfish pieces to turn it into a lovely fish braise, finished with a drizzle of garlicky Lemon Yoghurt Sauce. It works amazingly well! Of course you can use any white fish you like, but bread for mopping is mandatory!

---

600 g white fish fillets*[1], around 1.5–2 cm thick, cut into 8 portions or so (I used monkfish)

1 tsp salt*

½ tsp black pepper

SAUCE

2 tbsp extra-virgin olive oil, plus extra for drizzling

½ red onion, cut into 1 cm wedges

3 garlic cloves, finely sliced

1 small red bell pepper, deseeded and cut into 7 mm slices

¼ tsp cayenne pepper

2 tsp smoked paprika* (substitute regular paprika)

1½ tsp ground cumin

800 g can chopped tomatoes

1 tsp salt*

250 ml (1 cup) water

TO SERVE

1 batch Lemon Yoghurt Sauce (page 228)

Coriander leaves

Sauté sauce – Heat the oil in a large non-stick frying pan* over medium–high heat. Cook the onion, garlic and pepper for 5 minutes until the onion is softened. Add the cayenne pepper, paprika and cumin and stir for 1 minute.

Simmer – Add the tomatoes and salt. Use the water to rinse out the tomato cans, then tip it into the pan. Bring to a simmer, then lower the heat to medium and simmer for 5 minutes, stirring every now and then.

Cook fish – Sprinkle the fish with salt and pepper. Gently place the fish in the sauce – it doesn't need to be submerged. Cover the pan with a lid placed slightly ajar (or use another pan, foil or a baking tray) and cook for 5 minutes or until the fish is cooked through (it should flake).

Serve – Serve the fish with the sauce, drizzled with Lemon Yoghurt Sauce and sprinkled with coriander leaves. Toasted Easy Flatbread (page 325) for dunking/scooping is recommended!

NOTES

1 This recipe works best with white fish fillets about 1.5 cm thick. You can use thicker pieces but they will take longer to cook. Try monkfish (pictured), cod, snapper, tilapia, pollock, hake, haddock, John Dory, basa, hoki, perch, sea bass, turbot or flathead.

LEFTOVERS Fridge 3 days. Not suitable for freezing.

SPICY TUNA CRISPY RICE BOWLS

Sushi bowls with spicy mayo tuna, rebooted!

SERVES: 2 | PREP: 15 MINUTES | COOK: 10 MINUTES

Think of this as your favourite creamy tuna and avocado rolls from the sushi shop, but in bowl form! Only we go one better by frying cooked rice in a pan until the base is crunchy and golden for an extra textural slap. You can mix everything up for a big, satisfying bowl of deconstructed sushi. Or put on a DIY sushi 'taco' spread – let people pick and pile fillings into nori sheets as if they were tortillas. Kids love it and so do the grown-ups!

SPICY TUNA TOPPING

1½ tbsp sriracha*[1]

2 tbsp Kewpie* or whole-egg mayonnaise*

1 tsp light soy sauce*

185 g can tuna in oil, drained

CRISPY RICE

2 tbsp vegetable oil

280 g (2 cups) cooked white short-grain rice[2]

¼ tsp salt*

FOR THE BOWLS

½ avocado, peeled and cut into 6 wedges

½ cucumber*, cut in half lengthways, then cut diagonally into 5 mm thick slices

½ tsp black sesame seeds

2 tbsp finely sliced spring onion*

2 nori sheets[3], each cut into 4, toasted if required

Chilli crisp*, chilli sauce or sriracha* (optional)

Spicy tuna topping – Mix the sriracha, Kewpie and soy sauce in a bowl. Add the tuna and mix, breaking up the tuna to your desired consistency.

Crisp rice – Heat the oil in a large non-stick frying pan* over medium–high heat. Add the rice, spreading it out to cover the base of the pan and pressing down lightly to pack it together. Sprinkle with the salt and cook the rice for 5 minutes or until golden and crispy underneath. Flip the rice – it won't hold together in one piece, which is fine, but try to keep some large chunks together. Cook the other side for 5 minutes or until golden and crispy, then divide the rice between two serving bowls.

Assemble and serve – Top the crispy rice with the tuna mixture, then add the avocado and cucumber. Sprinkle with sesame seeds and spring onion, then tuck the nori sheets into the side. Finish with a dollop of your favourite chilli crisp, if desired. Dig in! (Really, try nori tacos. They are so good!)

NOTES

1 For a non-spicy option, substitute with 2½ teaspoons of ketchup* plus ½ teaspoon of rice vinegar.

2 While you can use any type of white rice (see page 318), short-grain rice works best because it's stickier than other types, so you get nice clumps of crispy rice.

3 Nori sheets are readily accessible these days in the Asian aisle of large grocery stores. They are usually sold pre-toasted and nice and crisp, so they can be used straight out of the packet. But if your nori seems a little chewy and floppy, just hold it with tongs and wave it back and forth over a gas stove burner, high enough above the flame so it doesn't catch fire. It will only take 20 seconds or so to crisp up.

LEFTOVERS Best served immediately once assembled. However, the tuna topping mixture will keep for 3 days in the fridge. Not suitable for freezing.

GOLDEN CHICKEN NOODLE SOUP

Ginger and a pinch of turmeric transform this chicken soup into a delicately fragrant bowl of nutrient-packed goodness.

SERVES: 4 | PREP: 15 MINUTES | COOK: 30 MINUTES

You might find a few additions to this chicken soup a tad surprising: ginger, turmeric, lemon juice. These three ingredients weave some welcome sunshine into a soothing but otherwise run-of-the-mill chicken soup. You don't need much for the sparkle they create. Sometimes less really is more (not something I'm known for saying often!). My other slightly unorthodox step here is searing the chicken to cook it, rather than poaching it – for extra flavour, naturally! (More is definitely more, in this case.)

---

500 g boneless, skinless chicken thighs (or breast[1])

½ tsp salt*

¼ tsp black pepper

2 tbsp olive oil

BROTH

3 garlic cloves*, finely minced

1 tbsp finely minced ginger*

1 brown onion, finely chopped

2 celery stalks, cut into 5 mm thick slices, thicker end cut lengthways

2 small carrots, cut into 5 mm thick half-moons

1.5 litres low-salt chicken stock*

1 bay leaf*

1 tsp ground turmeric

¾ tsp salt*

½ tsp black pepper

2½ tbsp lemon juice

1 tbsp finely chopped parsley

PASTA

2 tsp salt*, for cooking the pasta

150 g (1 cup) ditalini pasta (or other small pasta like risoni, star pasta, small shells)

Cook chicken – Sprinkle the chicken with the salt and pepper. Heat the oil in a large pot* over high heat. Cook each side of the chicken for 4 minutes or until golden – it doesn't matter if it's slightly undercooked. Transfer the chicken to a bowl. Once cool enough to handle, shred the meat using your fingers or two forks.

Sauté – In the same pot, cook the garlic, ginger, onion, celery and carrot for 5 minutes or until the onion is softened and translucent but not browned.

Broth – Add the stock, bay leaf, turmeric, salt and pepper. Bring to a simmer, then reduce the heat to low and simmer for 15 minutes. Skim off and discard any scum at about the 2-minute mark. Return the chicken to the pot at about the 8-minute mark, including any juices accumulated in the bowl.

Cook pasta[2] – Meanwhile, bring a large saucepan* of water to the boil. Add the salt and cook the pasta according to the packet directions. Drain in a colander.

Finish – Add the lemon juice and half the parsley to the soup broth. Stir, then taste. Add more salt or lemon juice, if you want.

Serve – Place some pasta in a soup bowl, then ladle the soup over the pasta and sprinkle with the remaining parsley. Serve immediately!

NOTES

1 If you use breast instead of thigh, you will need to add a splash of extra oil before sautéing the vegetables.

2 If you cook the pasta in the soup broth, you will need to add another 375 ml (1½ cups) of stock. Don't be tempted to use water instead of extra stock as it will dilute the flavour of the soup broth.

LEFTOVERS Fridge 3 days, freezer 3 months. Keep the cooked pasta separate from the soup broth.

CHICKEN & GRAVY ROLLS

Skip the trip to the charcoal chicken shop and make this Aussie favourite at home.

SERVES: 4 | PREP: 10 MINUTES | COOK: 15 MINUTES

A fixture at any charcoal chicken shop in Australia, a hot chicken roll is a soft bread roll stuffed silly with shredded rotisserie chicken and gravy (and stuffing, if you're going deluxe). Rustling one up at home, though, is easier than you think! For the gravy, adding a smidgen of soy sauce is my trick. It adds more depth than salt and tints the gravy just the right colour. Remember to overload the bread; if you don't make an absolute mess of your face eating it, it's not a proper hot chicken roll!

---

600 g boneless, skinless chicken breasts[1], each cut in half horizontally to form 2 thin steaks

½ tsp salt*

¼ tsp black pepper

1 tbsp vegetable oil

4 long crusty bread rolls

GRAVY

50 g unsalted butter

3 tbsp plain flour

500 ml (2 cups) low-salt beef stock*

¼ tsp dark soy sauce*[2]

¼ tsp salt*

¼ tsp black pepper

TO SERVE

Salted butter, for the rolls

Preheat the oven to 180°C (160°C fan).

Cook chicken – Sprinkle both sides of the chicken with the salt and pepper. Heat the oil in a large non-stick frying pan* over medium–high heat. Cook each side of the chicken for 3 minutes or until the chicken is fully cooked. Transfer the chicken to a pan or dish suitable for shredding and saucing.

Gravy – Reduce the heat to low and add the butter to the same pan. Once melted, add the flour and stir for 1 minute. While stirring, slowly pour in the beef stock. (With this technique, the gravy should be lump-free, though if you do get lumps, a quick swish with a whisk will get rid of them.) Add the soy sauce, salt and pepper. Increase the heat to medium and bring to a simmer. Simmer gently, stirring regularly so the base doesn't catch, for 3 minutes or until the mixture thickens into a gravy.

Warm rolls – Place the bread rolls in the oven for 5 minutes to warm and crisp them up. I just place them straight on the oven rack.

Shred and toss chicken – While the gravy is simmering, shred the chicken using your hands or two forks into fairly fine strands. Pour the gravy over the chicken and toss to coat.

Stuff and eat – Split the warm bread rolls open. Butter, then stuff with gravy-coated chicken. Take a huge bite and enjoy!

NOTES

1 Boneless, skinless chicken thighs and tenderloins work as well. Use the same weight.

2 This deepens the colour of the gravy and also adds more complexity to the flavour. (A little cooking secret to prop up a simple gravy!) Substitute with an extra pinch of salt.

LEFTOVERS The gravy-tossed chicken will keep in the fridge for 3 days or freezer for 3 months. Once assembled, the rolls are best eaten immediately as the gravy soaks the bread.

CRISPY RICE PAPER FISH ROLLS

No-fuss crispy spring rolls!

SERVES: 2 | PREP: 15 MINUTES | COOK: 6 MINUTES

This recipe might sound a little unusual. However, if you love fish and spring rolls, and hate long recipes and deep-frying, this is right up your alley! These crispy parcels filled with seasoned fish take just a few minutes to put together. It's literally as simple as dusting the fish pieces in flour, folding them in rice paper and throwing them into a frying pan to sizzle until the bases are golden and crunchy. Serve with the quick soy dipping sauce and watch them disappear!

---

350 g cod or other skinless white fish fillets*[1], up to 1.5 cm thick

8 x 22 cm round, dried rice paper sheets

3 tbsp vegetable oil

DIPPING SAUCE

1 tbsp light soy sauce*

1 tbsp rice wine vinegar

2 tsp sesame oil*

1 tsp sesame seeds

1 bird's eye chilli*, deseeded and finely minced (optional, for spiciness), plus extra slices for garnish

SEASONED FLOUR

1 tbsp plain flour[2]

1 tsp salt*

1 tsp Chinese five spice*

½ tsp white pepper

TO SERVE

Mixed leafy greens of your choice with Asian Sesame Dressing (page 313) sprinkled with crispy fried shallots*

Sauce – Mix the dipping sauce ingredients in a small bowl, then transfer to a little dipping bowl.

Cut fish – Cut the fish into eight 10 x 3 cm pieces. If necessary, bundle smaller offcuts together to make up extra pieces, as needed.

Dredge[2] – Mix the seasoned flour ingredients in a bowl. Coat the fish pieces in the flour, shaking off any excess. Transfer to a plate.

Wrap into rolls – Fill a large bowl with water. Dip a rice paper sheet in the water for 2 seconds, then transfer to a work surface. Place a piece of fish widthways on the sheet, 5 cm from the bottom. Fold the bottom of the rice paper up to enclose the fish, then fold the sides in. Roll up to enclose the fish – it will seal itself. Repeat with the remaining fish to make eight parcels.

Cook – Heat the vegetable oil in a large non-stick frying pan* over medium–high heat. Cook the rice paper rolls for 3 minutes on each side until crispy and golden.[3]

Serve – Transfer the rolls to a serving plate and serve immediately with the dipping sauce and the leafy greens!

NOTES

1. This recipe works best with white fish fillets about 1.5 cm thick. If your fillets are thicker, cut them in half horizontally to make thinner fillets. Try cod, monkfish, cod, snapper, tilapia, pollock, hake, haddock, John Dory, basa, hoki, perch, sea bass, turbot or flathead.
2. The flour is used to absorb a little of the fish juices, which helps make the rice paper become nice and crisp!
3. I only do two sides, but you can do four sides for extra-crispy if you want!

LEFTOVERS This dish is best eaten freshly made as the rice paper goes soggy.

TEXAS COWBOY CHICKEN

Marinated with chilli, lime and Southwest spices, my Tex-Mex chicken is as versatile as it is moreish!

SERVES: 4 | PREP: 10 MINUTES + 2–24 HOURS MARINATING | COOK: 15 MINUTES

This is the go-to chicken marinade I've been making every week during summer while writing this cookbook. I can't get enough of the smoky and spicy Tex-Mex flavours that this lime marinade crams into the chicken. The light brining effect it also has on the meat means epic juiciness is retained, while the chicken browns up in a hot pan. I've been using the chicken in wraps, bowls, loaded plates, tacos, salads (see page 200) – you name it. I've even been snacking on it cold from the fridge. Shameless!

---

3 x 200 g boneless, skinless chicken breasts[1, 2], pounded to 1.2 cm thickness

1 tbsp olive oil

TEXAS COWBOY CHICKEN MARINADE

1 tsp chipotle powder*[3]

2 tsp smoked paprika*

½ tsp garlic powder

½ tsp onion powder

½ tsp dried oregano, crushed between fingers to make it finer

½ tsp ground cumin

1 tsp white sugar

¾ tsp salt*

¼ tsp black pepper

1 tsp lime zest

2 tbsp lime juice (2 limes)

2 tbsp extra-virgin olive oil

Marinate chicken – Mix the marinade ingredients in a bowl. It will be like a paste. Add the chicken and use tongs to turn the chicken to ensure each piece is coated in the marinade. Cover with plastic wrap and marinate in the fridge for 24 hours (minimum 2 hours).

Cook – Heat the olive oil in a large non-stick frying pan* over high heat. Put the chicken in the pan and cook each side for 3 minutes or until deep golden[4].

Rest – Transfer to a plate and cover loosely with foil. Rest the cooked chicken for 3 minutes before serving.

Serve – Make my big, statement Cowboy Chicken Salad with Smoky Chipotle Dressing (page 200), or a dinner plate with a side of Creamy Mashed Potato (page 330), oven-roasted corn (see page 239) and chopped cos lettuce tossed with my House Salad Dressing (page 312). See the recipe introduction for more suggestions.

NOTES

1. To pound the chicken, cover with a sheet of plastic wrap or a freezer bag to protect it, then pound with the flat side of a meat mallet, a rolling pin or a heavy-based pan. The goal is to make the chicken a uniform thickness so it cooks evenly. It also tenderises the meat.
2. This recipe also works beautifully with boneless, skinless chicken thighs and tenderloins.
3. Chipotle powder has a terrific smoky, earthy flavour with a bit of a spice kick. It's a staple spice in Mexican cooking made from smoked jalapeños and is sold at some large grocery stores, Mexican and speciality stores. Substitute with ¾ teaspoon of smoked paprika plus ⅛ teaspoon of ground cumin plus ⅛ teaspoon of cayenne pepper (for spiciness).
4. Cook in batches if you can't fit all the chicken in your frying pan at the same time.

LEFTOVERS Fridge 3 days, freezer 3 months.

TOMATO PASTA WITH CRUNCHY GARLIC PARMESAN CRUMBS

excluding anchovies

Flavour-packed toasted breadcrumbs turn ordinary into extraordinary.

SERVES: 4 | PREP: 15 MINUTES | COOK: 20 MINUTES

Let's cut to the chase here ... the crunchy pangrattato crumbs on top absolutely make this pasta! Made by frying panko breadcrumbs with anchovies, parmesan and garlic until golden brown, they turn this modest red sauce spaghetti into a riot of textures and salty bursts of umami. Once you've made these crumbs you'll want to shower them over everything – roasted vegetables, stews, baked fish, creamy gratins, pan-seared chicken, soups ...

CRUNCHY CRUMB (PANGRATTATO)

60 g (1 cup) panko breadcrumbs*[1]

50 g (½ tightly packed cup) finely grated parmesan*

¼ tsp salt*

3 tbsp extra-virgin olive oil

1 tsp anchovy paste or finely chopped anchovies*[2] (highly recommended but can skip)

1 large garlic clove*, finely minced

2 tbsp finely chopped parsley (optional)

GARLIC TOMATO PASTA SAUCE

2 tbsp extra-virgin olive oil

1 tbsp finely sliced garlic

800 g can chopped tomatoes

1 tsp salt*

½ tsp black pepper

250 ml (1 cup) water

½ tsp white sugar[3], if needed

PASTA

2 tsp salt*, for cooking the pasta

400 g spaghetti (or other pasta of your choice)

Crunchy crumb – Toss together the breadcrumbs, parmesan and salt in a bowl. Heat the oil in a large non-stick frying pan* over medium heat. Add the anchovy paste and stir for 15 seconds. Add the breadcrumbs and stir for 3 minutes until light golden. Add the garlic and stir for another 2 minutes until the breadcrumbs are golden.[4] Transfer to a bowl, stir in the parsley (if using) and set aside to cool while you make the sauce.

Tomato pasta sauce – Heat the oil in a large pot* or large deep pan* over medium–high heat. Add the garlic and cook until light golden. Add the tomatoes, salt and pepper. Rinse out the tomato cans with the water, then add the water to the pan. Stir, bring to a simmer, then reduce the heat to low. Simmer for 15 minutes, stirring every now and then so the base doesn't catch. At the 10-minute mark, taste the sauce. If it's a bit sour, add the sugar[3], then keep cooking for another 5 minutes.

Cook pasta – Meanwhile, cook the pasta so it finishes at the same time as the sauce. Bring a large pot of water to the boil with the salt. Add the pasta and cook according to the packet directions. Just before draining, scoop out a large mugful of the pasta cooking water. Drain the pasta.

Finish and serve – Add the pasta to the pasta sauce along with 125 ml (½ cup) of the reserved pasta cooking water. Over medium–low heat, use two spatulas to toss the pasta until it's evenly coated with the sauce. Divide among four bowls. Cover with a generous mound of the crunchy crumb and eat immediately!

NOTES

1. Standard fine-milled breadcrumbs won't work here. We want chunky panko crumbs! Or impress me by making your own by blitzing sourdough, ciabatta or similar breads using a food processor. Don't use basic sandwich bread as it is too lightweight and will disintegrate on contact with the pasta.
2. Anchovies add terrific extra savoury flavour into the crumb and make this pasta memorable! You won't be able to taste any fishiness at all once it's cooked. Anchovy paste comes in tubes and can be found at delis and Italian speciality stores. Otherwise, use as many anchovies as needed from a can or jar so you have 1 tightly packed teaspoon of finely chopped anchovies.
3. Not all canned tomatoes are created equal. More economical ones tend to be a little sour. So only use the sugar if needed – see recipe directions for when to check.
4. The crumb won't be evenly golden because of the parmesan clumps.

LEFTOVERS Best eaten freshly made, though leftovers will keep for 3 days in the fridge. The crumb should be stored separately. Not suitable for freezing.

THAI CHICKEN WINGS

Finger-licking chicken wings in a punchy, turmeric-tinged Southern Thai–style marinade.

SERVES: 4 | PREP: 15 MINUTES + 2 HOURS MARINATING | COOK: 45 MINUTES

A plate of these sensational chicken wings is just the sort of thing I'd crave lounging by a pool somewhere in Phuket with a fruity cocktail in hand! This recipe is based on the grilled chicken found in the southern part of Thailand that's stained a warm yellow from the addition of turmeric. The spice gives the chicken a seductively earthy flavour quite unlike your usual Thai-style marinades. Serve these wings as a main, accompanied by fluffy steamed rice and a crisp salad, or pass around with the dipping sauce as a nibbly snack.

---

2 lemongrass* stalks[1], white part only

1.5 kg chicken wings – drumettes and winglets[2]

MARINADE

1 tbsp finely minced garlic*

3 tbsp oyster sauce

3 tbsp fish sauce

1 tbsp ground turmeric

3 tbsp brown sugar

2 tbsp vegetable oil

1 tsp white pepper

2 tbsp rice vinegar

DIPPING SAUCE (OPTIONAL)

3 tbsp sweet chilli sauce

2 tbsp lime juice

2 tsp fish sauce

TO GARNISH (OPTIONAL)

Coriander leaves

Lime slices

Lemongrass – Bash the lemongrass with a meat mallet, rolling pin or similar, to make it burst open slightly so it will release its flavour into the marinade. Slice it diagonally into 5 mm thick pieces.

Marinate – Mix the marinade ingredients in a small bowl. Place the wings in a large ziplock bag*[3]. Add the lemongrass and pour in the marinade. Close the bag, then massage the bag so the wings are coated in the marinade. Marinate for a minimum of 2 hours or up to overnight.

Preheat the oven to 200°C (180°C fan). Line a large baking tray with foil, then baking paper.

Bake – Remove the wings from the marinade (reserve the residual marinade for basting). Place the wings on the tray in a single layer. Bake for 45 minutes, basting with the reserved marinade at the 20-minute and 35-minute mark, until the wings are sticky and golden.

Dipping sauce – Meanwhile mix the dipping sauce ingredients in a bowl (if making). Pour into a small dipping bowl.

Serve – Pile the wings on a platter and place the sauce on the side. Sprinkle with coriander and serve with extra lime slices (if using).

NOTES

1. If you can't get fresh lemongrass, use 1 tablespoon of lemongrass paste.
2. I buy the chicken wings already cut up into drumettes and winglets – sometimes sold labelled as 'chicken wing nibbles'. You could use whole uncut chicken wings instead. Otherwise, cut your own using 1.6 kg of whole wings. Just cut through the joints and reserve the wing tips for stock (though in my case they go straight into Dozer's* mouth!).
3. If you prefer not to use a ziplock bag, you can marinate the wings in a bowl, but I recommend tossing several times.

LEFTOVERS Fridge 3 days, freezer 3 months.

INDIAN COCONUT PRAWN CURRY

If you love butter chicken, you'll love this velvety prawn curry spin-off!

SERVES: 4 | PREP: 15 MINUTES | COOK: 15 MINUTES

I've taken the building blocks of everyone's favourite butter chicken to create this velvety prawn curry that swaps out dairy cream for coconut milk. As an added bonus, there's no marinating time so you can make this now! Coconut retains the creaminess we all go mad for in butter chicken, and the sweet and nutty taste pairs so well with the prawns. Serve with a mound of steamed Basmati Rice (page 318) and a garden salad tossed with Lemon Dressing (page 313) with a sprinkle of finely chopped mint leaves.

---

500 g prawns*[1], peeled and deveined (800 g whole unpeeled)

1/2 tsp salt*

1 tbsp unrefined coconut oil*

CURRY PASTE

85 g (1/3 cup) plain yoghurt

2 tsp lemon juice

3/4 tsp ground turmeric

2 tsp garam masala*

1/2 tsp chilli powder*

1 tsp ground cumin

1 tbsp freshly grated ginger*

2 tsp freshly grated garlic*

CURRY SAUCE

260 g (1 cup) tomato passata*[2]

250 ml (1 cup) full-fat coconut milk*

125 ml (1/2 cup) water

4 tsp white sugar

3/4 tsp salt*

1 tbsp ghee* (or unsalted butter)

TO SERVE

Basmati Rice (page 318)

Roughly chopped coriander (optional)

Curry paste – Mix the curry paste ingredients in a bowl large enough to fit the prawns. Remove 3 tablespoons of the paste and set aside – this is for the sauce. Add the prawns and salt to the remaining curry paste and toss well to coat using a rubber spatula.

Cook prawns[3] – Melt the coconut oil in a large non-stick frying pan* over high heat. Working quickly, place half the prawns in the pan in a single layer. Cook for 1 minute, then turn and cook the other side for 1 minute. Don't cook them all the way through as we will finish cooking the prawns in the sauce. Transfer to a plate and repeat with the remaining prawns. Reserve the bowl with the prawn curry paste in it (we don't waste the curry paste!).

Curry sauce – Remove the pan from the stove to cool, then return to medium heat. Add the reserved curry paste, the tomato passata, coconut milk, water, sugar and salt. Scrape out any residual curry paste from the prawn bowl and add it to the pan. Stir, bring to a gentle simmer, then cook for 3 minutes or until the sauce thickens into a syrupy consistency. Add the ghee and stir until it melts.

Finish and serve – Add the prawns, including all the juices pooled on the plate, and toss to coat in the sauce. Cook for 2 minutes or until the prawns are cooked through. Immediately transfer to a serving bowl. Serve over basmati rice, sprinkled with coriander, if desired. A side of Easy Flatbread (page 325) for mopping bowls clean wouldn't be unwelcome either!

NOTES

1 White fish fillets* cut into large bite-sized pieces can also be used. Follow the same cooking method.

2 Substitute with canned chopped tomatoes, preferably pureed smooth.

3 The key here is to sear the surface quickly without cooking the inside all the way through, then finish cooking the prawns in the sauce. So work quickly – sear each side briefly, then get the prawns out of the pan!

LEFTOVERS Fridge 3 days, freezer 3 months.

NORMANDY PORK CHOPS

Pork, apples and cream make magical partners in this regional French classic.

SERVES: 4 | **PREP: 15 MINUTES** | **COOK: 15 MINUTES**

They say 'what grows together, goes together' and in the French region of Normandy, it's the apples and dairy the area is famous for. The two work in amazing harmony in savoury French recipes like these rustic pork chops in a creamy sauce. Apple finds its way into this dish in multiple forms – sautéed apple slices, cider and calvados, which is an apple brandy that gives it real depth and character. But don't fret if you can't find calvados, any regular brandy will work just fine here! If, like me, you're not usually much of a meat-with-fruit person, I strongly urge you to give this one a go. You'll be giving it an enthusiastic *très bon*, I promise!

SAUTÉED APPLE

20 g unsalted butter

1 granny smith apple, peeled, cored, then cut into 8 mm thick wedges

PORK CHOPS

4 x 220 g pork loin steaks or other pork chops

½ tsp salt*

¼ tsp black pepper

1 tbsp vegetable oil

NORMANDY CIDER-CREAM SAUCE

½ red onion, cut into 1 cm wedges

2 tbsp brandy (calvados apple brandy[1] if you can)

185 ml (¾ cup) dry apple cider[2] (alcoholic)

1 rosemary sprig (optional)

185 ml (¾ cup) double cream*

2 tsp dijon mustard

½ tsp salt*

¼ tsp black pepper

TO SERVE

Creamy Mashed Potato (page 330)

Cook apple – Melt the butter in a large frying pan* over medium–high heat. Cook the apple pieces for 4 minutes on each side until softened but not floppy, then transfer to a bowl.

Cook pork – Sprinkle the pork with the salt and pepper. Add the oil to the same pan and turn the heat up to high. Cook the pork chops for 3 minutes on each side, or until the surface is golden and the internal temperature is 60°C using a cooking thermometer*. Transfer to a plate and cover loosely with foil.

Cider-cream sauce – Cool the pan slightly, then return to the stove over medium–high heat. Add the onion and sauté for 2 minutes until slightly softened. Carefully add the brandy and stir, letting it simmer rapidly until mostly evaporated. Add the cider and rosemary (if using), then turn the heat up to high and let the sauce simmer rapidly for 2 minutes, scraping the base of the pan to dissolve any golden bits into the sauce. Add the cream, dijon mustard, salt and pepper. Stir to dissolve the mustard and simmer for 2–3 minutes or until the sauce reduces and becomes a thin syrup.

Finish and serve – Add the apple to the sauce, then add the pork along with any juices on the plate. Simmer for 1 minute to warm the pork through, then serve over mashed potato.

NOTES

1 Calvados is a French brandy made from apple. If it is difficult to find it in your supermarket, use regular brandy. Whichever you use, it will add 'restaurant-y' flavour to the sauce with just a small amount. Cognac or marsala can be substituted. As a last resort, it can be omitted as the cider does some heavy lifting in this sauce too!

2 Use a crisp, dry apple cider. A sweet one will overwhelm this sauce. Pear cider is also lovely! For non-alcoholic, use non-alcoholic apple cider.

LEFTOVERS Fridge 3 days, freezer 3 months.

CHICKEN BITES WITH MUSHROOM GRAVY

Comfort food at its people-pleasing best.

SERVES: 4 | PREP: 20 MINUTES | COOK: 15 MINUTES

I wasn't going to include this recipe because it seems to be such a tired and unexciting combination. I mean, chicken and mushroom? Every man and his dog has a recipe (this girl and her dog has many). But of the stack of meals I've shared with friends recently, this dish of bite-sized chicken with plump, rather than sliced, mushrooms in gravy received the most enthusiastic response. I was a little miffed at first. 'What about that amazing glazed pork belly I gave them?!' I thought. But, I realised, homestyle comfort food will always win people over – and what's wrong with that?

---

500 g boneless, skinless chicken thighs[1], cut into 2.5 cm pieces

1 tsp garlic powder

1 tsp salt*

½ tsp black pepper

1 tbsp vegetable oil

200 g very small mushrooms[2] (or larger ones halved or quartered)

1 brown onion, cut into 1 cm wedges

2 garlic cloves*, finely minced

25 g unsalted butter

3 tbsp plain flour

500 ml (2 cups) low-salt beef stock*

1 tsp Worcestershire sauce

70 g (½ cup) frozen peas

TO SERVE

Creamy Mashed Potato (page 330)

Steamed tenderstem broccoli drizzled with my House Salad Dressing (page 312)

Season chicken – Toss the chicken with the garlic powder, half the salt and half the pepper in a bowl.

Sear – Heat the oil in a large, deep non-stick frying pan* over high heat until very hot. Add the chicken and mushrooms and cook for 5 minutes, tossing occasionally, then add the onion and garlic. Continue to cook for another 5 minutes, stirring regularly, until the water released from the mushrooms has evaporated and the surface of the chicken is lightly coloured but the inside is still raw.

Gravy – Add the butter and let it melt. Sprinkle the flour across the surface of the pan (don't dump it in one place or the gravy will be lumpy). Stir for 1 minute. While stirring, slowly pour in the stock. Continue stirring as it comes to a simmer to dissolve the flour into the sauce. Stir in the remaining salt, the remaining pepper, Worcestershire sauce and peas.

Finish and serve – Bring to a simmer, then reduce the heat to medium. Simmer gently for 3–5 minutes, stirring regularly, until the sauce thickens into a thin gravy consistency. Serve over Creamy Mashed Potato with steamed tenderstem broccoli on the side.

NOTES

1 I prefer using chicken thighs because it's a juicier cut of chicken, but you can use breast if you prefer. You'll probably need to add a little extra oil to cook the mushrooms.

2 I like making this with whole mushrooms but they have to be small, about 2 cm diameter. Any larger and they should be halved or cut into quarters.

LEFTOVERS Fridge 3 days, freezer 3 months.

LEFTOVERS REVIVED! STUFFED SWEET POTATOES

Roasted sweet potatoes make a brilliant vessel for stuffing with leftovers, upcycling them into a delicious new meal. The sky's the limit for ideas!

SERVES: 1+ | PREP: 5 MINUTES | COOK: 45–60 MINUTES

As much as I love regular spuds, to me sweet potatoes have way more personality. Most people see roasted sweet potatoes as a side dish or maybe a street snack (Asia calling!). But I say they can be a brilliant dinner solution for using up leftovers. Think of them as jacket potato's sassier older sibling, and we can shoot well past the sour cream and bacon bits routine. Chopped up meatballs? Oh yes. Black bean chilli? Naturally. Shredded chicken? Excellent! You can stuff them with anything that you might serve sweet potatoes with, or put sweet potatoes in. It's thrifty, fun and, most of all, outrageously tasty!

1+ medium sweet potatoes, 250–300 g each, washed and dried

150 g (3/4 cup) per potato of leftovers[1], chopped as appropriate to make it stuffable

Toppings, sauces and garnishes to keep life interesting

Preheat the oven to 220°C (200°C fan).

Prick – Use a fork to prick the skin of each potato eight times, going about 3 mm deep.

Bake – Put the potatoes directly on the oven shelf. Place a foil-lined baking tray on the shelf underneath to catch the syrupy drips that will leak from the holes. Bake for 45–60 minutes, or until the potatoes are soft all the way through (use a butter knife to check). When the skin is puffed and you see syrup dripping from the holes, that's a good sign to start checking.

Warm filling – Meanwhile, warm the leftovers. I usually just do this in the microwave.

Stuffing – Use tongs or tea towels to remove the potatoes from the oven. Cool them a bit so you can handle them (I use a tea towel). Cut a wedge from the top lengthways to make room for the filling. Use a fork to mash the flesh lightly (add the flesh from the wedge you cut out). Pile in your fillings of choice, then add toppings and sauces. Serve!

Twice-baking option – If your filling or topping includes grated* cheese, I recommend popping the stuffed potato back in the oven for 10–15 minutes to make everything bubbly and oozy.

NOTES

1 I chop up the leftovers into small pieces so you can scoop them out with a spoon along with the potato flesh.

LEFTOVERS Cooked sweet potato will keep in the fridge for 5 days or freezer for 3 months.

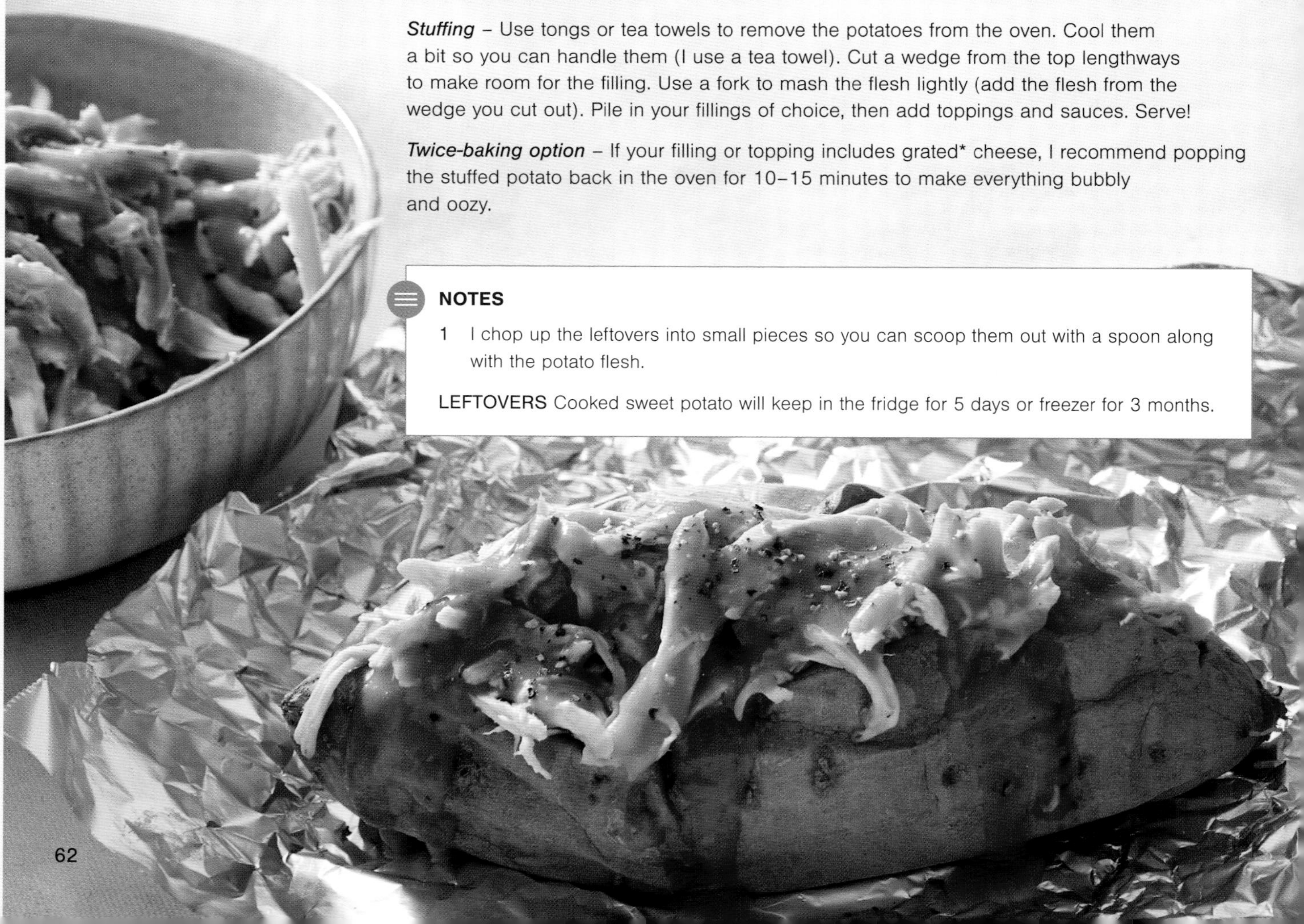

WHAT TO STUFF INSIDE SWEET POTATO

Other than soups (which pose logistical stuffing issues), stir-fries, pasta and noodles (which seem a little odd – but I wouldn't stop you!), virtually every other recipe in this cookbook can be used for stuffing inside sweet potatoes. Generally my rule of thumb is – if the food is something you'd eat with bread or flatbreads, then it'll be great with sweet potatoes!

PERSONAL FAVOURITES

- **Black Bean Chilli** (page 114) with grated* cheese piled on top, then baked to melt the cheese. Optional extras: pinch of chopped coriander leaves, sour cream, chopped avocado.
- **Slow-roasted Middle Eastern Lamb Shoulder** (page 251)
- Shredded chicken with gravy from **Chicken & Gravy Rolls** (page 46)

NOTABLE MENTIONS

- **Curried Chickpea Crunch** (page 119) **with Lemon Yoghurt Sauce** (page 228)
- **Tapas-y Chorizo Tray Bake** (page 194)
- **Baked Beef Koftas** (page 182)
- The stuffing from **Crispy One-pot Beef Burritos** (page 86)
- **Chicken Guinness Stew** (page 95)
- **Honey Sesame Ginger Beef** (page 31)
- **Chicken Bites with Mushroom Gravy** (page 61)

THINGS YOU MIGHTN'T HAVE THOUGHT OF

- **Vietnamese Coconut Lemongrass Pulled Pork** (page 284) with lots of chopped fresh coriander and mint, drizzled with a generous amount of the **Chilli Lime Dipping Sauce** (page 289) and a pile of the pickled vegetables, chopped for ease of eating.
- Goat's cheese and the **Maple Bacon Pecan Crumble** from the **Kale & Apple Salad** (page 205)

NON-LEFTOVER EASY OPTIONS

- Spicy canned tuna from the **Spicy Tuna Crispy Rice Bowls** (page 42)
- Shredded cooked chicken
- Feta, chopped tomato, olives, red onion and basil tossed with a drizzle of extra-virgin olive oil and a swish of balsamic glaze*
- Canned black beans and corn with an assertive dousing of the **Smoky Chipotle Dressing** from the **Cowboy Chicken Salad** (page 200)

THE FASTEST RECIPES

Eight recipes in 15 minutes or less.

One for every night of the week,
plus a spare!

HALLOUMI BURGERS

Halloumi is the star of the world's best meatless burger!

SERVES: 2 | PREP AND COOK TIME: 12 MINUTES

For an impressive and truly satisfying meat-free burger, halloumi is your BFF! Seared as a steak until a golden crust forms, this salty, firm cheese is every bit as good as a beef patty in my book. But wait, there's more! Cook down some cherry tomatoes in a hot pan and you've also got instant tomato salsa that's fresh, not out of a jar. Pile it all on buns with crushed avocado and you've got one epic burger that's fit for a vegetarian king (or your omnivorous friends).

½ avocado, in the skin

20 g salted butter, for buttering the bread

2 brioche buns or other soft bread rolls, split in half

1 tbsp olive oil

180 g halloumi[1] about 2 cm thick, cut in half horizontally to form 2 'steaks'

Pinch of salt*

50 g (2 lightly packed cups) baby spinach or other leafy greens

QUICK HOT TOMATO RELISH

1 tbsp olive oil

½ red onion, sliced

150 g (1 cup) grape or cherry tomatoes

¼ tsp salt*

⅛ tsp black pepper

1 tsp red wine vinegar[2]

Smashed avocado – Use a fork to roughly mash the avocado inside the avocado skin (why dirty a bowl?!). Lumps are fine! Just make it spread-able. Set aside.

Hot tomato relish – Heat the oil in a medium non-stick frying pan* over high heat. Add the onion, tomatoes, salt, pepper and vinegar. Cook, stirring regularly, for 3 minutes or until the tomatoes are lightly blistered, wrinkled and starting to collapse. Slide into a bowl.

Toast bread – Return the pan to the heat. Butter the buns, then put them cut-face down in the pan. Cook for 1 minute or until golden. Transfer to serving plates.

Fry halloumi – Heat the oil in the pan. Add the halloumi and cook each side for 1½ minutes or until deep golden. Transfer to a plate.

Assemble – Slather the base of the buns with avocado. Sprinkle with a pinch of salt. Pile on the spinach, top with the halloumi, then the tomato relish. Top with the bun lids and enjoy!

NOTES

1 Halloumi is the salty, firm cheese that looks like Greek feta. It's unique because it holds its form when fried so you get a gorgeous golden crust without the inside oozing everywhere. This means there are all sorts of wonderful eating options that aren't possible with typical cheeses. Like – burgers! There really is no substitute for halloumi, not even feta.

2 Substitute with lemon juice, white wine vinegar, balsamic vinegar or sherry vinegar.

LEFTOVERS Though all components in this recipe will keep for 3 days, burgers are just one of those things best eaten freshly made! Not suitable for freezing either.

QUICK SALMON RED CURRY

Pan-seared salmon smothered in everyone's favourite Thai red curry sauce.

SERVES: 2 | PREP AND COOK TIME: 15 MINUTES

I know, I know. Can you really pull off this richly flavoured Thai curry in 15 minutes? Yes! It all comes down to a handful of neat tricks. First, using thin slices of salmon speeds up cooking and boosts flavour with the fond[1] left in the pan. Adding fresh ginger and garlic also gives a freshness leg-up to store-bought curry paste. And using a wide pan accelerates sauce reduction to cut down on cooking time. Follow these tips and more and you'll be landing this irresistible one-pot curry complete with rice noodles on your dinner table in minutes!

NOODLES

100 g dried rice vermicelli noodles or other noodles of choice

SALMON

350 g salmon fillet(s)[1], skinless, cut lengthways into 4 equal thin pieces

¼ tsp salt*

⅛ tsp black pepper

1½ tbsp vegetable oil

RED CURRY SAUCE

3 tbsp Thai red curry paste*

1½ tsp finely grated garlic*

1 tsp finely grated ginger*

125 ml (½ cup) low-salt chicken stock*[2]

400 ml can full-fat coconut milk*[3]

2 tsp fish sauce

1 tsp white sugar

4 baby bok choy, ends trimmed, leaves separated

1–2 tbsp lime juice, plus wedges for serving

TO GARNISH (OPTIONAL)

Fresh coriander leaves

Red bird's eye chilli*, finely sliced

Noodles – Soak the noodles in boiling water according to the packet directions (usually 5 minutes). Drain and divide between two serving bowls.

Salmon – Sprinkle the salmon with the salt and pepper. Heat the oil in a large non-stick frying pan*[4] over high heat. Cook each side of the salmon for 1 minute until the surface is light golden but the inside is still raw, then transfer to a plate.

Curry sauce – Add the red curry paste, garlic and ginger to the pan. Cook, stirring constantly, for 1 minute. Add the chicken stock and simmer rapidly for 1 minute, stirring to dissolve all the golden bits stuck on the base of the pan into the liquid. Add the coconut milk, fish sauce and sugar. Simmer rapidly for 2 minutes.

Simmer – Return the salmon to the sauce and tuck the bok choy around the salmon. Simmer for 2 minutes, pushing the bok choy under the liquid as it starts to wilt. Once the salmon is fully cooked (check to ensure the flesh flakes in the centre), remove the pan from the stove.

Serve – Pour the lime juice over the fish. Serve over noodles, garnished with coriander and chilli (if using). Provide extra lime wedges so you can add more to taste.

NOTES

1. This recipe will work with any type of fish or raw, peeled prawns (same quantity). The idea is to cut the fish into thin pieces for maximum surface area for searing, which adds flavour into the sauce (by way of the golden bits left in the pan – the 'fond') and onto the fish itself, and also so it cooks quickly.
2. If you have homemade or a good-quality store-bought fish stock, by all means use that instead! However, give the basic grocery store carton fish stock a miss. Chicken stock is much better quality (in my humble opinion).
3. Your sauce thickness and coconut flavour will be affected by the quality of the coconut milk you use. Economical coconut milk is thinner and has less coconut flavour because it is typically more diluted with water.
4. The size of the pan matters here! Larger = faster sauce reduction = faster cook time. If you scale the recipe up, this will also affect the time it takes for the sauce to reduce.

LEFTOVERS Fridge 3 days, freezer 3 months.

CREAMY FETA ASPARAGUS PASTA

This fresh, no-cook sauce is as quick and easy as midweek pasta dinner gets!

SERVES: 2 | PREP AND COOK TIME: 15 MINUTES

Here's a handy way of making a ridiculously quick vegetable pasta. First boil the vegetables with the pasta to save time (and pots). Drain and mix with a simple no-cook sauce that acts as a kind of dressing. Toss well and you're done. It's essentially a warm pasta salad of sorts, sometimes known as pasta con salsa fresca ('pasta with fresh sauce') – yes, it's a real thing! I've used asparagus for this dish along with Danish feta, which melts to form a lovely creamy and tangy sauce. Feel free to use other vegetables; whatever you have on hand – that's the Italian way!

½ tsp salt*, for cooking pasta

200 g penne lisce[1] or other pasta of choice

2 bunches asparagus, woody ends trimmed, cut into 4 cm lengths

125 g Danish feta[2]

SAUCE

2 tsp lemon zest

2 tbsp lemon juice[3]

3 tbsp extra-virgin olive oil

1 garlic clove*, finely minced using a garlic crusher or knife

¼ tsp dried chilli flakes*

½ tsp dried oregano

¼ tsp salt*

Make sauce – Put the sauce ingredients in a jar and shake to combine. Do this while the pasta is cooking.

Cook pasta and asparagus – Bring a pot of water to the boil with the ½ teaspoon of salt. Add the pasta and cook according to the packet directions. Add the asparagus to the water for the last 2 minutes of cooking time.

Pasta cooking water – Just before draining, scoop out 3 tablespoons of the pasta cooking water and add it to the sauce. Drain the pasta and asparagus in a colander but do not rinse.

Finish and serve – Tip the hot cooked pasta and asparagus back into the same pot over medium–low heat. Add all the sauce and crumble in half the feta. Stir vigorously for 1 minute or until the feta is melted and coats the pasta. Pour the pasta into a serving bowl or divide between two bowls. Crumble the reserved feta over the top and dig in!

NOTES

1 Penne lisce is a type of penne that is on the smaller side and has a smooth surface. I like it because it's the perfect bite size and cooks in just 8 minutes. However, this recipe can be made with any type of pasta – short or long!

2 Danish feta is a type of feta that is creamier than Greek feta, which is more crumbly. Danish feta can be used to make creamy sauces, as in this recipe. Substitute with goat's cheese.

3 While fresh lemon really lifts this otherwise very simple dish, in the event of a dinner emergency, you can use wine vinegars (red, white, sherry, champagne vinegar) or apple cider vinegar.

LEFTOVERS Fridge 3 days. Not suitable for freezing.

CHICKEN BRUSCHETTA

Bruschetta can be dinner – just add chicken!

SERVES: 2 | PREP AND COOK TIME: 15 MINUTES

People can't seem to get behind the idea that bruschetta can be a meal. I say it all depends on what's on it! Shredded chicken works beautifully with fresh tomatoes and basil as a summery topping for these Italian toasts. It's delicious, healthy, wholesome and filling – what more could you want? A drizzle of sweet and intense balsamic glaze here is the perfect finishing touch that brings it all together, so don't skip it.

---

4 slices sourdough bread[1], each 1.3 cm thick

1 tbsp extra-virgin olive oil, for brushing (or olive oil spray), plus extra for drizzling

1 garlic clove, unpeeled, cut in half

BRUSCHETTA TOPPING

250 g (1½ cups) diced tomato* (4 big tomatoes), watery seeds scooped out, flesh cut into 1 cm cubes

½ tsp salt*

½ tsp black pepper

125 g (1 cup) cooked shredded chicken[2] (I use store-bought)

10 g (¼ tightly packed cup) basil leaves, finely sliced, plus extra for garnish

4 tbsp extra-virgin olive oil

TO FINISH

1 tsp balsamic glaze*

Bruschetta topping – Place the tomato, salt and pepper in a bowl and toss gently. Add the chicken, basil and olive oil, then toss again. Set aside for 5 minutes for the flavours to meld and the tomatoes to become juicy and soften slightly.

Toast bread – Preheat the oven grill to high and position an oven shelf 20 cm from the heat source. Brush each side of bread with the oil (or spray generously). Place on a baking tray, then grill until golden and crusty – about 3 minutes on each side. (Or just use your toaster, then brush with oil.)

Garlic rub – Use the cut face of the garlic to lightly rub one side of the hot toast.[3]

Assemble – Pile the topping onto the garlic-rubbed side of the bread, along with some of the juices accumulated in the bottom of the bowl. Drizzle with a swish of the balsamic glaze, more extra-virgin olive oil and add an extra scattering of basil, if desired. Serve immediately!

NOTES

1 Or other chewy, crusty bread. Standard white sandwich bread isn't sturdy enough to withstand juicy bruschetta toppings!

2 In the spirit of the speedy nature of the recipes in this chapter, I use a store-bought rotisserie chicken here. If you're a better person than me, poach your own chicken breast, shred, toss with a pinch of salt and pepper, then use as per recipe.

3 Just rub lightly to perfume the bread with garlic flavour – don't be too enthusiastic or the raw garlic flavour will overwhelm!

LEFTOVERS Best eaten freshly made.

SPICY KOREAN KIMCHI NOODLES

My pick of the chapter!

SERVES: 1 | **PREP AND COOK TIME: 15 MINUTES**

Kimchi pickling juice squeezed from kimchi cabbage is packed with umami and is a secret weapon used in Korean cooking. Here, I'm using it as the basis of a dynamite noodle sauce that explodes with fiery Korean flavour. A little vegetable chopping is the only other thing needed in what might just be the world's fastest spicy noodle stir-fry! Yes, it's spicy. But don't fret if your heat-o-meter caps out on the tamer side. You can always substitute some miso paste for the gochujang to dial down the spiciness.

---

200 g udon noodles[1], fresh or shelf-stable

1 tbsp vegetable oil

1 garlic clove*, finely minced

80 g (1 cup) bean sprouts

120 g (½ cup) cabbage kimchi[2], excess juice squeezed out

2 spring onions*, cut into batons, white part separated from the green part

Sesame seeds, for garnish (optional)

SAUCE

2 tbsp kimchi juice[2] from the kimchi jar (see above)

1 tbsp gochujang*[3]

1 tbsp honey

1 tbsp light soy sauce*[4] (or all-purpose soy sauce*)

Prepare noodles – Prepare the udon noodles according to the packet directions (usually soaked in boiling water for a few minutes), then drain in a colander. Time the noodles so they are tossed into the pan when hot – don't leave them sitting around in the colander.

Stir-fry – Heat the oil in a large non-stick frying pan* over high heat. Add the garlic, bean sprouts, kimchi and the white part of the spring onion. Cook for 1 minute until the bean sprouts are almost wilted. Add (in this order): the green part of the spring onion, the noodles and all the sauce ingredients. Toss for 2 minutes until the sauce stains the noodles.

Serve – Transfer to a bowl, sprinkle with sesame seeds (if using), then devour!

NOTES

1 I prefer to use udon noodles either from the refrigerator at grocery stores or vacuum-sealed packets sold in the aisles. I personally don't think dried udon noodles are that great. I'd rather substitute with other kinds of noodles, such as hokkien or egg noodles. Use 150 g fresh from the fridge or 100 g dried.

2 Kimchi is Korean fermented cabbage that is spicy and tangy. It is sold in jars and widely available these days. In this recipe, we're using the cabbage in the stir-fry (use your hands to squeeze out most of the liquid) and the liquid from the kimchi jar for the sauce. Excellent free flavour!

3 Gochujang is a Korean chilli paste made from soybeans. Loved for the spicy-sweet-savouriness it adds to anything, a little bit goes a long way. Excellent flavour shortcut! You can find it in most grocery stores these days, or in Asian/Korean grocery stores. It lasts 'forever' in the fridge.

4 Please do not substitute with dark soy sauce*. Too intense! It will ruin this dish.

LEFTOVERS Fridge 3 days. Not suitable for freezing.

ONE-PAN CHORIZO COUSCOUS

A Spanish-esque take on couscous!

SERVES: 2–3 | PREP AND COOK TIME: 15 MINUTES

Couscous is a staple in my pantry because it's a handy no-cook starch that has excellent sauce-soaking capabilities. Of North African origin, it can be used for dishes all over the world due to its neutral flavour. Here, I'm giving it a Spanish spin by teaming it with chorizo (hello, flavour shortcut!), a handful of juicy cherry tomatoes, frozen peas and a hint of smoky paprika flavour. The best part, though, is that the couscous is steamed in the same pan while the chorizo is still in it. Not only does that save on washing up, the couscous gets excellent flavour infusion from the tasty chorizo pan juices!

---

1 tbsp extra-virgin olive oil, plus extra for drizzling

220 g chorizo[1] (2 pieces), one cut into quarters lengthways, then into 1 cm thick pieces, the other sliced into 7 mm thick rounds[2]

1 garlic clove*, finely minced

1 small red onion, peeled, halved and finely sliced

1 tbsp tomato paste

190 g (1 cup) couscous[3]

½ tsp smoked paprika*[4]

¼ tsp black pepper

140 g (1 cup) frozen peas

250 ml (1 cup) low-salt chicken stock*

¾ tsp salt*

½ tbsp lemon zest

2 tbsp lemon juice

150 g (1 cup) cherry tomatoes, halved

5 g (¼ cup) roughly chopped parsley leaves (optional)

Sauté chorizo – Heat the oil in a large non-stick frying pan* over medium–high heat. Cook the chorizo for 3 minutes or until light golden. Add the garlic and onion and cook for a further 2 minutes until the chorizo is golden and the onion is softened. Turn the stove down to medium. Add the tomato paste and stir for 1 minute. Add the couscous, paprika and pepper and stir for 1 minute to coat the couscous in the tasty oil.

Steam couscous – Add the peas, stock and salt and let it come to a simmer. The couscous will soak up the stock straight away and that's okay! Trust the process! Spread the couscous out evenly and scrape down the sides of the pan. Cover the pan with a lid or another frying pan (or a baking tray) then turn the stove off. Leave the pan on the turned-off stove for 5 minutes to steam-cook the couscous.

Serve – Scatter the lemon zest and drizzle the lemon juice over the couscous. Add the cherry tomatoes. Gently fluff and mix the couscous with a spatula. Spoon into bowls and serve, sprinkled with parsley (if using) and drizzled with an extra swish of olive oil!

NOTES

1. Use chorizo that is cured – the type that is firm like salami, which can be sliced and eaten without cooking. Raw chorizo is like uncooked sausage. If you accidentally got raw chorizo, no problems! Squeeze the meat out of the casing and fry it up like mince, then proceed with the recipe.
2. I like to use a mix of smaller and larger pieces of chorizo so you get nice big meaty bites, as well as smaller pieces that release more tasty oil that flavours the couscous.
3. Couscous is made from small semolina grains and is a staple in North African cuisine. Widely available, it is usually found in the pasta aisle. Very handy starchy vehicle because it's no-cook – it just needs to be soaked in hot liquid!
4. Substitute with ordinary paprika.

LEFTOVERS Fridge 3 days, freezer 3 months.

MIGHTY SWISS MUSHROOM STEAK SANDWICH

Everything you dream a steak sandwich to be – done with speed!

SERVES: 1 | PREP AND COOK TIME: 15 MINUTES

This easy-to-make beauty is big, beefy and outrageously juicy, just like your favourite steak sanga! Layered with meaty golden mushrooms that almost double as a second steak, and blanketed by oozing Swiss cheese, the warm ciabatta bread is smeared with garlicky aioli, along with a handful of rocket for some perky bite. Remember, 2 minutes only for the sizzle steak – don't dare overcook it!

---

2 x 100 g thin (5 mm thick) slices rib-eye or other steak ('sizzle steak')[1]

¼ tsp salt*

¼ tsp black pepper

1 tbsp vegetable oil

AIOLI

1 tbsp mayonnaise*, preferably whole-egg

⅛ tsp finely grated garlic*

SANDWICH

Ciabatta or other bread of choice (the size of your steak), split in half

Handful of rocket or other leafy greens of choice

SWISS MUSHROOMS

½ tbsp vegetable oil

1 very large mushroom[2] (about 8 cm wide), cut into 7 mm thick slices

⅛ tsp salt*

⅛ tsp black pepper

1 slice Swiss cheese[3] or other melting cheese of choice

Aioli – Mix the aioli ingredients in a small bowl, then set aside to let the flavours meld.

Sear steak – Sprinkle the steak with the salt and pepper. Heat the vegetable oil in a cast-iron frying pan* over high heat until smoking. (You want to get it very hot for maximum browning in a very quick cook time!) Add the steaks and cook each side for just 1 minute, then transfer to a plate.

Toast bread – Remove the pan from the stove and let it cool for a bit, then return it to the stove over medium–high heat. Put the bread cut-face down in the pan and press down lightly so it soaks up the juices. Toast for 1 minute until light golden, then transfer to a serving plate.

Swiss mushrooms – Add the oil in the same pan still over medium–high heat, and swirl to spread. Add the mushroom and cook the first side for 1½ minutes until light golden. Turn and cook the other side for 1 minute. Sprinkle the mushroom with the salt and pepper, give it a quick toss, then push together into a pile that approximates the size of your sandwich. Place the cheese on top and cover the pan with a lid[4] for 30 seconds to melt the cheese. Once melted, remove the pan from the stove.

Assemble – Smear all the aioli on one slice of the bread. Top with the rocket, then both slices of beef. Use a spatula to scoop the pile of cheesy mushroom out of the pan and onto the beef. Top with the other slice of bread and sink your teeth in!

NOTES

1. These days, thin slices of steak are sold at both grocery stores and butchers and are relatively good value. If you can find rib-eye steak, I recommend using that, as it's a juicy cut with good beef flavour. However, even economical 'sizzle steak' works just fine here as long as you don't overcook it!
2. Large mushrooms have a lot going for them. They are faster to cut than a handful of small ones, and easier to cook as you just sear each side once like mini steaks! But by all means, you can use small mushrooms instead.
3. Use enough cheese to cover the pile of mushroom.
4. If you don't have a lid for your pan, use another pan or baking tray.

LEFTOVERS Best eaten freshly made, but leftovers will keep for 3 days in the fridge.

SPINACH & ARTICHOKE ANGEL HAIR PASTA

Meet angel hair pasta – the faster pasta!

SERVES: 2 | PREP AND COOK TIME: 15 MINUTES

Angel hair pasta is so fine it takes just a couple of minutes to cook, which means dinner on the table – fast! Marinated artichokes are my trick in this recipe for a load of briny flavour here, with a handful of spinach thrown in for colour and freshness. And finally, a shower of parmesan and a squeeze of lemon are the perfect finishing touches to bring this delicious (and meatless!) bowl of fork-twirling pasta together.

---

160 g angel hair pasta, or other long-strand pasta

½ tsp salt*, for cooking the pasta

Extra-virgin olive oil, for drizzling

SAUCE

30 g unsalted butter, or 2 tbsp extra-virgin olive oil

2 garlic cloves*, finely minced

⅛ tsp dried chilli flakes*, plus extra for sprinkling (or use black pepper)

100 g (2 tightly packed cups) baby spinach leaves

200 g (1 cup) marinated or brined quartered artichoke hearts[1], drained, petals partially separated using your fingers

½ tsp salt*

25 g (¼ cup) finely grated parmesan*, plus extra for serving

3 tbsp lemon juice, plus extra to taste

Boil pasta – Bring a large saucepan* or small pot* of water to the boil with the ½ teaspoon of salt. Add the pasta and cook according to the packet directions (usually 2 minutes). Scoop out a mugful of the pasta cooking water, then drain the pasta in a colander.

Pasta sauce – Return the same saucepan to the stove over medium–high heat. Toss the butter in and, once it melts, add the garlic and dried chilli flakes. Stir for 20 seconds until the garlic is light golden (don't let it burn!), then add (in this order): the spinach, artichokes, pasta, salt, parmesan and 60 ml (¼ cup) of the reserved pasta cooking water.

Toss – Using two spatulas, toss the pasta for 1 minute or until the spinach is mostly wilted. Add the lemon juice and toss again. Taste and add more salt, if needed. Use the extra reserved pasta cooking water to loosen the pasta if it starts to get sticky instead of being slippery with sauce!

Serve – Divide between two bowls. Drizzle with a little extra-virgin olive oil and garnish with more parmesan and a pinch of chilli flakes (if using), then dive in!

NOTES

1 Use artichoke hearts marinated in oil or brined in salted water rather than artichokes canned in plain water or plain frozen artichokes, as they will impart more free flavour into the dish. The artichokes you use will affect the salt levels in this recipe, so start with the conservative amount listed in the ingredients, then taste at the end before adding more. If your artichokes are whole, cut into halves or quarters before using.

LEFTOVERS Best made fresh but leftovers will keep for 3 days. A swish of extra-virgin olive oil will help bring it back to life.

MY FAVOURITES MADE EASIER

Meat pies! Hainanese chicken!
Guinness stew! Mega burritos!

BAKED SATAY CHICKEN

Everything you love about satay chicken minus the fiddly skewering!

SERVES: 4–6 | PREP: 10 MINUTES | COOK: 50 MINUTES

My Thai chicken satay skewers have been a reader-favourite recipe from the moment I published the recipe on my website. It's the peanut sauce! People go bonkers over the peanutty, sweet–savoury flavour. Skewering chicken pieces does take a bit of work, though, so I've come up with this oven-baked version using whole thighs, to make things easier and faster. Same taste, half the effort ... Now you can have chicken satay even more often! I dare say it's also possibly even better than the original, because of the flavour-boost the sauce gets from the delicious chicken juices that seep out as it bakes.

---

400 ml full-fat coconut milk*

6 x 250 g bone-in, skin-on chicken thighs[1]

SATAY PASTE FOR CHICKEN

1 tbsp curry powder[2]

1 tsp white sugar

½ tsp salt*

2 tsp red curry paste*

SATAY SAUCE

120 g (½ cup) natural unsweetened smooth peanut butter*

1½ tbsp caster sugar

2 tsp curry powder[2]

¾ tsp salt*

¼ tsp chilli powder* or cayenne pepper (optional)

2 tbsp apple cider vinegar

1½ tbsp red curry paste*

2 tsp dark soy sauce*[3]

310 ml (1¼ cups) water

TO SERVE

Jasmine Rice (page 318)

2 tbsp roughly chopped roasted peanuts, unsalted

Coriander leaves (optional)

Sliced red chilli (optional)

Lime wedges (optional)

Preheat the oven to 200°C (180°C fan).

Coat chicken – Put the satay paste ingredients in a bowl with 60 ml (¼ cup) of the coconut milk. Mix to combine. Add the chicken and turn to coat. Set aside while you prepare the sauce.[4]

Satay sauce – Place the remaining coconut milk and all the satay sauce ingredients in a 23 x 33 cm ovenproof casserole dish. Whisk to combine. Place the chicken in the sauce, skin-side up, arranging the pieces so that they are not touching each other (tuck the sides of the chicken under to make the footprint smaller, if needed).[5] Scrape all the satay paste out of the bowl and dab it onto the chicken skin.

Bake – Bake for 30 minutes. Remove from the oven and spoon the sauce over the chicken. Bake for a further 15 minutes. Spoon the sauce over the chicken, then bake for a further 5 minutes or until the chicken is golden. The sauce should have thickened into a thin, syrupy consistency – see note 6 if it's too thin.

Serve – Remove the dish from the oven and let it rest for 5 minutes. The sauce will thicken a little more during this time. Serve the chicken and sauce over rice, garnished with the chopped peanuts, and the coriander, fresh chilli and lime wedges (if using).

NOTES

1 Chicken drumsticks work just as well, use 8–10. Boneless chicken like thighs and breast will work but the sauce won't be as tasty because they don't release as many chicken juices. However, you can use 750 g of either of these. Bake the sauce only for 20 minutes, then add the chicken and bake for 15 minutes. Spoon the sauce over the top and bake for a further 5 minutes.

2 Just your regular curry powder from ordinary grocery stores.

3 Adds seasoning and deepens the colour of the sauce. Can substitute with light* or all-purpose soy sauce* but the sauce colour will be lighter.

4 The chicken does not need to be marinated, but you can if you want. Marinate for up to 24 hours in the fridge.

5 There needs to be space around each piece of chicken to allow the sauce to reduce and thicken in the oven.

6 If the sauce is looking a little too watery, take the chicken out of the dish and put it onto a plate for the resting time. Pop the dish, with just the sauce in it, back in the oven for 5–10 minutes to thicken the sauce.

LEFTOVERS Fridge 3 days, freezer 3 months.

CRISPY ONE-POT BEEF BURRITOS

Make the fillings together in one pot for the easiest burritos ever!

SERVES: 8 | **PREP: 20 MINUTES** | **COOK: 20 MINUTES**

Here's my ultimate trick for streamlining burritos when I'm short on time: cook all the fillings together in one pot! It's everything that goes inside my classic beef burritos – rice, corn, beans, seasoned beef – but cooked simultaneously instead of putting them out in separate bowls. Sure, the filling is all jumbled up instead of layered, but the savings on the time side are unbeatable. In some ways I also actually prefer the quick way. Not only does the filling hold together better, making it super easy to roll up, but you get consistently complete filling with every bite. Goodbye, mouthful-of-rice-and-not-much-else. Hello, perfect burrito bite!

---

2 tbsp vegetable oil

1 brown onion, finely chopped

2 garlic cloves, finely chopped

1 red bell pepper, deseeded and cut into 1 cm squares

500 g beef mince

2 tbsp tomato paste

200 g (1 cup) long-grain white rice, uncooked

560 ml (2¼ cups) low-salt chicken stock*

200 g (1½ cups) frozen corn (or 400 g can sweetcorn, drained)

400 g can black beans, drained

BURRITO SPICE MIX

½ tsp cayenne pepper

1½ tbsp dried oregano

1 tbsp ground cumin

1 tbsp ground coriander

1 tbsp onion powder

2 tsp paprika*

1½ tsp salt*

BURRITOS

8 jumbo (25 cm) tortillas*

16 slices cheddar cheese[1] (or other cheese of choice)

2 tbsp vegetable oil, for crisping (optional)

Avocado Crema (page 230)

Spice mix – Put the spice mix ingredients in a bowl and mix to combine. Set aside.

Prepare filling – Heat the vegetable oil in a large heavy-based pot* over high heat. Add the onion, garlic and pepper and cook for 3 minutes or until the onion is soft. Add the beef and cook, breaking it up as you go, until you no longer see pink. Add 3 tablespoons of the spice mix and stir for 1 minute. Stir in the tomato paste. Add the rice, chicken stock and the rest of the spice mix and stir them in. Scatter the corn and black beans across the surface – but do not stir them in.

Cook filling – Once the liquid comes to a simmer, put the lid on and reduce the heat to low. Cook for 14 minutes or until the liquid has been absorbed. Remove the pot from the stove and leave to rest for 12 minutes with the lid on. Remove the lid and mix the rice gently.

Roll burritos – Lay a tortilla on a work surface. Break two slices of cheese in half, then lay them on the bottom third of the tortilla. Loosely pack a 1 cup measure with the warm filling, then invert it on top of the cheese. Shape into a log, then roll up tightly, finishing with the seam-side down. Repeat with the remaining burritos to make eight.

Crisp it – Heat 1 tablespoon of the vegetable oil in a large non-stick frying pan* over medium–high heat. Pan-fry four burritos at a time to make the tortilla golden and crisp – about 1½ minutes on each side (I do four sides). Remove and repeat with the remaining burritos.

Serve – Serve the burritos with Avocado Crema for dunking!

NOTES

1 Standard pre-sliced cheese, about 10 cm square, is handy here. Otherwise slice or shred your own.

LEFTOVERS Fridge 3 days, freezer 3 months. If not consuming immediately, allow the burritos to fully cool, then wrap in plastic wrap to store in the fridge or freezer. To reheat, frozen burritos can be baked from frozen, wrapped in foil, at 160°C (140°C fan) for 1 hour, or 45 minutes if thawed.

SPICY SESAME GINGER NOODLE SOUP

A speedy spin-off of my all-time favourite spicy noodle soup.

SERVES: 1 | **PREP: 10 MINUTES** | **COOK: 15 MINUTES**

It's no secret I adore dan dan noodles. I just can't get enough of the intense, oily and rich sesame broth laced with *ma la* ('hot and numbing') flavours from the Sichuan pepper and chilli. Here's my speedier version of this Chinese classic. It's still got the layered flavours and a proper kick, but is way easier to make than the real thing! With strips of chicken and Asian greens, as well as a soft-boiled egg, it's actually a bit like tan tan ramen which, ironically, is a type of Japanese ramen adapted from dan dan noodles!

---

100 g boneless, skinless chicken thighs (or breast), cut in half lengthways, then finely sliced into 7 mm strips

5 Chinese broccoli (gai lan)[1] stems, cut into 8 cm lengths, stems separated from leaves, thick stems cut vertically to make them an even thickness

1 x 70 g ramen noodle cake[2]

1 soft-boiled egg*, halved

BROTH

3 tbsp Chinese sesame paste*[3]

2½ tbsp light soy sauce*[4]

½ tbsp Chinese chilli paste in oil[5] (or sriracha* or chilli crisp*, to taste)

1 tsp finely grated garlic*

1 tsp finely grated ginger*

1 tsp white sugar

½ tsp Chinese five spice*

1 tsp ground Sichuan pepper*[6] (substitute white pepper)

375 ml (1½ cups) low-salt chicken stock*

TO GARNISH

2 tsp Chinese chilli oil[7] (or chilli crisp* or your favourite chilli paste)

Pinch of black sesame seeds

Finely sliced spring onion*

Broth – Place all the broth ingredients in a small saucepan* and whisk to combine – small sesame lumps are fine as they will melt. Bring to a simmer over medium–high heat, then cook over low heat for 5 minutes, uncovered.

Cook chicken – Add the chicken to the broth and simmer for 2 minutes.

Cook vegetables and noodles – Meanwhile, bring a medium saucepan* of water to the boil. Add the Chinese broccoli stems and cook for 1 minute. Add the leaves and cook for 30 seconds. Using tongs, transfer the Chinese broccoli to a bowl. Cook the noodles in the same saucepan, according to the packet directions, then drain.

To serve – Place the noodles in a bowl and ladle all the broth and chicken over. Top with the Chinese broccoli and egg. Drizzle over the chilli oil (be liberal!), then sprinkle with sesame seeds and spring onion. Slurp away!

NOTES

1 Substitute with any other Asian greens, such as bok choy or choy sum.

2 Standard size dried ramen noodle cake. Substitute with the same amount of other dried egg noodles, 50 g dried vermicelli rice noodles or 100 g fresh noodles (from the fridge section of the grocery store).

3 Chinese sesame paste (zhi ma jiang) is like tahini* but has a more intense sesame flavour. Substitute with tahini or natural unsweetened smooth peanut butter*.

4 Substitute with all-purpose soy sauce*. Do not substitute with dark soy sauce* as the flavour is too intense.

5 Any spicy Asian sauce or chilli paste will work here. If you're unsure about spiciness, start with less, then add more at the end.

6 I just use pre-ground here, for convenience. If you toast and grind your own, reduce to ½ teaspoon as it will be spicier.

7 Find Chinese chilli oil at Asian grocery stores and the Asian aisle of large grocery stores.

LEFTOVERS Fridge 3 days. Keep the broth separate from the noodles. Not suitable for freezing.

ONE-POT HAINANESE CHICKEN & RICE

All the flavour and all the flair – but faster!

SERVES: 4 | PREP: 15 MINUTES | COOK: 20 MINUTES

Hainanese chicken rice is one of the world's greatest chicken-with-rice dishes. The idea of gently poaching a whole chicken, then using the stock to cook and flavour the accompanying rice is sheer brilliance! The only problem is it takes a good couple of hours. So when time is of the essence, forget the whole chicken and the poaching – use thighs instead and cook them together with the rice in a single pot! I also cook the rice in store-bought chicken stock, solving another common issue: bland rice. The whole recipe takes a fraction of the time of authentic chicken rice but is just as tasty. (PS: The ginger shallot sauce makes this dish, so don't even think about skipping it!)

---

4 x 220–250 g bone-in, skin-on chicken thighs[1]

3/4 tsp salt*

1/4 tsp white pepper

GINGER SHALLOT SAUCE[2]

55 g (1 lightly packed cup) finely sliced spring onion* (about 4 stems)

2 tbsp finely grated ginger*

1/4 tsp salt*

5 tbsp (75 ml) vegetable or grapeseed oil

CHICKEN RICE

15 g unsalted butter

1 tbsp finely julienned peeled ginger*

1 tsp finely minced garlic*

300 g (1 1/2 cups) long-grain rice, uncooked

2 x 2 cm slices unpeeled ginger

560 ml (2 1/4 cups) low-salt chicken stock*

1/4 tsp salt*

1 spring onion* stem, folded in half, then tied in a knot

TO SERVE

Sambal oelek* (or other chilli paste)

2 cucumbers*, sliced

Ginger shallot sauce – Place all the sauce ingredients in a bowl and mix to combine. Set aside for at least 5 minutes. The spring onion will soften. (I make this while the rice is cooking.)

Season chicken – Pat the chicken dry with paper towels. Sprinkle both sides with the salt and pepper.

Chicken rice – Heat the butter in a large heavy-based pot* over medium–low heat. Add the julienned ginger and garlic and sauté for 1 minute until light golden. Add the rice and stir to coat in the butter for 30 seconds.

Cook rice – Add the ginger slices, stock, salt and spring onion. Turn the heat up to high and bring to a simmer. Once there are bubbles all around the edge and the middle of the surface is rippling, gently place the chicken thighs in a single layer on the surface of the rice (tuck them into a ball shape, as needed, to fit). Don't push them into the liquid. When the water starts bubbling again, cover with a lid and reduce the heat to low. Cook for 14 minutes or until the liquid is absorbed.

Rest rice – With the lid still on, remove the pot from the stove and rest for 10 minutes.

Serve – Transfer the chicken to a cutting board. Fluff the rice. Remove the bone from the chicken and cut the meat into slices. Serve with the rice, ginger shallot sauce, sambal oelek and cucumber.

NOTES

1. You could also use 6–8 drumsticks or boneless, skinless chicken thighs. And, though the recipe will work with chicken breast, it's not recommended because the chicken will be drier than ideal and there won't be much chicken juice to flavour the rice.
2. 'Ginger spring onion sauce' doesn't have the same ring to it, so I'm sticking with the common name!

LEFTOVERS Fridge 3 days, freezer 3 months.

EASIER MEAT PIES

Homemade meat pies on a busy Monday night? Yes we can!

SERVES: 4 | PREP: 10 MINUTES + 45 MINUTES CHILLING | COOK: 1 HOUR

Australia is famous for its meat pies – and rightfully so! We're mad about these palm-sized portable meals, with their flaky pastry encasing beef mince bound with a rich gravy. A dollop of tomato sauce on top is practically Australian law. While no good Aussie would ever frown upon a frozen pie, the next time the craving hits, I implore you to turn to these homemade meat pie pastries! Easy enough to make even for a Monday night dinner, they still check off everything you love in a classic homemade meat pie.

---

2 tbsp extra-virgin olive oil

2 garlic cloves*, finely minced

½ brown onion, finely chopped

300 g beef mince

2 tsp Worcestershire sauce

150 g white mushrooms, sliced 5 mm thick

1 tbsp tomato paste

250 ml (1 cup) pinot noir or other dry red wine*[1]

1½ tbsp plain flour

250 ml (1 cup) low-salt beef stock*

¼ tsp salt*

½ tsp black pepper

1 beef bouillon cube*, crumbled

1 bay leaf*

½ tsp dried thyme

70 g (½ cup) frozen peas

PASTRY

2 x 25 cm square puff pastry sheets (preferably butter), barely thawed[2] (300 g)

1 egg, whisked

1 tbsp flour, for dusting the fork

TO SERVE

Tomato sauce or ketchup*

Cook beef and mushrooms – Heat the oil in a large non-stick frying pan* over high heat. Add the garlic and onion and cook for 2 minutes until the onion is softened. Add the beef and cook, breaking it up as you go, until you no longer see pink. Add the Worcestershire sauce and cook for 1 minute. Add the mushrooms and stir for 3 minutes until they start to soften – they will cook more in the next steps.

Finish filling – Add the tomato paste and cook for 1 minute. Add the red wine and let it simmer rapidly for 3 minutes, stirring every now and then, until mostly evaporated. Stir the flour in. Add the beef stock, salt, pepper, bouillon cube, bay leaf and thyme. Stir well and, once it comes to a simmer, reduce the heat to medium–high and let it simmer quite rapidly for 5 minutes, stirring regularly so the base doesn't catch, until the liquid reduces to a fairly thick gravy.

Cool – Remove the pot from the stove. Discard the bay leaf. Stir in the peas. Spread the filling out on a dinner plate or tray. Cool for 15 minutes, then place in the fridge, uncovered, for 30 minutes to fully chill.

Preheat the oven to 220°C (200°C fan). Put a baking tray in the oven to heat it up (crispier pie base!).

Assemble pies – Cut each piece of puff pastry into four equal squares.[3] Place each piece on a separate square of baking paper[4] on a work surface. Brush all four edges of the pastry with egg. Pile one-quarter of the filling on each piece of pastry. Smooth the surface and shape into a square, leaving a 1 cm border. Cover with another sheet of pastry. Dip a fork in the flour, then press along the edge to seal, re-dipping the fork in flour as needed so it doesn't stick to the puff pastry. Brush the surface with egg. Cut a 2 cm 'X' incision in the middle.

Bake – Remove the hot tray from the oven. Transfer the pies onto the baking tray, leaving them on the paper. Bake for 30 minutes or until deep golden. Serve with tomato sauce!

NOTES

1 Substitute with non-alcoholic red wine or more beef stock.

2 Puff pastry is easiest to work with when it is just thawed enough to cut without breaking. The more it thaws, the stickier and more difficult it is to handle. If it gets too sweaty and sticky, just pop it back in the freezer for 5 minutes to let it firm up a bit. Also – butter puff pastry is tastier than oil-based puff pastry!

3 The puff pastry pieces should be 12.5 cm squares, or thereabouts.

4 Putting each pie on a separate piece of paper makes it easier to press the edges with a fork to seal because you can rotate each piece as you press.

5 Make ahead: Uncooked assembled pies can be refrigerated for 24 hours, but do not brush with egg until just before baking.

LEFTOVERS Fridge 3 days, freezer 3 months.

CHICKEN GUINNESS STEW

The faster (and cheaper!) way to make everybody's favourite Irish Guinness stew!

SERVES: 4–5 | PREP: 10 MINUTES | COOK: 45 MINUTES

It might not be traditional, but chicken goes brilliantly with the dark and malty notes of Guinness in this much-loved Irish stew. Not only is it more affordable than the usual beef version, it's also far quicker to stew. I use bone-in pieces of chicken and simmer it all for just 30 minutes, keeping the chicken pieces lovely and juicy. Just add a side of mash to soak up all that rich-flavoured goodness!

CHICKEN

4 bone-in, skin-on chicken thighs[1] (or more drumsticks)

4 chicken drumsticks[1] (or more thighs)

½ tsp salt*

½ tsp black pepper

GUINNESS STEW

50 g unsalted butter

1 brown onion, halved, cut into 1 cm thick wedges

350 g button mushrooms, halved

2 garlic cloves*, finely minced

3 thyme sprigs

375 ml (1½ cups) Guinness beer[2]

3 tbsp plain flour

750 ml (3 cups) low-salt beef stock*

¼ tsp salt*

1 tsp black pepper

TO SERVE

Creamy Mashed Potato (page 330)

Fresh thyme sprigs (optional)

Season chicken – Sprinkle the chicken all over with the salt and pepper.

Brown chicken – Melt the butter in a large, deep heavy-based pan* or large pot*[3] over medium–high heat until foaming. Place the chicken in the pan. For the thighs, cook the skin side for 5–8 minutes or until golden, then turn and cook the flesh side for 1 minute. Transfer to a plate. For the drumsticks, do your best to brown them, rotating as needed – it's a bit hard because of the shape.

Sauté mushrooms – The butter in the pan is now browned, which means extra tasty sauce! Add the onion and cook for 1 minute. Add the mushrooms and cook for 5 minutes, until light golden. Stir in the garlic and thyme for the last 30 seconds.

Make sauce – Add the Guinness, turn the heat to high, and simmer rapidly until the sauce reduces by two-thirds, about 3 minutes. Add the flour and stir for 1 minute, then add the beef stock, salt and pepper. Stir until there are no flour lumps, then return the chicken to the sauce, pushing it down between the mushrooms so it is submerged as much as possible.

Simmer – Bring the sauce to a simmer, then reduce the heat to medium. Simmer gently for 30 minutes, stirring around the chicken every now and then so the base doesn't catch, until the sauce thickens into a gravy. The internal temperature of the chicken should be 72°C or slightly higher.

Serve – Place the mashed potato in bowls. Put a thigh and drumstick on top, then smother with the sauce. Sprinkle with thyme sprigs (if using), then dig in!

NOTES

1 Though this recipe can be made with boneless, skinless chicken thighs or breast, because they cook more quickly and are not as juicy, the sauce will not be quite as flavourful. However, to use these, simmer the sauce without the chicken for 10 minutes. Add the chicken and simmer on medium–low for 7–10 minutes or until the internal temperature reaches 72°C for thighs and 67°C for breast.

2 Guinness is a dark Irish beer (stout) that adds depth of flavour and complexity into the gravy, as well as giving it a deep, rich dark brown colour. Substitute with another stout or dark beer, or dry red wine.

3 The pan needs to be quite deep or you may have trouble containing all the sauce! The cast-iron pan pictured is 2.5 litres and 30 cm wide. A large pot* will also work. If your pan or pot is not big enough to fit all the chicken in a single layer, do this step in two batches.

LEFTOVERS Fridge 3 days, freezer 3 months.

AUBERGINE PARMIGIANA BOATS

No fussy frying or layering needed with these divine baked parmigiana aubergines.

SERVES: 4 | PREP: 15 MINUTES + 30 MINUTES SWEATING | COOK: 55 MINUTES

These aubergines are everything you cherish about aubergine parmigiana: creamy and juicy aubergine, garlicky Italian red sauce sandwiching gooey melted mozzarella, all blanketed with an irresistible crunchy breadcrumb crust. However, by baking the aubergine as halves, we save on a load of work! Weeknight aubergine parmigiana just became a reality. Each half also makes the perfect serving size for one – ideal for entertaining, especially as they're meat-free. Serves four with a side of Old-school Butter-oozing Garlic Bread (page 323), my 30-second Rocket Salad (page 315) and Hot Butterscotch Cake with Butterscotch Sauce (page 302) for dessert, or two as a (very!) hearty main without any sides.

AUBERGINE

2 x 400 g aubergines

½ tsp salt*

1 tbsp olive oil, plus extra to serve

CRUNCHY TOPPING

20 g (⅓ cup) panko breadcrumbs*

⅛ tsp salt*

1 tbsp extra-virgin olive oil

CHEESE

125 g mozzarella, grated*

50 g parmesan*, grated using a box grater[1]

SUGO (TOMATO SAUCE)

1 tbsp extra-virgin olive oil

3 garlic cloves*, finely minced

½ brown onion, finely chopped

800 g can chopped tomatoes

½ tsp salt*

½ tsp black pepper

10 g (¼ cup) basil leaves, plus extra to serve (recommended but not critical)

½ tsp white sugar[2], if needed

Sweat aubergines – Cut each aubergine in half lengthways, then use a small sharp knife to score 2 cm diamonds in the flesh – take care to not cut through the skin. Rub the flesh of each aubergine with the salt, opening the cuts to get a bit of salt into the crevices. Set aside for 30 minutes, then squeeze gently like a sponge to remove any excess water. (See note 3 to skip the salting.)

Toppings – Mix the crunchy topping ingredients in a bowl. Mix together the grated cheeses in another bowl.

Preheat the oven to 200°C (180°C fan).

Bake aubergine – Place the aubergine in a baking pan, flesh-side up. Pat the flesh dry using paper towels. Drizzle with the oil, then bake for 30 minutes or until the flesh is soft (larger and older aubergines will take longer).

Make sauce – Meanwhile, heat the oil in a large saucepan* over medium heat. Add the garlic and onion and cook until light golden. Add the remaining sauce ingredients, except the sugar, then stir and bring to a simmer. Reduce the heat to medium–low and cook, stirring regularly, for 20 minutes, until the sauce becomes thick and chunky. Halfway through, taste the sauce and if it seems sour, add the sugar.

Assemble – Spread the sauce on the surface of each aubergine. Cover with the cheese, then the panko mix. Bake for a further 25 minutes or until the cheese is melted.

Serve – Transfer to a serving plate. Drizzle with an extra swish of olive oil and sprinkle with fresh basil leaves, if desired, then dig in![4]

NOTES

1. You'll get the best flavour grating your own parmesan, but for this recipe it's okay to use parmesan that you buy grated.
2. Not all canned tomatoes are created equal. Better quality are sweeter, economical ones can be quite sour. If your sauce tastes a little sour, add the sugar.
3. No time for salting? Skip it. Bake as per the recipe (expect to add another 5–10 minutes – salting also reduces the cook time). Drain and discard any excess salty water, then proceed with the recipe.
4. I usually just eat the flesh out of the skin, but feel free to eat the skin if you wish (though bear in mind that sometimes the skin of older aubergines can be a little chewy).

LEFTOVERS Will keep for 3 days, but this is one of those dishes best made fresh. Not suitable for freezing.

JB'S 20-MINUTE LAKSA

Ridiculously fast. Irritatingly good.

SERVES: 4 | PREP AND COOK TIME: 20 MINUTES

This is a laksa recipe created by a chef in my team, Jean-Baptiste 'JB' Alexandre. It turns out that being trained in Michelin Star restaurants gives you nifty skills beyond plating microscopic piles of food with tweezers! Like: how to take my full-blown laksa recipe (from my first cookbook) – which takes over an hour to make involving a semi-homemade soup stock – and create a 20-minute version that is 90% as good. I was actually cross with him because this is irritatingly *too* good, and now I'm wondering whether anyone will bother using my best laksa recipe when you can make something nearly as good in less than half the time!! A key here is the use of prawns for the protein, which helps flavour the broth. You can substitute with fish, but if you use chicken or another animal protein, you'll find the depth of flavour in the broth is not quite as good.

---

1 tbsp vegetable oil

180 g (2/3 cup) laksa paste[1] (Por Kwan brand)

400 ml full-fat coconut cream*[2]

1 litre (4 cups) low-salt chicken stock*[3]

250 g dried rice vermicelli noodles

24 raw prawns*[4] (250 g), peeled and deveined (tails on or off)

4 baby bok choy[5], large stems cut in half lengthways so they're roughly the same size

8 fried tofu puffs[6], cut in half

3 tbsp fish sauce

1 tbsp+ lime juice

TO SERVE

120 g (1½ cups) bean sprouts

Fresh coriander leaves (highly recommended)

1 or 2 red bird's eye chillies*, finely sliced (optional)

2 tbsp crispy fried shallots* (optional)

Lime wedges

Soup broth – Heat the oil in a small pot* over medium heat. Add the laksa paste and cook for 3 minutes, stirring constantly, until the paste darkens in colour. Don't shortcut this step, it's key for good flavour in this fast laksa. Reduce the heat if it's catching on the base of the pot. Stir in the coconut cream. Once small bubbles appear, simmer for 5 minutes. Stir in the stock, bring back up to a simmer, then cook for a further 5 minutes.

Noodles – Meanwhile, prepare the noodles according to the packet directions. Drain well, shaking off any excess water, and divide among four bowls.

Finish soup – Add the prawns, bok choy and tofu puffs to the broth and simmer for 3 minutes. Stir in the fish sauce and lime juice.

Serve – Ladle the soup broth and all the add-ins over the noodles. Top with bean sprouts, coriander leaves, chilli and crispy fried shallots (if using) and serve lime wedges on the side. Dig in!

NOTES

1 My favourite brand is Por Kwan, which is sold at Asian stores and some independent grocery stores. The laksa pastes made by mainstream Westernised Asian brands sold at grocery stores tend to be too sweet and lack depth of flavour.

2 Coconut cream, rather than coconut milk*, is needed to give the broth sufficient flavour and richness to serve four people using just one can.

3 I know it sounds strange to use chicken stock for a prawn laksa, but it's far better than carton fish stock!

4 This quick laksa relies on the juices of the prawns to add flavour into the soup broth. Fish can also be used with a similar flavour result. Use medium or large prawns – total 250 g peeled weight, or 400 g before peeling (whole, including head and shell). I personally find chicken does not make the soup as tasty, but if you really want to make this with chicken, use strips of boneless, skinless chicken thigh.

5 Substitute with other leafy Asian greens, spinach or green beans.

6 Fried tofu puffs have a puffy, spongy texture and soak up the soup broth so it squirts in your mouth when you bite into them – one of the signature joys of laksa! Find them in some larger grocery stores and Asian grocery stores in the fridge section.

LEFTOVERS Fridge 3 days, freezer 3 months. Keep noodles separate from the broth and add-ins.

BEEF POT-FRIED RICE

No need for day-old rice, this ingenious fried-rice-in-a-pot starts with uncooked rice!

SERVES: 4–5 | PREP: 10 MINUTES | COOK: 30 MINUTES

Fried rice as a dish, in my opinion, is an overachiever. It's thrifty. It's easy. It's fast. It's flexible. And it's so tasty you'll find it in restaurants as often as homes. But it has one Achilles heel. To make it you need day-old cooked rice already kicking around. My solution: a fried rice recipe that starts with uncooked rice. Once the base ingredients are cooked off, I add raw rice plus stock, then 15 minutes later, voilà: pot-fried rice! I've added a good amount of vegetables as well as protein so I can serve it as a meal. I like the beefy flavour of beef mince in this, but it works just as well with chicken, turkey, lamb or pork – or even just double up the vegetables.

---

2 tbsp vegetable oil

2 garlic cloves*, finely minced

½ brown onion, finely chopped

500 g beef mince[1]

300 g (1½ cups) long-grain white rice[2], not rinsed

335 g (2½ cups) frozen mixed diced vegetables (carrots, peas and corn)[3]

625 ml (2½ cups) low-salt chicken stock*

SAUCE

2 tbsp Chinese cooking wine*[4]

3 tbsp oyster sauce

1½ tbsp light soy sauce*

1½ tsp dark soy sauce*[5] (or more light soy sauce)

¼ tsp white pepper (or black pepper)

SESAME EGGS

1 tbsp sesame oil*

3 eggs, lightly whisked

⅛ tsp salt*

TO SERVE

2 spring onion* stems, finely sliced

Sauce – Mix the sauce ingredients in a bowl. Set aside.

Cook beef – Heat the vegetable oil in a large heavy-based pot* over high heat. Add the garlic and onion and cook for 1 minute, stirring constantly. Add the beef and cook, breaking it up as you go, until you no longer see pink. Add 3 tablespoons of the sauce and cook for a further 3 minutes, stirring every now and then, or until the beef is nicely browned.

Cook rice – Add the rice and frozen vegetables. Stir for 1 minute or until the rice grains become translucent and coated with the oil. Add the stock and remaining sauce. Stir, then let it come to a simmer. Reduce the heat to low, cover with a lid, then cook for 15 minutes or until the liquid is absorbed (quickly lift the lid and tilt the pot to check).

Sesame eggs – While the rice is cooking, heat the sesame oil in a large non-stick frying pan* over medium–low heat. Add the eggs and salt. Use a rubber spatula to leisurely stir the eggs as they set, until barely cooked. Transfer to a bowl and set aside.

Rest and serve – Remove the pot of rice and vegetables from the stove. Leave to rest, with the lid still on (no peeking!), for 10 minutes. Remove the lid and add the scrambled eggs and spring onion. Use a fork to fluff the rice (which will chop up the eggs), then serve.

NOTES

1. Or chicken, turkey, lamb or pork.
2. Substitute with medium-grain white rice or basmati rice. Short-grain rice (sushi rice) will also work but the cooked rice will be a little stickier. This recipe is not suitable for jasmine rice, brown rice, risotto rice or wild rice. There is no need to rinse the rice if you purchase it in packets from the grocery store, this recipe uses the right ratio of rice to liquid so the rice will not be mushy and sticky. But if you insist on rinsing the rice (or are concerned about cleanliness), reduce the stock by 2½ tablespoons (to account for the water-logging in your rice).
3. I have always used a frozen vegetable mix for my fried rice, and I'm pretty sure my local Chinese restaurant does too! It's the right mix of vegetables and it's handy. If you're a better person than me, dice your own and add an extra 2 tablespoons of chicken stock (fresh vegetables don't leach as much water as frozen vegetables).
4. Or mirin* or dry sherry. If you can't consume alcohol, omit and add an extra 1 tablespoon of light soy sauce.
5. Dark soy sauce stains the beef and rice a mahogany colour, as well as adding a richer soy flavour than light soy sauce.

LEFTOVERS Fridge 2 days, freezer 3 months.

MINI MEATBALL SOUP

A chunky minestrone-vibe soup starring super fast, no-roll meatballs!

SERVES: 5 | PREP: 15 MINUTES | COOK: 30 MINUTES

I love meatballs (who doesn't?). But the tedious task of shaping them for me is more 'eye roll' than 'I roll', especially if they're best made small, like in this charming pot of minestrone-inspired soup. But there's an answer, and it couldn't be simpler! Just use thin sausages, cut into small chunks. Instant meatballs! They make the perfect size for scooping up in a spoon alongside the pasta, beans and vegetables that pack this tomato-rich soup. I like to add a splash of cream to give this soup a lovely rounded finish, but feel free to leave it out.

---

2 tbsp olive oil

500 g thin beef sausages[1] (or chicken, pork or lamb sausages), cut into 2 cm pieces

1 brown onion, finely chopped

2 garlic cloves*, finely minced

½ tsp dried oregano

½ tsp dried basil

½ tsp dried chilli flakes* (optional)

80 ml (⅓ cup) chardonnay or other dry white wine*[2]

1 litre (4 cups) low-salt chicken stock*

250 ml (1 cup) water

400 g can chopped tomatoes

400 g can red kidney beans, drained

½ tsp sugar (any type), if needed[3]

¾ tsp salt*

¼ tsp black pepper

135 g (1 cup) ditalini, small macaroni, small shells or similar

50 g (2 lightly packed cups) kale leaves*, torn into bite-sized pieces

60 ml (¼ cup) double cream*

TO SERVE

Freshly grated parmesan*

Brown sausage meatballs – Heat the oil in a large pot* over high heat. Add the sausage and cook, stirring constantly, for 3 minutes or until browned on the surface but still raw inside. Transfer to a bowl using a slotted spoon.

Simmer soup – Add the onion, garlic, oregano, basil and chilli flakes (if using) to the same pot. Cook for 3 minutes or until the onion is softened. Add the white wine and let it simmer rapidly, stirring to loosen any golden bits stuck to the base of the pot, until the wine is mostly evaporated. Add the stock, water, tomatoes, beans, sugar (if using), salt and pepper. Add the meatballs, including any juices pooled in the bowl. Stir, bring to a simmer and cook for 5 minutes.

Add pasta – Add the pasta, stir, then cook for the time required as per the packet directions. Stir every now and then so the base doesn't catch. Just before the pasta is ready, stir in the kale and cream until the kale is slightly wilted.

Serve – Ladle the soup into bowls and serve sprinkled with parmesan, then dive in with a spoon!

NOTES

1 Skip the really economical sausages that are a uniform pink colour. Look for good-quality ones made with more meat and less fillers, with specks of fat. Read the ingredients label or ask your butcher – aim for 90%+ meat. I like to use beef because it browns the best. However, sausages made from other meats work just as well! Just make sure they are thin sausages because they work much better for this mini meatball shortcut than fat sausages.

2 For a non-alcoholic version, use non-alcoholic white wine or substitute with water.

3 Not all canned tomatoes are created equal. Economical brands tend to be on the sour side so adding a touch of sugar is recommended. If you're using good-quality tomatoes, you won't need the sugar.

LEFTOVERS Fridge 3 days, freezer 3 months. Either way, drain the soup using a colander set over a large bowl and store the pasta and meatballs separate from the liquid (or the pasta will bloat).

SINGAPORE CHILLI PRAWNS

Everything you love about Singapore chilli crab, done with prawns!

SERVES: 4 | PREP: 15 MINUTES | COOK: 20 MINUTES

Singapore's famous chilli crab deserves its reputation. Who doesn't love getting their hands filthy tearing into mighty hunks of mud crab smothered with that phenomenally moreish chilli sauce? Of course, this is a dish for special rather than everyday occasions. So here's a version with the signature chilli sauce, using prawns instead. It's (way!) easier and (way!) more accessible. Note I've deliberately left the shells on the prawns, so you still get the same shell-sucking, finger-licking feasting experience and the soul of the dish remains intact, plus the sauce needs all the juices from whole prawns! All that's left to do now is gather a stack of napkins and a bunch of your favourite people ...

---

60 ml (1/4 cup) vegetable oil

1 tbsp dried belachan paste[1], chopped into 5 mm pieces

260 g (1 cup) tomato passata*

125 ml (1/2 cup) sweet chilli sauce

2 tbsp ketchup* or tomato sauce

250 ml (1 cup) water

3 tbsp white vinegar

1.2 kg large tiger or king prawns, whole, raw[2]

CHILLI PASTE

5 long red (cayenne) chillies*, deseeded and roughly chopped

2 tbsp miso paste (red or white), or taucu paste[3] if you can find it

6 garlic cloves, roughly chopped

3 eschalots*, peeled and roughly chopped

30 g (1/4 cup) roughly chopped ginger

TO SERVE

2 tbsp roughly chopped coriander leaves

2 tbsp finely sliced spring onion*

12 mantou buns[4], heated as per the packet directions, or small brioche buns

Chilli paste – Place the chillies, miso or taucu paste, garlic, eschalot and ginger into a jug wide enough to fit the head of a stick blender. Blitz into a paste for about 10 seconds on high, then set aside.

Toast belachan – Heat the oil in a large pot* over medium–high heat. Add the belachan and cook, stirring constantly, for 2 minutes. The smell will not be pleasant at this stage but have faith! I wouldn't put you through this if it wasn't worth it!

Sauce – Add the chilli paste and cook, stirring constantly, for 3 minutes, until it changes from red to crimson. Add the passata and stir for 2 minutes. Add the sweet chilli sauce, ketchup, water and vinegar and stir to combine. Once it comes to the boil, add the prawns. Toss to coat in the sauce, then put a lid on the pot. Cook for 5 minutes (for medium prawns) or 8 minutes (for very large prawns).

Serve – Tip all the prawns and sauce into a large serving bowl. Sprinkle with the coriander and spring onion. Pile the mantou buns in a bowl and serve on the side.

Eating – To eat, spoon some prawns and plenty of sauce into a bowl. Use your hands to remove the prawn head and shell, then dunk the prawn meat into the sauce and eat! Use the mantou buns to mop up the sauce in your bowl.

NOTES

1 Dried shrimp paste sold in crumbly blocks, available at large grocery stores or Asian grocery stores.

2 I like to use large-ish prawns around 8–10 cm long, though this recipe works with smaller or larger prawns.

3 Traditional Singapore chilli crab sauce is made with taucu paste, which is a sweet and savoury soybean paste. Find it in Asian grocery stores. But then I substituted it with miso paste and I couldn't tell the difference at all. So the miso paste version has become my base recipe because it's sold 'everywhere' these days. You can use red or white (shiro) miso paste.

4 Mantou buns are soft, white, steamed Asian bread rolls that are sold in the freezer section of Asian grocery stores. Don't freak out if you can't find them! You just need any soft white bread to dunk into the sauce. I usually just use small brioche buns.

LEFTOVERS Fridge 2 days. Not suitable for freezing.

BPA FREE
BPA FREE

WHAT YOU'VE GOT ON HAND

Make dinner tonight without going to the store!

INDIAN LENTIL COCONUT STEW-SOUP

A cosy, spice-infused bowl of deliciousness with dal vibes.

SERVES: 4 AS A SOUP, 8 AS A STEW OVER RICE | PREP: 10 MINUTES | COOK: 20 MINUTES

This is absurdly tasty for something I made up on a whim purely from what I had in the pantry! Think dal meets Indian coconut curry, and you're somewhere in the ballpark. I couldn't decide if it was more a thick soup for dunking flatbreads, or a stew for serving over rice. So a bet each way: I call it stew-soup! If you use coconut oil instead of ghee, this dish is also suitable for vegans. (I mean, is there anything this recipe can't do?)

---

400 ml coconut milk*

2 tbsp ghee*[1] or coconut oil*

3 garlic cloves*, finely minced

1 brown onion, finely chopped

400 g can chopped tomatoes

750 ml (3 cups) water

200 g (1 cup) dried split red lentils[2]

400 g can chickpeas, drained

SPICES

½ tsp cayenne pepper or chilli powder*[3]

½ tsp ground ginger[3]

1 tsp ground turmeric[3]

1 tsp curry powder[4]

1 tsp ground cumin

1½ tsp salt*

2 tsp ground coriander

TO SERVE (OPTIONAL)

Pinch of dried chilli flakes*

Coriander leaves

Rice (see pages 318–21)

Reserve coconut milk – Set aside 60 ml (¼ cup) of the coconut milk for drizzling.

Sauté aromatics – Melt the ghee in a large pot* over medium–high heat. Add the garlic and onion and cook for 3 minutes until the onion is translucent. Add the spices and stir for 1 minute.

Simmer – Add the tomatoes, remaining coconut milk, water, lentils and chickpeas. Stir, then once it comes to a simmer, reduce the heat to medium–low/low. Simmer gently for 15 minutes, uncovered, stirring every now and then to ensure the base doesn't catch, until the lentils are soft and creamy and mostly broken down.

Serve – Ladle into bowls if you see this as a soup (pictured), or over rice if you consider it a stew. Either way, drizzle generously with the reserved coconut milk, a pinch of dried chilli flakes, if you like (I do), and coriander leaves if you have them (I did). Devour!

NOTES

1 Use whichever of these fats you have. Ghee adds an intense buttery-ness, while coconut oil adds fabulous extra coconut flavour. I alternate between the two. Substitute with butter or any plain oil.

2 Yellow split lentils and split peas will also work here as a direct substitute, but the colour of your dish will be different. Whole dried green or brown lentils are also great but will take 10–15 minutes longer – add extra water if it gets too thick. Puy lentils (aka French lentils) don't work as well here because they are firmer.

3 Cayenne pepper – just adds a background warmth; feel free to omit or dial it up! Ginger – substitute with 1½ teaspoons of finely minced fresh ginger*; sauté with the garlic. Turmeric – substitute with ½ teaspoon of finely grated fresh turmeric; sauté with the garlic.

4 Just regular curry powder from grocery stores is fine here. Mild – or spicy, if you want!

LEFTOVERS Fridge 4 days, freezer 3 months.

PEA PESTO PASTA

The humble frozen pea turned showstopper!

SERVES: 5 | PREP: 10 MINUTES | COOK: 20 MINUTES

Frozen peas are hands down the greatest frozen vegetable ever invented. Sweet, colourful, cheap and easy to prepare, there are a million uses for these little green wonders. One of my favourite things to make is pea pesto. It's luscious and visually striking, while the flavours echo the familiar flavours of pesto. I love using short pasta tubes because the creamy pea pesto fills the inside, so you almost feel like you're eating ravioli with each bite! But long pastas like spaghetti or fettuccine work just as well.

PASTA

1 tbsp salt*, for cooking the pasta

500 g penne or other short pasta of choice

PEA PESTO

280 g (2 cups) frozen peas

50 g (⅓ cup) pine nuts, toasted*[1]

2 garlic cloves, peeled (kept whole)

80 ml (⅓ cup) extra-virgin olive oil

4 tbsp lemon juice[2]

100 g (2 very tightly packed cups) baby spinach (or frozen spinach, thawed and lightly squeezed to remove excess water)

50 g (½ tightly packed cup) finely grated parmesan*[3]

1 tsp salt*

½ tsp black pepper

TO SERVE

Parmesan*, shaved using a vegetable peeler

Cook pasta – Bring a large pot* of water to the boil with the 1 tablespoon of salt. Add the pasta and cook according to the packet directions. Just before draining, scoop out 500 ml (2 cups) of the pasta cooking water, then drain the pasta in a colander.

Boil peas – While the pasta is cooking, make the pea pesto. Bring a large saucepan* of water to the boil. Add the peas, bring the water back up to the boil, then turn off the heat and leave to cool for 2 minutes. Drain in a colander. Measure out 35 g (¼ cup) of peas and set them aside for garnish.

Pea pesto – Transfer the remaining hot peas to a jug large enough to fit the head of a stick blender. Add 35 g (¼ cup) of the pine nuts (reserve the rest for garnish), the garlic, oil and lemon juice. Blitz on high for 10 seconds, moving the stick blender around as needed, until the peas are pureed – it will not be completely smooth. Add the spinach in two or three batches and blitz until smooth.[4] Add the remaining pesto ingredients, then blitz until smooth, though there will be some tiny bits of pine nuts, which is nice for a little soft crunch. Set aside.

Toss – Return the pasta to the pot. Add all the pea pesto plus 250 ml (1 cup) of the reserved pasta cooking water. Toss well until the pasta is coated with the pesto, using extra pasta cooking water if required to loosen the pasta.

Serve – Divide among bowls and serve garnished with the reserved peas, pine nuts and parmesan shavings.

NOTES

1. Walnuts are a great alternative here. Almonds and pecans also work well.
2. Substitute with apple cider vinegar, white wine vinegar or champagne vinegar.
3. Store-bought grated parmesan (the sandy type) will work in this recipe, though I encourage you to grate your own if you can, as freshly grated has better flavour.
4. Scrunch the spinach up in your hand before pushing it tightly into the jug. This stops the spinach from flying everywhere when you start to blitz.

LEFTOVERS Fridge 3 days, freezer 3 months.

SPICY PEANUT NOODLES

An Excellent Emergency Spicy Asian Food Fix. (Caps intentional.)

SERVES: 1 | PREP: 10 MINUTES | COOK: 10 MINUTES

As people in my life will tell you, 'Can we have spicy Asian food?' is a plea that comes out of my mouth a lot. Chilli hotpots, curries, sambals, spicy soups – I crave it all! There's something about the wild and bold flavours of tongue-scorching Asian dishes that has me hopelessly hooked. My itch for a hit can raise its head without warning, so when it needs scratching at home in a hurry these spicy peanut noodles are what I turn to. I always make sure I stock everything I need to make these in a snap. Make these once, and I dare say you will too!

---

100 g dried noodles[1] (I use wide ribbon wheat noodles – dao xiao mian – but any type works)

SAUCE

1 tbsp natural unsweetened smooth peanut butter*[2]

½ tsp finely grated garlic*

2 tsp oyster sauce

2 tsp light soy sauce*[3]

2 tsp rice wine vinegar[4]

2 tsp chilli crisp*[5] or sriracha*, plus extra to serve

SIZZLING OIL

1½ tbsp sesame oil*

EXTRAS (RECOMMENDED)

15 g (¼ cup) finely sliced spring onion* (about 1 stem)

2 tbsp finely chopped salted peanuts

Cook noodles – Cook the noodles according to the packet directions. Just before draining, scoop out 125 ml (½ cup) of the noodle cooking water, then drain the noodles in a colander. Rinse very briefly under tap water to remove the excess starch, then shake off any excess water.

Sauce – Meanwhile, put the sauce ingredients in a medium bowl in the order listed. No need to mix.

Sizzling oil – Heat the oil in a small saucepan* or small frying pan* over medium heat. Once hot, pour the oil over the sauce in the bowl. Enjoy the (small!) sizzle, then stir to combine.

Toss – Add the spring onion, hot noodles and 60 ml (¼ cup) of the reserved noodle cooking water to the bowl. Toss well, using more reserved noodle cooking water as needed to loosen. Serve sprinkled with peanuts and extra chilli crisp, if desired.

NOTES

1. I've used wide, dried flat wheat noodles (pictured) from an Asian grocery store – my current obsession! But this dish is excellent with any dried noodles or ramen you have, such as egg or rice noodles. Even pasta works! If you've got fresh noodles (i.e. from the fridge section of the grocery store), you'll need 150 g.
2. Substitute with (in order of recommendation): Chinese sesame paste*, regular sweetened peanut butter spread or tahini*.
3. Can be substituted with all-purpose soy sauce*. Do not use dark soy sauce* as the flavour is too intense.
4. Substitute with apple cider vinegar.
5. Use any Asian chilli sauce or paste you want. Just be mindful of spiciness! You can always add more to taste at the end.

LEFTOVERS Fridge 3 days. Not suitable for freezing.

BLACK BEAN CHILLI

Beans baked in my chilli con carne sauce under a blanket of cheese. Hello, delicious!

SERVES: 5 | **PREP: 10 MINUTES** | **COOK: 40 MINUTES**

I wondered what would happen if I made my chilli con carne using cans of black beans hiding in the back of my pantry instead of beef mince. As it turns out ... very good things indeed! These earthy beans marry with the richly spiced chilli sauce like soulmates from birth. The whole thing is topped with a blanket of cheese to make everything better and then baked. Serve the chilli with corn chips or warm tortillas for dunking and scooping. Otherwise it's perfect over rice and pasta, or stuffed into jacket potatoes and big soft rolls as sloppy joes. Have black beans ever sounded so damned fabulous?

CHILLI CON CARNE

2 tbsp olive oil

½ brown onion, finely diced

2 garlic cloves*, finely minced

2 tsp dried oregano

½ red bell pepper, deseeded and chopped into 1 cm squares

2 tbsp tomato paste

250 ml (1 cup) low-salt vegetable stock*

400 g can chopped tomatoes

1 tsp salt*

1 tsp white sugar

2 x 400 g cans black beans, drained

200 g (2 cups) grated* cheddar cheese

SPICES

1 tsp cayenne pepper[1] (reduce for less spicy)

1 tsp garlic powder[1]

1 tsp onion powder[1]

3 tsp smoked paprika* (or ordinary paprika)

2 tsp ground cumin

TO SERVE (CHOOSE)

Sour cream or plain yoghurt

Corn chips, warmed tortillas*, rice, cooked pasta, pita pockets, soft rolls, baked potatoes

Preheat the oven to 180°C (160°C fan).

Sauté – Heat the oil in a 26 cm cast-iron frying pan* or large ovenproof pan* over medium–high heat. Add the onion, garlic and oregano and cook for 2 minutes. Add the pepper and cook for 1 minute. Add the tomato paste and cook for 2 minutes, stirring constantly, until the colour of the tomato paste becomes a dark red.

Sauce – Add the stock, stir, then simmer for 5 minutes or until reduced by about one-quarter. Add the tomatoes, salt, sugar and spices. Stir, then simmer for a further 5 minutes, stirring every now and then, until the sauce has reduced and thickened.[2]

Bake – Turn the stove off. Add the beans and stir. Cover with the cheese, then bake in the oven for 25 minutes or until the cheese is melted and golden.

Serve – Remove from the oven. Rest for 5 minutes, then place the pan on the table so everyone can help themselves!

NOTES

1 Spice substitution options: cayenne pepper can be substituted with chilli powder*. Garlic powder can be switched with more onion powder, and vice versa.

2 The sauce will not reduce further in the oven, so get it to the desired thickness on the stove before you bake.

LEFTOVERS Fridge 4 days, freezer 3 months.

VIETNAMESE PIZZA

Go wild on toppings and make it your own with this super quick, classic Vietnamese street food!

SERVES: 1 | PREP: 3 MINUTES | COOK: 5 MINUTES

No, I didn't invent this! It's a home-friendly riff on the popular Vietnamese street food bánh tráng nướng – rice paper sheets covered with egg, toppings and sauce, grilled over charcoal until the rice paper turns crispy. Basically a Vietnamese 'pizza'! Like pizza, the toppings are a bit of a free-for-all. Traditionally you might see pork floss, sausage, dried prawns and corn. I'm using canned tuna here but go with whatever you like. Finish it with a drizzle of mayonnaise plus a spicy or sweet sauce like sriracha, hoisin or sweet chilli. These little babies are irresistible, I tell you! And done in 8 minutes flat.

---

1 x 22 cm round, dried rice paper sheet[1]

1 egg, whisked

90 g can tuna, preferably in oil, drained (or any other scatterable thing of choice)[2]

Sriracha*[3], for drizzling

Kewpie mayonnaise*, for drizzling

1 tbsp finely sliced spring onion*[4]

Crisp rice paper – Heat a non-stick frying pan over medium–high heat. Place the rice paper sheet in. Leave for 1 minute to start crisping (white patches will begin appearing). If it curls, use spatulas to flatten it as best you can, but don't fret too much as it will get weighed down by the toppings.

Egg – Slowly pour the egg into the middle of the rice paper, using a rubber spatula to push it back onto the rice paper if it starts to run off. As the egg starts to set, coax it to spread over the rice paper like pizza sauce, leaving a border around the edge of the rice paper for gripping. No need to be meticulous here – it's fine if there's leakage!

Toppings – Turn the heat down to medium–low. Sprinkle with tuna chunks. Cook until the egg is set and the base is crisp, about 2 minutes.

Serve – Slide onto a cutting board. Cut into wedges, then immediately slide onto a serving plate. Drizzle with sriracha and mayonnaise, then sprinkle with spring onion. Eat immediately while the base is crispy!

NOTES

1 Readily available these days in the Asian or noodle aisle of grocery stores. An excellent way to use up left-over rice paper after making Crispy Rice Paper Fish Rolls on page 48.

2 Think cooked sausage, bacon, chicken, ham, left-over roast meat, prawn, flaked fish. There are no rules!

3 Or hoisin, sweet chilli sauce or other hot sauce of choice.

4 Substitute with finely chopped red onion, eschalots*, coriander leaves or chives.

LEFTOVERS This recipe is intended to be eaten freshly cooked as the base goes soggy as it cools.

CURRIED CHICKPEA CRUNCH

Better, faster, crispier chickpeas without deep-frying!

SERVES: 2 | PREP: 5 MINUTES | COOK: 12 MINUTES

I adore fried chickpea snacks. My arm will pump those crunchy balls from packet to mouth like a factory robot until they're all gone. But I've never been able to make a truly crispy home version without deep-frying. That is until I discovered a secret: rolling them in cornflour before pan-frying! This gives the chickpeas an extra-crunchy and craggy surface that's as close to deep-fried as you can get. I've headed in a curry-flavoured direction with mine, though feel free to change it up (see note 3). I love these chickpeas as is for snacking, but if you add a garlic yoghurt sauce and sautéed vegetables, you've got a terrific meal.

---

400 g can chickpeas[1]

3 tbsp cornflour, or rice flour

1 tsp curry powder[2]

½ tsp salt*

¼ tsp black pepper

2 tbsp extra-virgin olive oil

GARLIC YOGHURT SAUCE

260 g (1 cup) plain yoghurt

1 large garlic clove*, finely grated

¼ tsp salt*

VEG SIDES – AS PICTURED, BUT MAKE IT YOUR OWN!

1 tbsp extra-virgin olive oil

12 cherry tomatoes, halved

¼ tsp salt*

¼ tsp black pepper

80 g (2 heaped cups) baby spinach

TO SERVE (OPTIONAL)

Flatbreads, tortillas* or toast – anything for piling on/dunking/scooping

Garlic yoghurt sauce – Mix the sauce ingredients in a bowl. Set aside while you cook the chickpeas, to allow the flavours to meld.

Coat chickpeas – Drain the chickpeas in a colander. Still in the colander, sprinkle the cornflour over them, then shake to coat, allowing the excess cornflour to shake out through the colander. Transfer to a bowl. Add the curry powder, salt and pepper and toss to coat.

Crisp them – Heat the oil in a large non-stick frying pan* over medium–high heat. Add the chickpeas and cook for 7 minutes, tossing/shaking regularly, until golden and crispy. Pour into a bowl.

Sauté veg sides – Return the pan to the stove and add the oil – it should get hot very quickly. Add the cherry tomatoes, salt and pepper. Toss for 2 minutes, then add the spinach and toss for another 30 seconds or until the spinach is wilted and the tomatoes are wrinkly.

Serve – Smear yoghurt sauce onto serving plates. Pile the chickpeas on the yoghurt, then place the vegetables on the side. Eat with a spoon! Add Easy Flatbread (page 325) on the side, if desired.

NOTES

1 I use canned chickpeas for convenience. To cook your own, use 130 g (¾ cup) of dried chickpeas. This will make the equivalent of 400 g canned.

2 Just your regular curry powder from ordinary grocery stores. Use hot if you dare!

3 Feel free to use other flavours. Try paprika* with garlic and onion powder, or a store-bought mix, such as Moroccan seasoning. If you're uncertain about quantities, just start frying up plain chickpeas, then add seasoning little by little, tasting as you go.

LEFTOVERS Best made fresh as the chickpeas do lose crispiness as they cool. But they will keep for 4 days in an airtight container in the pantry. Not suitable for freezing.

CREAMY, CHEESY SPAGHETTI

An instant bowl of creamy, dreamy spaghetti in the time it takes to boil pasta.

SERVES: 2 | PREP: 8 MINUTES | COOK: 12 MINUTES

Chances are you've already got everything you need to make this bowl of slippery spaghetti smothered in a cheesy white sauce. No cream needed! We go for a simple béchamel sauce instead, and throw in handfuls of cheese until the sauce turns rich and gooey. By the time the sauce is done, so is the pasta. Toss it all together and listen to the ooooohs start around you. Decadent? Undeniably. So feel free to also add some greens or vegetables to assuage your guilt! (I declined ...!)

---

2 tsp salt*, for cooking the pasta

200 g spaghetti, or any other pasta of choice

CHEESY SAUCE

30 g unsalted butter

2 garlic cloves*, finely minced

1½ tbsp flour*

250 ml (1 cup) milk, preferably full-fat

125 g (1¼ cups) grated* cheddar cheese or other cheese of choice[1]

¼ tsp salt*

¼ tsp black pepper

TO SERVE

Freshly grated parmesan*

1 tsp finely chopped parsley (optional)

Cook pasta – Bring a large saucepan* or small pot* of water to the boil with the 2 teaspoons of salt. Cook the pasta according to the packet directions. Just before draining, scoop out 250 ml (1 cup) of the pasta cooking water, then drain the pasta in a colander.

Sauce – While the pasta is cooking, melt the butter in a large saucepan* over medium heat. Add the garlic and cook for 1 minute, stirring with a wooden spoon. Add the flour and stir for 1 minute. Switch to a whisk. While whisking, slowly pour in about half the milk, then whisk until thickened and lump-free (it will thicken fairly quickly). Pour in the remaining milk and whisk to combine. Cook for 3 minutes, whisking every now and then, until the sauce starts to thicken, which will happen as the milk heats up. Whisk more frequently as the sauce thickens.

Thicken sauce – Once the sauce is the thickness of pouring cream and coats the back of a spoon, add the cheese, salt and pepper. Stir with the wooden spoon until the cheese melts – this will further thicken the sauce.

Toss – Add the pasta and 80 ml (⅓ cup) of the reserved pasta cooking water.[2] Toss for 30 seconds or until the pasta is coated in the sauce – use the extra reserved pasta cooking water to loosen if needed.

Serve – Divide between warmed pasta bowls. Sprinkle with parmesan and parsley (if using) and serve immediately!

NOTES

1 Any melting cheese will work here. I always seem to have cheddar these days, which is an excellent all-rounder. Store-bought grated cheese is not recommended as it has anti-caking agents that may cause the sauce to be grainy.

2 The starch in the pasta cooking water will thicken the cheese sauce slightly and make it cling to the pasta strands instead of remaining in a watery pool at the bottom of the saucepan.

LEFTOVERS The sauce (before tossing with pasta) will keep for 3 days in the fridge, or 3 months in the freezer. Once the cheese sauce is tossed with the pasta, it is best eaten fresh, though leftovers will keep for 3 days in the fridge. Not suitable for freezing.

STICKY PANTRY CHICKEN – MY MAIDEN RECIPE

A clever use of pantry staples for a delicious sticky chicken!

SERVES: 4 | PREP: 5 MINUTES | COOK: 10 MINUTES

I found myself writing the introduction for this cookbook on the 10-year anniversary of my website, reminiscing about the very first recipe I ever published – this sticky chicken!! It's not strictly a pantry recipe because it includes a refrigerated protein, but there's just no way I was not going to include it in this book. And it's the only website recipe I'm including in this book, at that! This dish reflects the heart and soul of the type of recipes I like to share. Quick to make. Easy to put together. Clever use of pantry staples. Maximum flavour. And everybody loves it! It has a country-style glaze that gives the chicken a bronze glow when you fry it up. I like to make extra sauce with it too, for dousing everything on my plate. Sauce this good should be used for smothering extensively! I've used chicken here but it's brilliant with pork chops too.

---

6 pieces boneless, skinless chicken thigh[1] (800 g–1kg)

½ tsp salt*

½ tsp black pepper

1 tbsp vegetable oil

125 ml (½ cup) water

SAUCE

90 g (⅓ cup) ketchup* (or tomato sauce)

2 tbsp light or all-purpose soy sauce*[2]

1 tbsp dijon mustard

2 tbsp sriracha* (optional)

2 tbsp white vinegar or other clear vinegar

2½ tbsp honey[3]

2 garlic cloves*, finely minced

TO SERVE

Finely chopped parsley (optional)

Creamy Mashed Potato (page 330)

30-second Rocket Salad (page 315)

Sauce – Whisk the sauce ingredients in a medium bowl to combine.

Season chicken – Sprinkle each piece of chicken with the salt and pepper.

Coat chicken – Heat the oil in a large non-stick frying pan* over medium–high heat. Quickly dip a piece of chicken in the sauce, shake off the excess, then place in the pan. Repeat with the remaining chicken and sauce, cooking as many pieces at a time as you can fit in the pan. Reserve the remaining sauce.

Cook – Cook the first side of the chicken for 3 minutes until it caramelises and is dark golden. Turn and cook the other side for 2 minutes until the chicken is almost cooked through.

Simmer sauce – Add the water and the remaining sauce. Bring to a rapid simmer, stirring occasionally, scraping the bottom of the pan to get all the brown bits stuck there – free extra flavour! When the sauce has thickened (around 1–2 minutes), remove the pan from the stove. Turn the chicken in the sauce to coat.

Serve – To serve, place the chicken on a plate and spoon the sauce over. Sprinkle with parsley (if using). I like to serve this chicken over Creamy Mashed Potato to soak up the tasty sauce, with my 30-second Rocket Salad on the side.

NOTES

1 You can also use 750 g boneless, skinless chicken breast. Cut each piece in half horizontally (to make thinner 'steaks') and proceed with the recipe as written – though I recommend reducing the cook time by a couple of minutes to ensure the chicken breast does not overcook.

2 Do not use dark soy sauce* (too intense) or sweet soy sauce.

3 Substitute with maple syrup or brown sugar.

LEFTOVERS Fridge 3 days, freezer 3 months.

CRISPY SWEETCORN TUNA FRITTERS

A crunchy crust makes these miles better than the tuna fritters you know!

SERVES: 3–4 (MAKES 14 FRITTERS) | PREP: 20 MINUTES | COOK: 10 MINUTES

I had to resist adding 'awesome' to this recipe's title because I'm on the wrong side of twenty to be leaning on this word. But this one really deserves it! Canned tuna fritters are usually ho-hum at best. I think it's because they suffer from the same problem as most fritters: they're a textural yawn. Enter panko breadcrumbs! Crusting the fritters with a sprinkle of panko gives them an addictive crunch, and along with the snappy pops of sweetcorn, the am-I-eating-airline-food affliction is instantly shaken off. Tuna fritters, reborn. (Maybe that should've been the title, on second thoughts ...!)

PINK DIPPING SAUCE

185 g (¾ cup) plain yoghurt

1 garlic clove*, finely grated

1 tbsp sriracha* (for grown-ups) or ketchup* (family-friendly)

1 tbsp extra-virgin olive oil

¼ tsp salt*

FRITTERS

3 eggs

400 g can sweetcorn, drained[1]

1 tsp paprika*

1 tbsp dried parsley[2]

¼ red onion, finely chopped[3]

2 garlic cloves*, finely grated or crushed using a garlic crusher

½ tsp salt*

¼ tsp black pepper

425 g can tuna in oil, well drained

35 g (¼ cup) plain flour

COATING AND COOKING

20 g (⅓ cup) panko breadcrumbs*[4], for coating

5 tbsp olive oil, for cooking

Preheat the oven to 100°C (all oven types).

Sauce – Whisk the sauce ingredients together in a bowl. Set aside.

Fritter mixture – Place the eggs, corn, paprika, parsley, onion, garlic, salt and pepper in a bowl and mix to combine. Add the tuna and roughly mash it using a fork before mixing to combine with the other ingredients. Finally, add the flour and gently mix it through.

Form patties – Measure out tightly packed 40 g (¼ cup) portions of the mixture and tap them out onto a tray (we will flatten them later). You should get 14 patties. Sprinkle the surface with a pinch of breadcrumbs and press them in.

Cook – Heat 3 tablespoons of the olive oil in a large non-stick frying pan* over medium–high heat. Place five patties in the pan, breadcrumb-side down, then lightly flatten them using a spatula to a 1.5 cm thickness. Sprinkle the surface with breadcrumbs and lightly press them in. Cook for 2 minutes until the underside is golden and crispy. Turn carefully, using a spatula in one hand and a butter knife in the other, to stabilise the flip, then cook the other side for 2 minutes until golden and crisp. Transfer the fritters to a tray and keep them warm in the oven. Cook the remaining fritters, adding 1 tablespoon of oil per batch, wiping out loose burnt bits if needed.

Serve – Transfer the fritters to a serving plate. Serve with the sauce for dipping.

NOTES

1 Or 200 g (1½ cups) frozen sweetcorn, thawed.

2 Or dried basil, or 1½ teaspoons of dried thyme or oregano.

3 Or any onion, spring onion* or eschalots*.

4 Regular breadcrumbs can also be used, but panko work better. Better crunch!

LEFTOVERS Best made fresh, though they will keep in the fridge for 3 days. Not suitable for freezing.

LION WHITE BEANS

Originally called Lemon White Beans, the name is part of the charm!

SERVES: 3 AS A MAIN, 5–6 AS A SIDE | PREP: 10 MINUTES | COOK: 15 MINUTES

I sent this lemony stewed bean recipe to a friend with a typo in the name – Lion White Beans instead of Lemon White Beans. She never questioned it. Instead she raved: 'My mother-in-law is obsessed with your Lion Beans!' So the name has stuck. I like to include a hit of chilli in these beans – if not just because I feel a bit of attitude befits any dish with 'Lion' in the name! Feel free to omit it though. Whether you include the chilli or not, this recipe is a killer way to turn pallid canned beans into a gorgeous stew singing with citrus.

LION LEMON OIL

- 1 tbsp lemon zest
- 1/2 tsp dried chilli flakes*[1]
- 2 tbsp extra-virgin olive oil
- 1/8 tsp salt*

LION LEMONY WHITE BEANS

- 2 tbsp olive oil
- 4 garlic cloves*, minced
- 1/4 brown onion, finely chopped
- 3 fresh thyme sprigs (or 1 tsp dried thyme)
- 125 ml (1/2 cup) chardonnay, or other dry white wine*[2]
- 2 x 400 g cans cannellini beans, including all the liquid in the cans[3]
- 250 ml (1 cup) low-salt chicken stock*
- 1/4 tsp salt*
- 1/4 tsp black pepper
- 120 g (3 heaped cups) baby spinach
- 25 g (1/4 tightly packed cup) finely grated parmesan*, plus extra for serving
- 2 tbsp lemon juice

GARLIC TOAST

- 4–8 slices sourdough bread, or other bread of choice
- 1 garlic clove, cut in half
- Extra-virgin olive oil, for drizzling

TO SERVE

- 2 tbsp lemon juice

Lion lemon oil – Mix the ingredients in a small bowl and set aside.

Sauté aromatics – Heat the olive oil in a large non-stick frying pan* over medium heat. Add the garlic, onion and thyme and stir for 3 minutes or until the onion is translucent. Add the wine, stir, then turn the heat up to high and simmer rapidly for 2 minutes or until the wine is mostly evaporated.

Simmer – Add the beans (including all the liquid in the cans), the chicken stock, salt and pepper. Once it starts simmering, turn the heat down to medium–high and simmer rapidly for 5 minutes or until the sauce reduces and thickens to a thin syrup consistency. Stir in the baby spinach until it wilts. Add the parmesan and lemon juice and stir until the parmesan melts, which will thicken the sauce a little more.

Garlic toast – Meanwhile, toast the bread using whatever method suits. Lightly rub one side of the hot toasted bread with the cut face of the garlic clove, then drizzle with extra-virgin olive oil – be as liberal as you want!

Serve – Remove the pan from the stove and stir the lemon juice into the beans. Divide among serving bowls, drizzle with the lion lemon oil and sprinkle with extra parmesan. Serve with the garlic toast for dunking.

NOTES

1 The warm buzz of chilli can elevate anything, but feel free to omit or reduce. You can always sprinkle some on at the end.

2 Substitute with non-alcoholic white wine or more chicken stock.

3 Any type of canned beans will work for this recipe – large or small, any colour, any shape. Using the liquid in the can is a neat trick to thicken the sauce because it's already slightly thickened – plus, it has free bean flavour in it!

LEFTOVERS Fridge 4 days, freezer 3 months. A squeeze of lemon will help perk it up.

THE MOST AMAZING PANTRY TOMATO SOUP

Cooking down and caramelising the tomato paste is my game-changing trick.

SERVES: 4 | PREP: 5 MINUTES | COOK: 35 MINUTES

I've got a few power-tricks in this recipe that take a pantry tomato soup from 'meh' to 'mmmm!'. First, patiently cooking down the tomato paste until it caramelises, mellows and deepens the tomato taste. I also sauté the oregano to bloom the flavour, then deglaze it all with white wine. And finally, a spoonful of honey is essential for harmony by balancing the acidity. The result? A tomato soup so good you may never use fresh tomatoes again! Bonus: Skip the cream garnish and swap honey for sugar, and this soup is also 100% vegan.

- 60 ml (1/4 cup) extra-virgin olive oil
- 3 garlic cloves*, finely minced
- 1 brown onion, finely chopped
- 1 tsp dried oregano
- 100 g (1/3 cup) tomato paste
- 125 ml (1/2 cup) chardonnay wine*[1], for deglazing (optional)
- 1 tsp salt*
- 1/2 tsp black pepper, plus extra to serve
- 400 g can chopped tomatoes
- 1 litre (4 cups) low-salt vegetable stock*
- 1 tbsp honey or 2 tsp sugar (any type)

TO SERVE (OPTIONAL)

- 4 tbsp thick cream*[2]
- Parmesan Toasties (page 328)

Sauté aromatics – Heat the oil in a large pot* over medium–high heat. Add the garlic, onion and oregano and cook for 3 minutes until the onion is translucent.

Caramelise tomato paste – Reduce the heat to medium. Add the tomato paste and cook, stirring constantly, for 8 minutes or until it changes from red to dark crimson. Use a rubber spatula to prevent the tomato paste from catching and burning on the base or side of the pot, adjusting the heat as needed.[3]

Simmer – Add the wine (if using). Stir, turn the heat up to high and bring to a rapid simmer. Simmer for 2 minutes or until the wine has mostly evaporated. Add everything else. Stir, bring to the boil, then reduce the heat to medium and simmer for 20 minutes.

Serve – Blitz until smooth in the pot using a stick blender.[4] Simmer for a further 5 minutes, then ladle into bowls. Serve with a pinch of pepper and, if desired, a drizzle of cream and Parmesan Toasties for dunking.

NOTES

1. Substitute with any other dry white wine that's not too sweet or woody, or a dry red wine. Omit for a non-alcoholic version.
2. Alternatives: a drizzle of extra-virgin olive oil, coconut milk* or a shower of freshly grated parmesan*.
3. If the tomato paste gets stuck to the side or base of the pot and starts burning, dissolve it using a small splash of the vegetable stock. Once the stock has evaporated, you can recommence sautéing the tomato paste.
4. Alternatively, transfer to a jug blender. Blend in batches, with the feeder tube removed and the hole covered with a folded tea towel.

LEFTOVERS Fridge 4 days, freezer 3 months.

CHEESY BREAD CASSEROLE (STRATA)

Think custardy quiche meets cheesy French toast, tossed with anything you've got!

SERVES: 6 | PREP: 10 MINUTES | COOK: 40 MINUTES

American strata is a gem of a dish that's still undiscovered in Australia and the UK and should get way more love. Think of it as a savoury bread pudding that tastes like a quiche. It's dead simple and is also the perfect destination for fridge-dive finds. Chuck in whatever you like: left-over roast scraps, deli meats, frozen peas, random veg bits, olives, canned tuna are all great ... I've even thrown in spaghetti bolognese (yep, pasta and all!). No matter what you put into it, the bubbling, cheesy, eggy bake that emerges from your oven will be nothing short of a masterpiece, I guarantee it!

---

8 large or 10 small slices sandwich bread (350 g in total)[1], preferably slightly stale, cut in half diagonally

200 g (2 cups) grated* cheddar cheese[2] or other cheese of choice

EGG CUSTARD

½ tsp mustard powder or 1 tsp dijon mustard

1 tsp garlic powder (or 1 finely minced garlic clove*)

375 ml (1½ cups) milk, preferably full-fat

6 large eggs*

½ tsp salt*

¼ tsp black pepper

WHAT I USED – SEE NOTE 3 FOR ALTERNATIVES

150 g (1½ cups) deli ham, cut into 1.5 cm x 7 mm batons

2 spring onion* stems, finely sliced (about 55 g/1 cup)

250 g frozen spinach, thawed, then squeezed to remove excess liquid

Spray a 1.5 litre (20 x 25 cm) ceramic or glass baking dish with oil or grease it with butter.

Egg custard – Put the mustard and garlic powder in a large bowl with a small splash of the milk. Whisk until lump-free.[4] Add the remaining egg custard ingredients and whisk until combined.

Layer – Line the base of the baking dish with one-third of the bread slices, trimming/tearing as needed. Sprinkle with one-third of the ham and spring onion, then dot with one-third of the spinach. Sprinkle with one-third of the cheese, then pour over one-third of the custard. Repeat twice more. Press down firmly to ensure all the bread gets soaked with the egg mixture. Set aside to soak on the counter while the oven preheats.

Preheat the oven to 180°C (160°C fan).

Bake – Bake the strata for 40 minutes or until puffed and golden.

Serve – Remove from the oven. Heads up – it will deflate! Cut slices like frittata, or scoop out hunks and place on serving plates. Enjoy!

NOTES

1. I always seem to have regular sliced sandwich bread left over, so that's what I'm using here. If I have bread slices with a curved edge, I like to reserve those pieces for the top layer to create a decorative surface, overlapping like fish scales, as pictured. Regular sandwich bread, soft rolls and baguettes work best. Avoid chewy, crusty bread like sourdough as it does not absorb the custard well and the finished dish is not as custardy as it should be.
2. Any melting cheese will work here, though mozzarella is a little light on flavour so I'd recommend adding 50 g (½ cup) of grated parmesan* or ¼ teaspoon of extra salt into the egg mixture. Crumbled feta, goat's cheese and brie also work. Mix-and-match cheeseboard leftovers!
3. Oh, the possibilities! Cooked meats, deli meats, canned tuna, potato, corn, roasted red peppers, canned artichokes, olives. Anything that needs to be cooked (like raw meat and vegetables that require cooking) should be cooked before adding into the strata as they will not cook in the oven.
4. If your mustard or garlic powder is lumpy, crumble it between your fingers to remove the lumps.
5. Make ahead: This is ideal for preparing 24 hours ahead! Assemble and refrigerate, then bake according to the recipe directions.

LEFTOVERS Fridge 4 days, freezer 3 months. I swear it's even better the next day!

CHARLIE

By popular demand, a whole chapter of recipes dedicated to Charlie, my beloved all-purpose Chinese stir-fry sauce!

CHARLIE – MY ALL-PURPOSE STIR-FRY SAUCE

Forever change your dinner game.

MAKES: 375 ML (1½ CUPS) | PREP: 5 MINUTES

Charlie is my all-purpose stir-fry sauce. It's a classic, glossy Chinese brown sauce (hence 'Charlie' ... as in Charlie Brown!). I use it as both a sauce and flavour foundation for more dishes than you can shake a chopstick at. Whip up a jar, keep him for weeks, and you've got oodles of Chinese stir-fries (and beyond) at your fingertips! Hokkien noodles? Yum. Crispy sweet and sour pork chops? Oh yes. Sizzling beef? Charlie's all over it. Even soup? You bet!

- 125 ml (½ cup) light soy sauce*[1]
- 125 ml (½ cup) oyster sauce
- 60 ml (¼ cup) Chinese cooking wine*[2]
- 30 g (¼ cup) cornflour
- 1 tbsp white sugar
- 2 tbsp sesame oil*
- 1 tsp white pepper

Make Charlie – Place all the ingredients in a jar and shake well to combine. Store Charlie in the fridge and shake well before use. Use for any of the recipes in this chapter.

To use – Mix 3 tablespoons of Charlie with 80 ml (⅓ cup) water to make a stir-fry or stir-fried noodles for two people. Or see page 137 for **My Stir-fry Formula!**

Quantity – Makes 375 ml (1½ cups) of Charlie, enough for 16 serves of stir-fries or noodles.

NOTES

1 Can be substituted with all-purpose soy sauce*, though the sauce will be darker in colour.

2 Can be substituted with low-salt chicken stock* though this will reduce the shelf life of the sauce to 1 week.

STORAGE Fridge 6+ weeks (subject to the shelf life of the ingredients used). Shake the jar every couple of days to prevent the cornflour from settling and hardening on the base of the jar. Not suitable for freezing.

Charlie!

BUILD YOUR OWN STIR-FRIES & NOODLES

SERVES: 2 | PREP: 5 MINUTES | COOK: 5 MINUTES

Be sure to have all your ingredients measured out and ready to toss into the pan because, once you start cooking, things move fast! See overleaf for stir-fries and stir-fried noodle recipes.

---

2 tbsp vegetable oil

3 tbsp Charlie Stir-fry Sauce (page 134)

80 ml (1/3 cup) water

BASE FLAVOURINGS

1 garlic clove*, finely minced[1]

1 tsp finely minced ginger*

Fresh chillies*, finely minced

INGREDIENTS FOR A STIR-FRY

180 g (1 cup) sliced raw protein of choice[2], tenderised (optional)

450 g (4 cups) vegetables[3], cut as per pages 172–73

INGREDIENTS FOR STIR-FRIED NOODLES

180 g (1 cup) sliced raw protein of choice[2], tenderised (optional)

375 g (3 cups) vegetables[3], cut as per pages 172–73

480 g (3 cups) cooked noodles[4] of choice (250 g fresh or 150 g dry)

EXTRA FLAVOURINGS

Sriracha*, chilli crisp*, sambal oelek* or other spicy condiment

Sweet chilli sauce

Sesame oil*

Substitute the water with pineapple juice or orange juice

Thai basil*, garlic chives* or coriander leaves

Chinese five spice*

Sauté base flavourings – Heat the oil in a large frying pan* or wok over high heat. Add your choice of base flavourings (all or just one!) and stir for 10 seconds until light golden.

Stir-fry – Add the stir-fry ingredients in order of the time they take to cook, starting with the ingredients that take the longest (e.g. onion, proteins and carrot first, leaving leafy greens like cabbage and Asian greens until the end). See pages 172–73 for a guide to how long different vegetables take to cook. Stir constantly or they will become watery.

Noodle option – If making stir-fried noodles, add them now.

Add Charlie stir-fry sauce – Add Charlie, the water and any extra flavourings you're using.

Reduce sauce – Gently toss to combine and cook for around 1 minute. The sauce will become a thick, glossy sauce that coats your stir-fry.

Serve immediately! Serve stir-fries over rice. If making stir-fried noodles, divide between bowls and serve as is.

NOTES

1 Always mince garlic with a knife for stir-fries, rather than using a garlic crusher, which makes the garlic paste-like so it burns, spits and sticks to the wok!

2 Protein suggestions: chicken, pork, beef or lamb (tenderised as per pages 170–71), medium whole prawns or even minced meat.

3 Vegetable suggestions: see pages 172–73 for how to cut and how long to cook common vegetables used in stir-fries.

4 Noodle options: 250 g fresh noodles (from the fridge), such as hokkien noodles; 150 g dried noodles (egg, wheat or rice noodles); 2 instant noodle or ramen cakes. Note that these are the weights straight out of the packet. Prepare them as per the packet directions. Fresh noodles are my favourite – best flavour and texture.

LEFTOVERS Fridge 3 days. Not suitable for freezing.

MY STIR-FRY FORMULA

Here's the formula I use to make stir-fries and noodles using Charlie and whatever I've got in the fridge. The shiny brown sauce will coat everything beautifully and is excellent for rice soakage or coating noodles.

START HERE ...

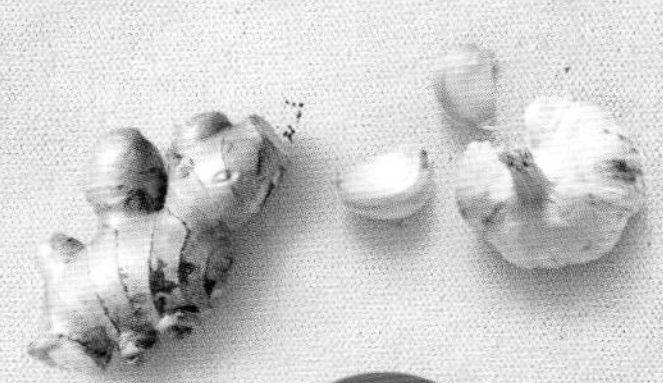

1 tsp
BASE FLAVOURINGS

+

1 cup (180 g)
PROTEIN[1, 2]

+

4 cups (450 g)
VEGETABLES[3]

3 tbsp
CHARLIE STIR-FRY SAUCE

+

$\frac{1}{3}$ cup (80 ml)
WATER

+

EXTRA FLAVOURINGS

STIR-FRY NOODLES

Use above **STIR-FRY** ingredients and add:

3 cups (380 g)
COOKED NOODLES

NOTES

1. Tenderise your meat using the handy information on pages 170–71.
2. Use firm tofu or tempeh to keep it meat-free. Or use more vegetables.
3. Cutting and cooking vegetables: Use the table on pages 172–73 as a guide for how to cut the vegetables and how long to cook them for.

EVERYDAY STIR-FRY

Charlie in action in a quick choose-your-own-adventure stir-fry.

SERVES: 2–3 | PREP: 10 MINUTES + 20 MINUTES TENDERISING | COOK: 6 MINUTES

Think of this stir-fry as a template more than a recipe. I've used beef and a selection of colourful everyday vegetables here. But the idea is to make it your own using whatever protein and vegetable combos you like or have on hand – there are no rules! I really recommend velveting (tenderising) your meat if you have the time (see pages 170–71) – if you've ever wondered about the silky, juicy meats in Chinese restaurant stir-fries, this is the secret! The vegetable cutting guide on pages 172–73 is also handy.

TENDERISED MEAT[1]

180 g beef rump, boneless, skinless chicken breast or pork loin, cut into 7 mm thick slices, 5 cm long

½ tsp bicarbonate of soda*[2]

STIR-FRY

2 tbsp vegetable oil

½ onion, cut into 1 cm wedges

1 garlic clove*, finely minced

1 small carrot, cut into 3 mm slices diagonally

½ large red bell pepper, cut into 7 mm strips

2 spring onion* stems, cut into 5 cm lengths, white and green parts separated

3 tbsp (45 ml) Charlie Stir-fry Sauce (page 134)

80 ml (⅓ cup) water

TO SERVE

Rice (see pages 318–21)

Tenderise meat – Place the meat in a bowl and sprinkle the bicarbonate of soda over the top. Toss with your fingers to coat all the pieces evenly, then set aside for 20 minutes. Rinse in a colander under tap water for 5 seconds, shake off the excess water, then pat the meat dry with paper towels.

Stir-fry – Heat the oil in a wok or large non-stick frying pan* over high heat until smoking. Add the onion and cook for 1 minute. Add the meat and toss for 1 minute until the surface is almost cooked. Add the garlic and toss for 15 seconds. Add the carrot, pepper and white part of the spring onion. Stir constantly for 1 minute.

Sauce – Add Charlie, the water and the green part of the spring onion. Toss for 1½–2 minutes or until the sauce thickens and coats the stir-fry ingredients. Pour into bowls and serve with rice.

NOTES

1. This recipe can also be made using any protein listed on pages 170–71, tenderised using the marinating times provided. You could also make this with firm tofu. There's no need to tenderise. Just slice 1 cm thick, then cut into bite-sized rectangles and cook in place of the meat as per the recipe.
2. Also known as baking soda, this tenderises the meat so it's soft and velvety, just like you get at Chinese restaurants. Without tenderising, the meat would be overcooked and dry within 3 minutes! See pages 170–71 for more information, including the marinating time for other cuts and proteins.

LEFTOVERS Fridge 3 days, though stir-fries are always best made fresh because the sauce goes watery due to water leaching out of the vegetables. Not suitable for freezing.

STIR-FRIED NOODLES

The Charlie formula working magic with noodles!

SERVES: 2 | PREP: 8 MINUTES | COOK: 10 MINUTES

With just a handful of ingredients and the help of Charlie, here's a great way to toss together a pile of noodles quickly that covers your carb, protein and vegetable bases. Chicken thighs are always a favourite for stir-fries because there's no need to tenderise them. I love tenderstem broccoli because it's easy to chop, cooks fast and tangles nicely with the noodles.

CHICKEN

180 g boneless, skinless chicken thighs[1], cut into bite-sized pieces

½ tbsp Charlie Stir-fry Sauce (page 134)

STIR-FRIED NOODLES

250 g fresh hokkien noodles, from the fridge section[2]

1 tbsp vegetable oil

½ onion, cut into wedges

1 garlic clove*, finely minced

2 bunches tenderstem broccoli (about 10 stems), ends trimmed, cut in half, thicker stems cut in half lengthways[3]

3 tbsp Charlie Stir-fry Sauce (page 134)

80 ml (⅓ cup) water

Chicken – Put the chicken in a bowl. Add Charlie, then toss to coat. Set aside until ready to cook.

Noodles – Prepare the noodles according to the packet directions. Do this just prior to cooking.[4]

Cook – Heat the oil in a wok or large non-stick frying pan* over high heat. Add the onion and stir for 30 seconds. Add the chicken and stir for 1½ minutes or until the surface changes from pink to white. Add the garlic and tenderstem broccoli and stir for 2 minutes.

Add noodles – Add the noodles, Charlie and water. Toss well for 2 minutes to coat with the sauce and until the broccoli is crisp-tender. Divide between bowls and serve immediately!

NOTES

1 I prefer using chicken thighs because they're juicier, but chicken breast will work here too. No need to tenderise for this recipe because we're using bite-sized pieces. This recipe can also be made using any protein listed on pages 170–71, tenderised using the marinating times provided.

2 You can substitute the noodles with 250 g of other fresh noodles from the fridge section, or 150 g of dried noodles.

3 Cut the tenderstem broccoli stems all roughly the same width so they cook in the same time. And feel free to substitute with any other vegetables of choice. Use the cutting and cook time guide on pages 172–73.

4 If you soak or boil the noodles too far in advance, they will be more susceptible to breaking when you cook them.

LEFTOVERS Fridge 3 days. Not suitable for freezing.

IT'S NOT MAPO TOFU (BUT IT IS!)

An express take on the world's greatest tofu dish.

SERVES: 3–4 | PREP: 15 MINUTES | COOK: 10 MINUTES

The iconic Sichuanese dish mapo tofu is arguably the world's greatest tofu dish. That luscious combination of silky tofu cubes bathed in a spicy and intensely savoury pork mince sauce, layered with classic Sichuan flavours, is impossible to forget once tasted. It's at heart a simple dish. But as the real deal takes time, effort and at least one trip to the Chinese grocery store, here's my streamlined version for us mere mortals. It's made with easy-to-source ingredients with a leg-up from Charlie for extra depth of flavour. Tune your chilli levels to how you like them!

SAUCE

1 tbsp Charlie Stir-fry Sauce (page 134)

2 tsp cornflour

1 tsp sesame oil*

1 tsp ground Sichuan pepper*[1] (or ¾ tsp freshly ground)

250 ml (1 cup) water

MAPO TOFU

2 tbsp vegetable oil

1 tbsp finely minced ginger*

2 tsp finely minced garlic*

150 g pork mince[2]

1 tbsp red miso paste

1 tbsp sambal oelek*

500 g silken tofu[3], drained and cut into 2 cm cubes

1–3 tbsp chilli oil

TO SERVE

2 tbsp sliced spring onion* (optional)

Rice (see pages 318–21)

Sauce – Mix Charlie and the cornflour in a jug until lump-free. Add the remaining sauce ingredients and mix to combine.

Sauté – Heat the oil in a wok or large non-stick frying pan* over medium–high heat. Add the ginger and garlic and stir for 20 seconds. Add the pork and cook, breaking it up as you go, until you no longer see pink. Add the miso and sambal oelek and cook for 1 minute.

Simmer – Add the sauce, then stir. Gently add the tofu. Stir very gently (I use a rubber spatula), spooning the sauce over the tofu pieces. Simmer for 3 minutes until the sauce thickens into a syrupy consistency.

Finish – Gently transfer into a bowl. Drizzle with as much chilli oil as you dare (remember, mapo tofu is supposed to be spicy!). Sprinkle with spring onion (if using) and serve with rice on the side.

NOTES

1. Also spelled Szechuan pepper. Easily found at Asian grocery stores and some fresh produce stores. For convenience, I use pre-ground in this recipe. If grinding your own, I applaud you – but I recommend reducing to ¾ teaspoon or you may find it a tad too spicy!
2. Or beef or chicken.
3. Silken tofu is very delicate, so handle with care.

LEFTOVERS Fridge 3 days. Not suitable for freezing.

SIZZLING BEEF

On the table – smoking and sputtering hot!

SERVES: 2–3 | PREP: 10 MINUTES + 40 MINUTES TENDERISING AND MARINATING | COOK: 8 MINUTES

If there ever was a Chinese dish to make a proper show of beef, this is it! Sizzling beef is a signature at Chinese restaurants; a dish where the beef arrives at the table on a screaming-hot iron plate, the beef and sauce still spitting and smoking. It's easy to recreate the mesmerising drama at home – just tip the cooked beef onto a hot cast-iron serving plate or cast-iron frying pan*[1] and rush it to the table. It will sizzle and sputter, just like the real thing! Don't skip the steps to tenderise, which keeps the thin slices of beef lusciously tender, even using economical cuts of steak.

BEEF

250 g beef rump or rib-eye steak[2], cut into 3 mm thick strips, about 6 cm long

3/4 tsp bicarbonate of soda*[2]

1 tbsp Charlie Stir-fry Sauce (page 134)

SAUCE

2 tbsp Charlie Stir-fry Sauce (page 134)

1/4 tsp dark soy sauce*

80 ml (1/3 cup) water

STIR-FRY

1 1/2 tbsp vegetable oil

1 garlic clove*, finely minced

2 tsp julienned ginger*

3 spring onions*, cut into 6 cm lengths, white and green parts separated

TO SERVE

Rice (see pages 318–21)

Tenderise beef – Place the beef in a bowl and sprinkle the bicarbonate of soda over. Toss with your fingers to coat, then set aside for 20 minutes. Rinse in a colander under tap water for 5 seconds, shake off the excess water, then pat the beef dry with paper towels.

Marinate beef – Transfer the beef into a clean bowl. Add the 1 tablespoon of Charlie and toss, then set aside for 20 minutes to marinate.

Sauce – Mix the sauce ingredients in a small bowl.

Heat serving plate – Heat a cast-iron serving plate or cast-iron frying-pan* over high heat until hot. Keep it hot while you cook the beef.

Cook – Heat the oil in a large non-stick frying pan* over high heat until very hot and starting to smoke. Spread the beef in the pan in a single layer, then leave for 20 seconds. Add the garlic, ginger and the white part of the spring onion and toss for 1 1/2 minutes. Add the sauce and the green part of the spring onion. Toss quickly for 30 seconds or until the sauce becomes syrupy.

Sizzle! – Place the hot cast-iron serving plate or frying pan on the table. Pour the beef in and enjoy the sizzle! Serve with rice.

NOTES

1. Don't use a regular non-stick frying pan to serve the beef. Heating a non-stick frying pan until it's so hot it is smoking, as required in this recipe, can ruin the non-stick coating.
2. The bicarbonate of soda tenderises the beef so it's soft and velvety, just like you get at Chinese restaurants. Without tendering, the beef would be overcooked and dry within 2 minutes! See the meat tenderising information on pages 170–71 for more information, as well as directions for using other cuts of beef for this recipe.

LEFTOVERS Fridge 3 days. Not suitable for freezing.

CHILLI GARLIC AUBERGINE

A killer sauce powers this Sichuan vegetarian classic.

SERVES: 3–4 | PREP: 7 MINUTES | COOK: 8 MINUTES

Another Sichuan-inspired dish made weeknight-friendly! This recipe is inspired by Sichuan's famous 'fish fragrant aubergine' – though ironically it contains no fish in any form. Instead the name refers to the flavours of the sauce, commonly paired with fish. The traditional dish consists of melt-in-the-mouth deep-fried aubergine, swimming in an alluring sweet–sour sauce laced with chilli and garlic. My version swaps frying the aubergine for an easy pan-steaming method. Charlie gets a boost thanks to fresh garlic, plus a healthy spoonful of chilli paste. Result? An easier but equally delicious take, with a sauce you'll want to smother on everything – from chops to greens to, well, fish!

---

4 Asian aubergines[1], 17 cm long, cut in half lengthways, then each piece cut in half

Vegetable oil spray

¼ tsp salt*

2 tbsp vegetable oil

80 ml (⅓ cup) water

2 tsp finely minced garlic*

SAUCE

1½ tbsp Charlie Stir-fry Sauce (page 134)

1 tbsp cornflour

250 ml (1 cup) water

2 tsp Chinkiang Chinese black vinegar[2]

1½ tsp sambal oelek*[3], or more! (or less)

TO SERVE

2 tbsp finely sliced spring onion*

Rice (see pages 318–21)

Sauce – Mix Charlie with the cornflour and a splash of the water in a large jug or bowl until lump-free. Stir in the remaining water plus the vinegar and sambal oelek.

Sear aubergine – Spray the cut face of the aubergine with the oil, then sprinkle with the salt. Heat 1 tablespoon of the oil in a large non-stick frying pan* (preferably with a lid) over high heat. Place the aubergine in the pan, cut-face down. Cook for 2 minutes or until the surface is golden. Turn and cook the other side for 2 minutes.

Pan-steam aubergine – Slowly pour the water into the pan (careful, it will steam!), then cover with a lid. Cook for 2 minutes or until the aubergine is soft. (See note 4 for what to do if the aubergine is not cooked.) Remove the lid and let any remaining water evaporate. Transfer the aubergine onto a serving platter, mostly spread out in a single layer.

Sauce – Remove from the heat to cool the pan slightly, then add the remaining 1 tablespoon of oil. Return the frying pan to medium–high heat. Once the oil is hot, add the garlic and sauté it for 20 seconds or until golden. Add the sauce, then simmer for 2 minutes or until it thickens into a honey consistency. Pour the sauce over the aubergine, garnish with spring onion, then serve over rice!

NOTES

1. These are the smaller aubergines known by a variety of names, including Chinese aubergine, Japanese aubergine or Lebanese aubergine. Available from Asian grocery stores and some large grocery stores. To make this with regular aubergine, cut into 2 cm rounds, then cut each piece in half. Cook as per the recipe.
2. A dark brown vinegar made from black rice with a slightly sweet, malty taste. Less sharp than ordinary white vinegar. Though the Sichuanese will have my head for saying this, you can substitute with regular balsamic vinegar (not balsamic glaze*).
3. Sambal oelek provides the spiciness in this dish. I like how it stains the sauce a red colour and that you get authentic-looking bits of red chilli in the sauce. Feel free to reduce, omit or increase the amount, or use another type of chilli paste (just add to taste at the end).
4. If the aubergine is still not cooked, add a splash of extra water and keep cooking until it is soft in the middle.

LEFTOVERS Fridge 3 days, though the aubergine does tend to get a little softer than ideal for my taste. Not suitable for freezing.

CHINESE CHICKEN WITH MUSHROOM SAUCE

Think chicken with mushroom gravy – Chinese-style!

SERVES: 4 | PREP: 7 MINUTES | COOK: 15 MINUTES

This is by no means authentic! But mushrooms go brilliantly with both chicken and with Charlie sauce, so I thought, why not? It's incredibly simple to make (NO MEAT CUTTING) and works a treat. I love how the mushrooms release flavour into the sauce as it simmers. The sauce also naturally clings to them, meaning extra sauce hitches a ride as you spoon it over the chicken for maximum smotherage! (I know that's not a real word but it absolutely should be.)

SAUCE

2½ tbsp Charlie Stir-fry Sauce (page 134)

1½ tbsp cornflour

375 ml (1½ cups) water

CHICKEN

750 g boneless, skinless chicken thighs[1] (6 small)

¾ tsp salt*

½ tsp white pepper (substitute black pepper)

1 tbsp vegetable oil

MUSHROOMS

1 tbsp vegetable oil

150 g sliced white mushrooms

2 garlic cloves*, finely minced

TO SERVE

1 tbsp finely minced spring onion* (optional)

Rice (see pages 318–21)

Sauce – Mix Charlie with the cornflour and a splash of the water in a large jug or bowl until lump-free. Stir in the remaining water.

Cook chicken – Sprinkle the chicken with the salt and pepper. Heat the oil in a large non-stick frying pan* over high heat. Cook the chicken for 3 minutes on each side until golden and cooked through, then transfer to a plate. (Do this in batches if your pan is too small.)

Mushroom sauce – Add the oil into the same pan, still over high heat. Tumble the mushrooms in and cook for 4 minutes or until they soften. Add the garlic and stir for 30 seconds. Pour the sauce in, stir, then bring to a simmer. Reduce the heat to medium–low and simmer for 2 minutes or until the sauce thickens into a syrupy consistency.

Serve – Transfer the chicken and any juices pooled on the plate into the mushroom sauce. Let it bubble for a minute to re-warm the chicken. Place the chicken on serving plates and spoon the mushroom sauce over the top. Garnish with the spring onion (if using) and serve over rice.

NOTES

1 This recipe is also ideal made with chicken breast, sliced in half horizontally to form thin 'steaks'.

LEFTOVERS Fridge 3 days. Not suitable for freezing.

SAUCY, CRUNCHY NOODLE STIR-FRY

How I get my midweek crunchy chow mein noodle fix, fast.

SERVES: 4 | PREP: 10 MINUTES + 20 MINUTES TENDERISING | COOK: 10 MINUTES

One of my all-time favourite suburban Chinese restaurant classics is crunchy chow mein noodles, where a bed of deep-fried crispy egg noodles is smothered with a saucy stir-fry. The riot of textures is what this dish is all about. But when the craving hits, who really wants to deep-fry a giant wad of fresh noodles? Leave it to the restaurants and use my trick instead: a packet of store-bought crispy fried noodles. Cheap 'n' cheerful, when stirred through the stir-fry, they're 90% as good with 10% of the effort!

TENDERISED CHICKEN

360 g boneless, skinless chicken breast[1], cut into thin strips about 7 mm thick, 4 cm long

1 tsp bicarbonate of soda*[2]

2 tsp light soy sauce* or all-purpose soy sauce*[3]

STIR-FRY SAUCE

60 ml (¼ cup) Charlie Stir-fry Sauce (page 134)

2½ tbsp cornflour

560 ml (2¼ cups) water (yes, you really need this much!)

STIR-FRY

1 tbsp vegetable oil

1 brown onion, halved, cut into 7 mm thick slices

2 garlic cloves*, finely minced

1 red bell pepper[4], cut into thin strips, 7 mm wide, 5 cm long

100 g baby spinach[4]

200 g thin crispy fried noodles[5]

Tenderise chicken – Place the chicken in a bowl and sprinkle the bicarbonate of soda over. Toss with your fingers to coat, then set aside for 20 minutes. Rinse in a colander under tap water for 5 seconds, shake off the excess water, then pat the chicken dry with paper towels.

Season chicken – Place the chicken in a bowl and toss with the soy sauce.

Stir-fry sauce – Place Charlie in a medium bowl with the cornflour and a splash of the water. Mix until lump-free, then stir in the remaining water.

Stir-fry – Heat the oil in a large non-stick frying pan* over high heat. Add the onion and stir for 1 minute. Add the chicken and cook, stirring constantly, for 2 minutes or until the surface changes from pink to white. Add the garlic and pepper and stir for 1 minute.

Sauce – Pour in the sauce and stir, then simmer for 1½ minutes or until the sauce thickens and becomes glossy.

Crunchy noodles – Turn the heat off to stop the sauce thickening further. Add the spinach and toss for 20 seconds or until just wilted. Add the crunchy noodles and toss them through, then serve immediately!

NOTES

1. Feel free to use any protein listed on pages 170–71, tenderised using the marinating times provided.
2. The bicarbonate of soda tenderises the chicken breast so it's soft and velvety, just like you get at Chinese restaurants – see page 170 for more information. There's no need to tenderise chicken thighs if you use those instead.
3. Any soy sauce is fine here, as it's just to flavour the chicken a little. If you use dark soy sauce*, the meat will be a darker brown.
4. Substitute with other vegetables of choice. Use the information on pages 172–73 for how to cut and cooking times.
5. Any thin crispy noodles will work here. You can find a variety at most Asian grocery stores. Otherwise, use 200 g dried ramen noodles. Crumble and spread them on a baking tray, spray with oil and bake at 180°C for 10 minutes, tossing once halfway through cooking, until crispy.

LEFTOVERS Fridge 3 days, though the noodles will lose crunchiness. Not suitable for freezing.

CHINESE SWEETCORN SOUP

Complete with the signature egg ribbons.

SERVES: 2 | PREP: 5 MINUTES + 20 MINUTES TENDERISING | COOK: 10 MINUTES

As a kid I always loved sweetcorn soup at Chinese restaurants. And I never grew out of it! I still love this soup for the hearty and slightly thickened broth, the sweet pops of corn and the gorgeous marbling effect from the egg ribbons. Although it's usually an appetiser, I scale it up and add chicken bits to make it a filling but healthy meal. Recently I discovered adding a little Charlie makes an even better soup base!

TENDERISED CHICKEN

150 g boneless, skinless chicken breast[1], cut into 5 mm thick slices, 3 cm long

½ tsp bicarbonate of soda*[2]

SOUP

500 ml (2 cups) low-salt chicken stock*

400 g can creamed corn

2 tbsp Charlie Stir-fry Sauce (page 134)

1 garlic clove*, finely grated

1 tsp finely grated ginger*

⅛ tsp white pepper, plus extra for finishing

TO FINISH

1 egg, whisked in a jug

2 tbsp finely sliced spring onion*

½ tsp sesame oil*, for drizzling

Tenderise chicken – Place the chicken in a bowl and sprinkle the bicarbonate of soda over the top. Toss with your fingers to coat, then set aside for 20 minutes. Rinse in a colander under tap water for 5 seconds, shake off the excess water, then pat the chicken dry with paper towels.

Soup – Place all the soup ingredients in a medium saucepan over medium–high heat. Bring to a simmer, then reduce the heat to medium and simmer gently for 3 minutes. Add the chicken and simmer for a further 2 minutes.

Egg ribbons – Turn the heat up to medium–high so the soup is simmering rapidly. Use a wooden spoon to swirl the soup slowly to create a lazy whirlpool. Slowly pour the egg into the middle. The swirling motion of the soup will set the egg into ribbons within seconds of the egg hitting the hot broth!

Serve – Ladle into bowls. Finish with spring onion, a pinch of white pepper and a swish of sesame oil.

NOTES

1 Feel free to use any protein listed on pages 170–71, tenderised using the marinating times provided. However, use the meat and bicarbonate of soda quantity specified for this recipe.

2 The bicarbonate of soda tenderises the chicken breast so it's soft and velvety, just like you get at Chinese restaurants – see page 170 for more information. It's particularly recommended for this recipe because the small, thin strips of chicken overcook quickly in steamy soups.

LEFTOVERS Fridge 3 days. Not recommended for freezing as cornflour-thickened soups tend to go watery once frozen.

FIRECRACKER BEEF & CABBAGE

This is how you make mince and cabbage ROCK!

SERVES: 4 | PREP: 10 MINUTES | COOK: 10 MINUTES

I've always said that mince is underrated in stir-fries! Affordable, flavourful and ready to go with no chopping required, it's so handy. The trick with this dish is to cook the beef aggressively to get good browning and build flavour. Cabbage strips, meanwhile, give sweet crunch and catch all the beef, almost like pasta! Bringing it all together is the firecracker sauce – Charlie, soy and a good wallop of sriracha for an explosion of fiery, bold flavour. Boom!

SAUCE

3 tbsp Charlie Stir-fry Sauce (page 134)

4 tbsp sriracha*[1], plus extra to serve

2 tbsp rice vinegar

2 tbsp brown sugar

1 tbsp dark soy sauce*

STIR-FRY

1 tbsp vegetable oil

2 garlic cloves*, finely minced

1 onion, halved, then finely sliced

500 g beef mince[2]

300 g (4 cups) sliced green cabbage[3] (7 mm thick) (or other vegetables of choice)

1 small carrot[3], peeled, then finely julienned or grated[4]

TO SERVE

Rice (see pages 318–21)

Finely sliced spring onion* (optional)

Finely sliced red chilli (optional)

Sauce – Mix the ingredients in a small bowl.

Stir-fry beef – Heat the oil in a large non-stick frying pan* over high heat. Add the garlic and onion and stir for 1 minute. Add the beef and cook, breaking it up as you go, until it mostly changes from red to brown. Add 4 tablespoons of the sauce. Cook for a further 5 minutes until the sauce is evaporated and the beef is a bit caramelised (don't shortcut this step, it's key for flavour!).

Cabbage and sauce – Add the cabbage and the remaining sauce. Cook, stirring constantly, for 2 minutes until the cabbage is wilted. Add the carrot and stir it through until wilted, about 30 seconds. Serve over rice, garnished with spring onion and chilli (if using), and extra sriracha if you dare!

NOTES

1 Or other chilli sauce of choice. If you're concerned about spiciness, start with less, cook, taste just before you finish, then add more if you like.

2 Chicken and pork mince will also work great in this recipe.

3 Substitute these with other vegetables using the guide on pages 172–73 for how to cut and cooking times.

4 I use my julienne grater for the carrot. I picked it up for a few dollars from my local Asian store. You could also just use a box grater.

LEFTOVERS Fridge 3 days, freezer 3 months.

SMOTHERED CHINESE OMELETTE

Eggs for dinner, the Chinese way.

SERVES: 1 GENEROUSLY, OR 2 WITH RICE (SEE PAGES 318–21) | PREP: 10 MINUTES | COOK: 10 MINUTES

Chinese-style omelettes around the world come in all shapes and sizes. Big and small, neat and free-form, sauced and plain! The choice of fillings also seems to be endless. So I've taken these cues to make my own, using eggs and Charlie! This is a lovely, low-fat Chinese omelette stuffed with pork and bean sprouts, then drenched generously with sauce (because I love sauce!). You can easily adapt this recipe to whatever meat and vegetables you have in the fridge.

SAUCE

1½ tbsp Charlie Stir-fry Sauce (page 134)

2 tsp cornflour

185 ml (¾ cup) water

1 tsp sesame oil*

OMELETTE

3 eggs

1 tsp Charlie Stir-fry Sauce (page 134)

1 tbsp vegetable oil

SAUCY PORK STUFFING

1 tbsp vegetable oil

75 g pork mince (or 150 g/1 cup any diced meat or vegetables[1])

1 tsp Charlie Stir-fry Sauce (page 134)

1 garlic clove*, finely minced

45 g (½ heaped cup[1]) bean sprouts[2]

2 tbsp finely sliced spring onion* (optional)

TOPPING

20 g (¼ heaped cup) extra bean sprouts[2]

1 spring onion* stem, finely sliced diagonally (optional)

Finely sliced red chilli (optional)

Sauce – Mix Charlie and the cornflour in a jug until lump-free. Add the water and sesame oil and mix them in.

Eggs for omelette – Whisk the eggs and Charlie in a bowl, then set aside.

Saucy pork stuffing – Heat the oil in a medium non-stick frying pan* over medium–high heat. Add the pork and cook, breaking it up as you go, until it changes from pink to white. Add the 1 teaspoon of Charlie and stir for 30 seconds. Add the garlic and bean sprouts and stir for another 30 seconds. Add the sauce, then simmer for 1 minute or until thickened and glossy. Stir in the spring onion (if using). Remove from the heat and set aside while you make the omelette.

Omelette – In a separate small to medium non-stick frying pan*, heat the oil over medium–low heat. Add the egg, wait 30 seconds or until the edges are set, then start to stir leisurely, using a rubber spatula. Keep stirring for about 45 seconds, scraping up the set egg from the base of the pan until it is half set, almost like jam. Spread it out across the pan and smooth the surface.

Stuff and serve – Use a slotted spoon to spoon half the pork filling onto one side of the omelette (not too much sauce). Fold the omelette over, then slide onto a plate. Pile on the extra bean sprouts, then pour all the remaining pork and sauce over the top. Garnish with spring onion and chilli (if using), then serve!

NOTES

1. Use 150 g (1 cup) in total of any raw meat cut into small pieces or diced vegetables (like carrots, courgettes, onion, Chinese greens, peas, cabbage).
2. I know bean sprouts are a little hard to measure in a cup. Just gently put them in a cup measure without packing them in so they don't break.

LEFTOVERS Fridge 3 days. Not suitable for freezing.

SUPREME SOY HOKKIEN NOODLES

I just adore the intense soy flavours with these thick noodles.

SERVES: 2 | PREP: 12 MINUTES + 20 MINUTES TENDERISING | COOK: 7 MINUTES

I like to think of this dish as the big sister to the Stir-fried Noodles on page 141. Stained a dark mahogany colour with a bolder soy flavour, they are similar to classic Shanghai-style noodles. But I have taken to calling them 'Supreme Noodles' instead so I'm not captive to any authenticity! I find beef works great with the stronger flavours, but it's also terrific with chicken, pork or even lamb. Whatever you use, tenderising the meat is recommended so it stays soft and juicy (see note 1).

TENDERISED BEEF (OR OTHER PROTEIN)

180 g beef rump steak, cut into 5 mm thick slices, 6 cm long

½ tsp bicarbonate of soda*[1]

SAUCE

3 tbsp Charlie Stir-fry Sauce (page 134)

1 tbsp dark soy sauce*

60 ml (¼ cup) water

STIR-FRIED NOODLES

250 g fresh hokkien noodles, from the fridge section[2]

2 tbsp vegetable oil

2 garlic cloves*, finely minced

2 spring onions*, cut into 6 cm lengths, green and white parts separated

80 g (1 cup) bean sprouts[3]

150 g (2 tightly packed cups) sliced green cabbage[3] (7 mm thick)

Tenderise beef – Place the beef in a bowl and sprinkle the bicarbonate of soda over. Toss with your fingers to coat, then set aside for 20 minutes. Rinse in a colander under tap water for 5 seconds, shake off the excess water, then pat the beef dry with paper towels.

Sauce – Mix the sauce ingredients in a jug or bowl.

Noodles – Prepare the noodles according to the packet directions.

Cook beef – Heat the oil in a wok or large non-stick frying pan* over high heat. Add the beef and stir for 1 minute until it mostly changes from red to brown. Add the garlic and white part of the spring onion. Stir for 30 seconds or until the surface of all the beef is no longer red, but it's still raw inside.

Vegetables and noodles – Add the bean sprouts and cabbage and toss for 1½ minutes or until mostly wilted. Add the noodles, sauce and green part of the spring onion. Toss well for 2 minutes until the sauce thickens and stains the noodles a mahogany colour.

Serve – Divide between bowls and serve immediately!

NOTES

1. The bicarbonate of soda tenderises the beef so it's soft and velvety, just like you get at Chinese restaurants. Without tenderising, the beef would be overcooked and dry within 2 minutes! You can substitute the beef with chicken, lamb or pork. Whatever protein you choose, use 180 g with ½ teaspoon of bicarbonate of soda, as per the recipe. But use the marinating times set out on pages 170–71.
2. You can substitute the noodles with 250 g of other fresh noodles from the fridge section, or 150 g of dried noodles.
3. Substitute these with other vegetables using the guide on pages 172–73 for how to cut and cooking times.

LEFTOVERS Fridge 3 days. Not suitable for freezing.

SWEET & SOUR CRISPY PORK CHOPS

Everything you love about sweet and sour pork – but half the work!

SERVES: 4 | PREP: 15 MINUTES | COOK: 15 MINUTES

This one's for everyone who loves sweet and sour pork (which is ... everyone)! Traditional sweet and sour pork is a labour of love, double-frying cubes of pork and all that jazz. We're taking the easy road! Shallow-frying the pork as steaks and serving them whole saves a bunch of work and uses far less oil. As for Charlie, he's doing double duty – both in the sweet and sour sauce and for seasoning the batter. Truly the little hero that keeps on giving!

CHARLIE

SWEET AND SOUR SAUCE

2 tbsp Charlie Stir-fry Sauce (page 134)

65 g (1/3 cup) white sugar

60 ml (1/4 cup) white vinegar

70 g (1/4 cup) ketchup*, or tomato sauce

60 ml (1/4 cup) pineapple juice[1], unsweetened

60 ml (1/4 cup) water

2 tsp cornflour

CRISPY PORK

4 x 150 g (600 g total) pork loin steaks[2]

1 1/2 tbsp Charlie Stir-fry Sauce (page 134)

1 1/2 tbsp Chinese cooking wine*

60 g (1/2 cup) cornflour

Vegetable oil, for frying (1 cm depth)

TO SERVE

Rice (see pages 318–21)

Mixed leafy greens of choice

Ginger Dressing (page 313)

Sauce – Place all the sauce ingredients in a small saucepan* over medium heat and mix to combine. Simmer for 5 minutes until the sauce thickens into a syrupy consistency. Remove from the stove and keep warm.

Pound pork – Using the spiky side of a meat mallet, pound the pork to an even 7 mm thickness.[3]

Coat pork – Mix Charlie and the Chinese cooking wine in a medium bowl. Add the pork and turn to coat each piece in the sauce. Spread the cornflour on a dinner plate, then coat the pork, ensuring to thoroughly shake off any excess cornflour.[4] Repeat with the remaining pork, then lay the pork pieces on a cutting board.

Crispy pork – Heat 1 cm of oil in a non-stick frying pan* over high heat. Carefully place two pieces of pork in the pan and cook each side for 1 1/2 minutes until golden and crispy. Transfer to a paper towel–lined tray. Repeat with the remaining pork.

Serve – Place the pork on serving plates with a side of rice and leafy greens tossed with the Ginger Dressing. Spoon the sweet and sour sauce over the top, then serve immediately!

NOTES

1 Pineapple juice will give the sauce an authentic flavour. However, it can be substituted with apple juice.

2 Other pork steaks, such as pork tenderloin cut into medallion steaks, can also be used. Because we pound the meat, it will tenderise more economical steaks so you don't need to worry about getting premium pork. However, do not use slow-cooking cuts of pork, such as shoulder. You could also use pork that's already been pounded or sliced into thin steaks. Chicken breast can also be used. Use 2 x 250 g boneless, skinless chicken breasts, cut in half horizontally to form four thin 'steaks'. Pound as per the recipe, but cover with plastic wrap or the meat mallet will tear the chicken as it is more delicate than pork.

3 If you don't have a meat mallet, you can use a rolling pin or heavy frying pan but cover the meat with a freezer bag or similar before doing so.

4 Cornflour is what gives the pork a crispy coating, so you want full coverage. But be sure to avoid excessive white patches of cornflour because it will be powdery and will stay white after cooking. Shake the excess cornflour off very well.

LEFTOVERS Fridge 3 days or freezer 3 months, though the pork will lose its crispy coating. Store the sauce separately.

SIMPLE, TASTY VEGETABLE STIR-FRY

Essential rules for a lifetime of delicious stir-fried vegetables!

SERVES: 2–3 | PREP: 10 MINUTES | COOK: 6 MINUTES

The golden rules of stir-frying vegetables are simple. First, cook them hard and fast over high heat so they char and stay tender-crisp instead of steaming slowly and turning mushy. Second, add vegetables in the order of cooking time needed so everything is perfectly done by the end of cooking (see pages 172–73 for more information on the order). Third, don't crowd the pan – cook in batches if necessary, so high heat is maintained and you're stir-frying not braising. And finally, vegetables are dead boring without a great sauce. Luckily, you've got Charlie on hand!

SAUCE

3 tbsp Charlie Stir-fry Sauce (page 134)

80 ml (1/3 cup) water

STIR-FRY

2 tbsp vegetable oil

1/2 small onion, cut into 1 cm thick wedges

1 garlic clove*, finely minced

ANY VEGETABLES YOU LIKE[1] – I USED:

130 g (2 heaped cups) small broccoli florets

1 small carrot, peeled, sliced diagonally 3 mm thick

1/2 red bell pepper, cut into 7 mm wide strips

60 g (1 cup) white mushrooms, cut into 5 mm thick slices

TO SERVE

Rice (see pages 318–21)

Sauce – Mix the sauce ingredients in a jug or bowl.

Stir-fry – Heat 1 tablespoon of the oil in a wok or large non-stick frying pan* over high heat. Add the broccoli and stir for 1 minute. Add the remaining 1 tablespoon of oil and the onion. Stir constantly for 1 minute. Add the garlic, carrot, pepper and mushrooms and stir for another 2 minutes until the vegetables are just about cooked.

Add sauce – Add the sauce, then stir constantly for a further 1 minute just until the sauce thickens into a syrupy consistency and coats the vegetables, and the vegetables are tender-crisp.

Serve – Pour all the vegetables and sauce onto serving plates. Serve with rice!

NOTES

1 The whole point of stir-fries is to make them your own! So substitute the suggested veg with about 325 g (5 cups) of any vegetables you want. See the information on pages 172–73 for how to cut the vegetables and when to add them into the wok/pan.

LEFTOVERS Fridge 3 days, though stir-fries are always best made fresh because the sauce goes watery due to water leaching out of the vegetables. Not suitable for freezing.

STIR-FRIED PRAWNS WITH MANGETOUT

Everyone should know this classic combination stir-fry.

SERVES: 2 | PREP: 7 MINUTES | COOK: 8 MINUTES

Prawns with mangetout is a classic stir-fry that you see on the menu of many Chinese restaurants. Usually teamed with a light and fragrant ginger or garlic sauce, the dish is all about shining the spotlight on beautiful fresh prawns at their best. Sweet and tender mangetout meanwhile add lovely texture, colour and freshness. Try to get large prawns if you can. Not only are they meatier and grander, but they don't overcook as easily.

SAUCE

$1\frac{1}{2}$ tbsp Charlie Stir-fry Sauce (page 134)

1 tsp cornflour

125 ml ($\frac{1}{2}$ cup) water

STIR-FRY

2 tbsp vegetable oil

250 g peeled and deveined raw prawns*[1] – larger is better (500 g unpeeled prawns)

100 g mangetout[2], trimmed and string removed ($\frac{3}{4}$ cup standing upright)

$1\frac{1}{2}$ tsp finely minced ginger*

1 tsp finely minced garlic*

TO SERVE

Rice (see pages 318–21)

Sauce – Mix Charlie with the cornflour and a splash of the water in a jug or bowl until lump-free. Stir in the remaining water.

Sear prawns – Heat the oil in a large non-stick frying pan* over high heat. Place the prawns in the pan in a single layer and let them cook, undisturbed, for 1 minute. Turn each prawn over, cook for a further 1 minute until just almost cooked, then transfer to a plate – they will cook more in the sauce.

Stir-fry – Reduce the heat to medium–high. Add the mangetout to the same pan and toss for 1 minute. Add the ginger and garlic and toss for 15 seconds. Return the prawns to the pan and pour the sauce in. Stir and bring the sauce to a simmer. Cook for 2 minutes until the sauce thickens. Pour onto a serving plate and serve with rice on the side.

NOTES

1 Your cheap and cheerful local Chinese restaurant would be using frozen, pre-peeled prawns, which is fine for everyday convenience. Seafood-freezing technology has come a long way! But try this with fresh prawns that you peel yourself. The difference is remarkable – the prawn meat texture is soft and meaty, whereas frozen pre-peeled prawns tend to be firmer and more rubbery. I like to use prawns on the larger side, about 25 g each before peeling (15 cm long including the head and tail), 15 g and 11 cm long after peeling (meat only, with tail, straightened).

2 Substitute these with other vegetables using the guide on pages 172–73 for how to cut and cooking times.

LEFTOVERS Fridge 2 days. Not suitable for freezing.

HONEY PEPPER CHICKEN

A winning flavour combination that's super fast and super easy.

SERVES: 4 | PREP: 10 MINUTES | COOK: 8 MINUTES

Inspired by everybody's favourite honey pepper beef, I've used chicken instead and added peppers for lots of vegetable goodness and colour. Serve with plenty of rice – everyone will be mopping up that sticky, savoury honey sauce! The bites of cracked pepper littered through the just-sweet-enough sauce is where the magic is.

---

2 tbsp vegetable oil

1 onion, cut into 1.5 cm squares

500 g boneless, skinless chicken thighs[1], cut into bite-sized pieces

2 garlic cloves*, finely minced

1 each small red and green bell pepper[2], cut into 2 cm squares

HONEY PEPPER SAUCE

60 ml (1/4 cup) Charlie Stir-fry Sauce (page 134)

2 tsp cornflour

85 g (1/4 cup) honey

1 1/2 tsp coarsely cracked black pepper

60 ml (1/4 cup) water

TO SERVE

Rice (see pages 318–21)

Sauce – Mix Charlie with the cornflour in a jug or bowl until lump-free. Mix in the remaining sauce ingredients.

Cook – Heat the oil in a large non-stick frying pan* over high heat. Add the onion and stir for 1 minute. Add the chicken and cook for 2 minutes or until the surface mostly changes from pink to white. Add the garlic and pepper and cook, stirring constantly, for another 1 minute.

Honey pepper sauce – Add the sauce, stir and simmer for 2 minutes until it thickens slightly and becomes syrupy. Pour onto a plate and serve with rice.

NOTES

1 Boneless, skinless chicken breasts can be used, though the meat won't be as juicy. To tenderise the chicken breast, cut the chicken into thin strips instead of bite-sized pieces and follow the directions on pages 170–71. (Chicken thighs don't need to be tenderised.)

This recipe can also be made with beef or pork, cut into thin strips and tenderised as per the directions on pages 170–71.

2 Substitute with other vegetables (like carrots and courgettes), either cut into 2 cm squares or into thin bite-sized rounds.

LEFTOVERS Fridge 3 days, freezer 3 months.

RAINBOW GINGER FISH

Pan-fried fish smothered with a vegetable rainbow sauce.

SERVES: 3–4 | PREP: 12 MINUTES | COOK: 8 MINUTES

I named this dish 'Rainbow Fish' for the bright jumble of colourful vegetable ribbons strewn over white fish when it's served with the glossy brown sauce, then scattered with a good amount of fresh ginger. Cutting the vegetables into thin strips also speeds up the cooking time, so the sauce comes together in just a couple of minutes. I've chosen a mix of vegetables for their colour variety but feel free to experiment!

SAUCE

2 tbsp Charlie Stir-fry Sauce (page 134)

5 tsp cornflour

1/4 tsp white pepper

375 ml (1 1/2 cups) water

FISH

500 g skinless white fish fillets*[1], about 1.5 cm thick (I used John Dory)

1/2 tsp salt*

1/8 tsp white pepper (substitute black pepper)

1 tbsp vegetable oil

RAINBOW VEGETABLES

1 tbsp vegetable oil

2 tbsp finely julienned ginger*

30 g (1/4 cup) finely sliced brown onion (5 mm thick)

40 g (1/4 cup) each courgette, carrot and red bell pepper[2], cut into thin strips about 4 mm wide, 6 cm long

1/2 stem spring onion, finely sliced diagonally

TO SERVE

Rice (see pages 318–21)

Sauce – Mix Charlie, the cornflour, white pepper and a splash of the water in a jug or bowl until lump-free. Stir in the remaining water.

Cook fish – Cut the fish into rectangles about 10 x 5 cm (no need to be exact here). Sprinkle both sides with the salt and pepper. Heat the oil in a large non-stick frying pan* over medium–high heat. Cook the fish for 2 minutes on each side, or until cooked through, then transfer to a plate.

Rainbow vegetable sauce – Add the oil to the same pan, still over medium–high heat. Once hot, add the ginger and onion. Stir for 1 minute, then toss in the courgette, carrot and pepper. Stir constantly for 1 minute, then pour in the sauce. Bring to a simmer, then let it bubble away gently for 1 minute until the sauce is glossy and clear, lowering the heat slightly if needed. Stir through the spring onion.

Serve – Carefully transfer the fish into the sauce, including any juices pooled on the plate. Spoon the sauce over the top and let it simmer for 30 seconds. Serve over rice!

NOTES

1. This recipe works best with white fish fillets about 1.5 cm thick. You can use thicker pieces but they will take longer to cook on the stove. Thinner is better because there is more surface area to smother with the tasty sauce! Try cod, monkfish, cod, snapper, tilapia, pollock, hake, haddock, John Dory, basa, hoki, perch, sea bass, turbot or flathead.
2. Substitute with any other vegetables that can be cut in a similar shape, such as cabbage, green beans, mangetout, tenderstem broccoli, and even the stalks of broccoli (peeled to remove the tough outer layer). A handful of bean sprouts also makes for a handy, no-chop alternative! I know it's a bit hard to measure 40 g (1/4 cup) of these vegetables.
   You can sort of bend the vegetables to fit them in. But truthfully, I just eyeball it!
3. This recipe can also be made with thinly pounded boneless, skinless chicken breasts and thighs or pork chops (like loin). Just use in place of the fish in this recipe and increase the cook time as needed.

LEFTOVERS Fridge 3 days. Not suitable for freezing.

TENDERISING MEAT FOR STIR-FRIES

Never suffer dry, chewy, overcooked meat again!

SERVES: 2 | PREP: 5 MINUTES + 20–45 MINUTES MARINATING | COOK: NIL

Ever notice how the meat in stir-fries at Chinese restaurants is incredibly tender? That's because it's tenderised using a method called *velveting*, in reference to the soft velvet-like texture of the meat. There are a few different ways to do it, but I find the easiest method at home is to use a smidgen of bicarbonate of soda. Simple, easy and highly effective!

Tenderising can be used for any protein, but it's particularly good for lean boneless, skinless chicken breast and beef steaks like rump, which become dry and overcooked easily in stir-fries, and tenderising economical slow-cooking cuts of meat like shoulder. *This will change your stir-fry game!*

---

250 g boneless, skinless chicken breast, beef rump steak, pork loin chops[1] or any other cut listed in the boxes

3/4 tsp bicarbonate of soda*[2]

Cut – Cut the meat into thin strips about 7 mm thick and 5 cm long.

Tenderise – Place the meat in a bowl and sprinkle the bicarbonate of soda over. Toss with your fingers to coat, then set aside for the time specified for the protein you are using.

Rinse – Rinse in a colander under tap water for 5 seconds, shake off the excess water, then pat the meat dry with paper towels.

Use – The tenderised meat is now ready for cooking! It can be cooked like any meat – wok-tossed or pan-seared, steamed or braised in soups – and will stay soft and juicy even when it would otherwise become completely overcooked and dry.

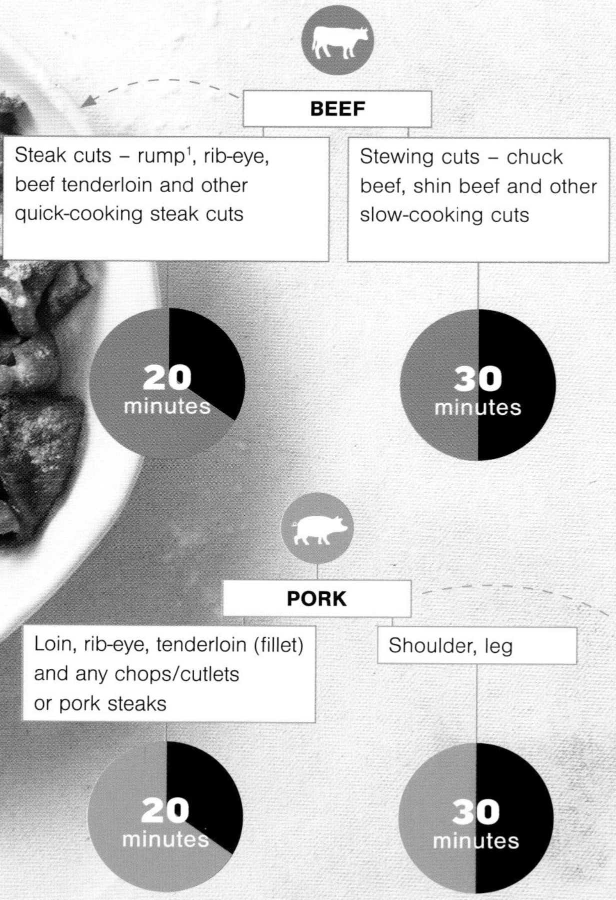

NOTES

1 Boneless, skinless chicken breast and thighs, rump steak and pork loin chops are the cuts I use most often.

2 Not to be confused with baking powder, which does not have the same effect.

3 General rule to follow in case a particular protein is not listed: Marinate steaks and other quick-cooking cuts for 20 minutes, and tougher slow-cooking cuts for 40 minutes.

4 Meat I don't tenderise:

- Boneless, skinless chicken thighs – juicy enough as is, no need to tenderise.
- Pork belly – because of the high fat ratio.
- Lamb cutlets – too expensive!
- Lamb shanks, beef shanks, beef ribs, pork knuckle and other slow-cooking cuts of meat with large bones inside.

5 No need to buy premium-quality meat for tenderising – it's actually kind of wasted. Cheap and cheerful steaks are ideal!

HOW TO CUT VEGETABLES FOR STIR-FRIES

This is the typical way I cut vegetables that I commonly use in stir-fries. It's only a guide – sometimes I like to live life on the edge and cut them differently!

Put vegetables into your wok or pan in the order in which they take to cook, starting with vegetables that take the longest.

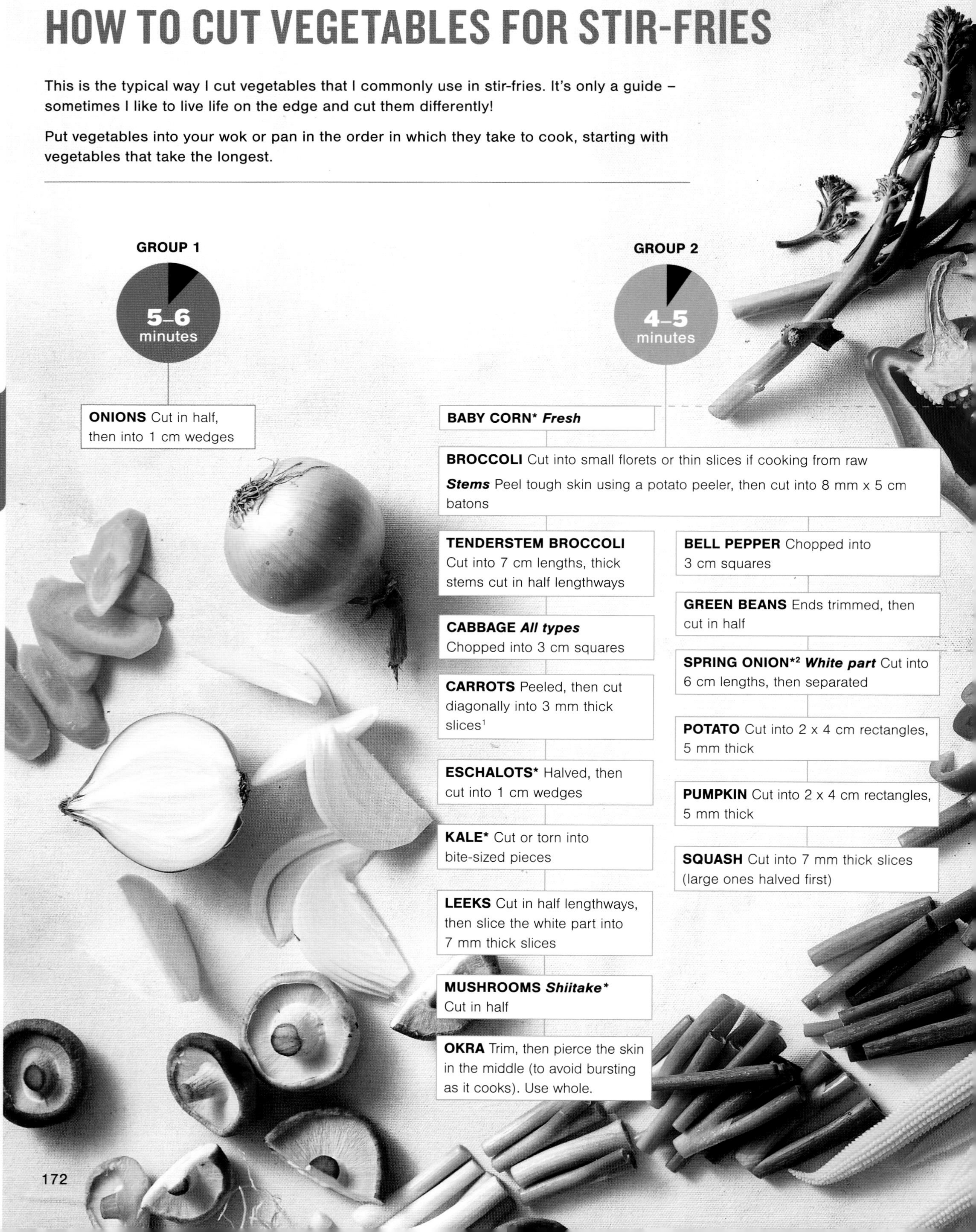

GROUP 1

5–6 minutes

ONIONS Cut in half, then into 1 cm wedges

GROUP 2

4–5 minutes

BABY CORN* ***Fresh***

BROCCOLI Cut into small florets or thin slices if cooking from raw

Stems Peel tough skin using a potato peeler, then cut into 8 mm x 5 cm batons

TENDERSTEM BROCCOLI Cut into 7 cm lengths, thick stems cut in half lengthways

CABBAGE ***All types*** Chopped into 3 cm squares

CARROTS Peeled, then cut diagonally into 3 mm thick slices[1]

ESCHALOTS* Halved, then cut into 1 cm wedges

KALE* Cut or torn into bite-sized pieces

LEEKS Cut in half lengthways, then slice the white part into 7 mm thick slices

MUSHROOMS ***Shiitake**** Cut in half

OKRA Trim, then pierce the skin in the middle (to avoid bursting as it cooks). Use whole.

BELL PEPPER Chopped into 3 cm squares

GREEN BEANS Ends trimmed, then cut in half

SPRING ONION*[2] ***White part*** Cut into 6 cm lengths, then separated

POTATO Cut into 2 x 4 cm rectangles, 5 mm thick

PUMPKIN Cut into 2 x 4 cm rectangles, 5 mm thick

SQUASH Cut into 7 mm thick slices (large ones halved first)

GROUP 3

2 minutes

ASIAN GREENS – CHINESE BROCCOLI (GAI LAN), PAK CHOY, CHOY SUM *Stems* Cut into 7 cm lengths, stems separated from leafy end. Cut thick stems in half lengthways.

ASPARAGUS Woody ends trimmed, then cut into 7 cm lengths. Very thick stems cut in half lengthways so all stems are approximately the same width.

BOK CHOY *Stems* Leafy end cut off the stems, then the stems cut lengthways so they are the same width

CABBAGE *All types* Shredded or cut into 1 cm thick slices

BABY CORN* *Canned (drained)*

BROCCOLI Cut into florets, then steamed or blanched

CAULIFLOWER Cut into florets, then steamed or blanched

BELL PEPPER Sliced into 7 mm strips

CELERY Cut diagonally into 5 mm thick slices

AUBERGINE *Chinese / Japanese* Cut in half lengthways, then diagonally into 5 mm thick slices

Western (small is better) Cut into 1.2 cm thick chips

KALE* Sliced into 1 cm strips

SUGAR SNAP PEAS Trimmed and string removed

MUSHROOMS *White and Swiss brown* Sliced 5 mm thick

King oyster Sliced 5 mm thick (cut extra-large ones in half first)

Enoki and shimeji Trim stem, break into clumps

COURGETTE Peeled, then cut diagonally into 4 mm thick slices[1]

GROUP 4

Barely a minute. Just toss until they wilt or warm through

ASIAN GREENS – CHINESE BROCCOLI (GAI LAN), PAK CHOY, CHOY SUM *Leafy part*

BOK CHOY *Leafy part*

BABY SPINACH Use as is

BEAN SPROUTS Use as is

SPRING ONION*[2] *Green part* Cut into 6 cm lengths, then separated

MANGETOUT Trimmed and string removed

NOTES

1. If one end of the carrot or courgette is substantially thicker than the other, cut the wider end in half lengthways before slicing.
2. For garnish, I typically finely slice the green part. Save the white part and use in place of onion in recipes.

ONE

... pot, pan, tray. Less washing up!

ONE-POT CHICKEN TOMATO PASTA

Cooking the pasta in this garlicky tomato sauce cuts the work and time in half!

SERVES: 4 | PREP: 10 MINUTES | COOK: 25 MINUTES

Over the years I've become an enthusiastic fan of cooking pasta directly in sauce. It's a brilliant shortcut. Not only does it save on washing up, but the starch from the pasta naturally thickens the sauce while absorbing the tasty flavours as it cooks. This pot is bursting with tasty, garlicky tomato flavours and Italian mixed herbs. A handful of fresh basil is a great finishing touch but by no means essential. Chicken's my protein pick here for its fast and easy cooking, and because I think chicken goes with just about any pasta sauce. Yes, it's true that Italians traditionally don't mix chicken and pasta, but the rest of the world thinks it's a completely delicious combo, so the Italians should really get on board!

---

500 g boneless, skinless chicken thighs[1], cut into thin strips (about 1 x 4 cm)

½ tsp salt*

¼ tsp black pepper

2 tsp Italian mixed herbs[2]

2 tbsp olive oil

PASTA AND SAUCE

1 brown onion, finely chopped

3 garlic cloves*, finely minced

3 tbsp tomato paste

80 ml (⅓ cup) chardonnay or other dry white wine* (optional)

400 g can chopped tomatoes

1 litre (4 cups) low-salt chicken stock*

½ tsp white sugar, if needed[3]

½ tsp salt*

½ tsp black pepper

345 g (3 cups) penne (or other similar-sized pasta)

100 g (1 cup) grated* cheddar[4]

TO SERVE

Finely grated parmesan*

Handful of basil leaves (optional)

Sear chicken – In a bowl, toss the chicken with the salt, pepper and Italian mixed herbs. Heat the oil in a large heavy-based pot* with a lid over high heat until very hot. Add the chicken and cook until the surface changes from pink to white, but is still raw inside. Transfer to a bowl using a slotted spoon, leaving the fat behind in the pot.

Make sauce – In the same pot, cook the onion and garlic for 2 minutes. Add the tomato paste and stir for 1 minute. Add the white wine (if using) and let it simmer rapidly for 2 minutes, stirring the base of the pot until it is mostly evaporated. Add the tomatoes, stock, sugar[3] (if using), salt and pepper. Stir, then once the sauce comes to a simmer, add the pasta and return the cooked chicken to the pot (along with any juices pooled on the plate). Stir, then reduce the heat to medium–high so the sauce is bubbling energetically but not rapidly boiling.

Cook pasta – Cook for 15 minutes, stirring regularly so the pasta cooks evenly. Towards the end, as the sauce gets thicker, reduce the heat to medium–low and stir more regularly so the base doesn't catch. Once the penne is tender (pick one out to check), remove the pot from the stove. It should seem a little more watery than you expect – the liquid will be absorbed in the next step. Add the cheese and stir it through.

Rest and serve – Leave the pasta for 3 minutes. The cheese will melt and the excess liquid will be absorbed by the pasta. Serve, topped with parmesan and a good handful of basil (if using).

NOTES

1. Boneless, skinless chicken breast also works but will not be as juicy as thighs.
2. Just your everyday Italian herb mix from regular grocery stores. Substitute with a mix of dried parsley, basil and oregano (equal quantities).
3. Not all canned tomatoes are created equal. Economical brands tend to be on the sour side so adding a touch of sugar is recommended. If you're using good-quality tomatoes, you won't need the sugar.
4. Or other melting cheese of choice, such as monterey jack. Mozzarella isn't recommended as it doesn't add flavour. If you do use it, add an extra 50 g (½ cup) of grated parmesan.

LEFTOVERS Fridge 3 days, freezer 3 months.

LEMON SALMON WITH POTATO GRATIN

This one's a bit of a showstopper, if I do say so myself!

SERVES: 4 | **PREP: 15 MINUTES** | **COOK: 1 HOUR 45 MINUTES**

This dish is truly amazing in every sense! After assembly, the potato gratin gets a head start in the oven while the salmon gets marinating in lemon and garlic. You then pop the flavoured fish fillets on top and, as the salmon cooks, the delicious juices seep down into the creamy, cheesy layers of potato below, working all kinds of mouthwatering magic. By the time the gratin is done, the fish is perfectly cooked. And as if the sheer convenience of two dishes in one wasn't enough, the recipe makes more gratin than you need. So you'll have lunch leftovers to fight over the next day. Didn't I say amazing?

---

4 x 180 g skinless salmon fillets[1]

POTATO GRATIN

1.25 kg sebago* potatoes[2]

250 ml (1 cup) double cream*

1½ tsp salt*

¼ tsp black pepper

1 tsp finely chopped thyme leaves, plus extra for serving

2 garlic cloves*, finely minced

100 g (1 cup) grated* gruyere (or other cheese[3] of choice)

2 tbsp (30 g) unsalted butter, cut into 1 cm cubes

LEMON GARLIC MARINADE

1 garlic clove*, finely grated or minced using a garlic crusher[4]

1 tsp dijon mustard

2 tbsp extra-virgin olive oil

1 tsp lemon zest

1 tbsp lemon juice

½ tsp salt*

¼ tsp black pepper

Preheat the oven to 200°C (180°C fan).

Slice potatoes – Peel the potatoes, then cut into 3 mm thick slices. A mandoline* will make short work of this, otherwise, show off your knife skills!

Bake gratin – Spread one-third of the potato slices in a 23 x 33 cm baking dish. Drizzle with one-third of the cream, sprinkle with one-third of the salt, pepper, thyme, garlic, and finally, one-third of the cheese. Repeat twice more, then dot the surface with butter. Cover with foil and bake for 80–90 minutes until the potato is soft (check with the tip of a knife).

Marinate salmon – Meanwhile, mix the marinade ingredients in a small bowl – it should be a smearable paste that will stay on the salmon. Brush/spoon the marinade on the top and sides of each salmon fillet (not the underside). Set aside on a plate while the potato is cooking.

Brown gratin – When the potato is cooked, switch the oven grill to high with the shelf 25 cm from the heat source. Remove the foil and grill the potato gratin until the surface is light golden, about 3 minutes.

Cook salmon – Place the salmon on the surface of the gratin, then place the dish back under the grill. Grill for 10 minutes or until the salmon is cooked and the exposed gratin surface is nicely golden. The internal temperature of the salmon should be 50°C for medium–rare (optimum juiciness), or 60°C for medium, measured using a cooking thermometer*[5].

Serve – Remove from the grill and immediately transfer the salmon to serving plates. Rest for 3 minutes, then serve with slices of the potato gratin, sprinkled with extra fresh thyme, if desired.

NOTES

1. Any thick fish fillets similar in size to salmon will also work. Don't worry if your salmon has skin, leave it on for cooking, then just eat the flesh off the skin if you don't want to eat it.
2. Or other all-purpose or starchy potatoes. Waxy potatoes are not recommended.
3. Any good melting cheese will work fine here, but gruyere certainly gives the best flavour for gratin! Cheddar and Swiss are both suitable alternatives. If using mozzarella, mix it up with 30 g (⅓ cup) finely grated parmesan* (for extra flavour).
4. If you don't have a garlic crusher, finely mince the garlic, then smear into a paste with the side of a knife.
5. After resting, the internal temperature will rise from 50°C to 53°C, which is medium–rare (for optimum juiciness). This is the default doneness at which restaurants serve salmon. For medium, target an internal temperature of 60°C, which will rise to 63°C after resting – still juicy, but it will be juicier if medium–rare! (You can tell which camp I'm in ...)

LEFTOVERS Fridge 3 days, freezer 3 months.

ARABIC CHICKEN & POTATOES

Exotic spices lift chicken and potatoes in this complete Middle Eastern meal-in-a-tray!

SERVES: 5 | PREP: 15 MINUTES | COOK: 45 MINUTES

My trick for packing as much spice and flavour as possible onto baked chicken? Coat it with something wet first so it sticks even better! I like to use either a sticky glaze (like Sticky Soy Chicken with Sesame Tenderstem broccoli on page 193) or yoghurt. Here I'm using the technique for an Arab-inspired chicken and vegetable tray bake. My spice mix is loosely based on zaatar – I just love the earthy, herbal flavours of this Middle Eastern spice blend. One tip: Don't skip the sumac here! This tangy red spice tastes a bit like lemon in powder form. It both lifts the dish and gives it an authentic edge.

5 x 250 g bone-in, skin-on chicken thighs[1]

Extra-virgin olive oil spray, or 2 tsp extra-virgin olive oil

VEGETABLES

1 kg potatoes[2], scrubbed clean, cut into 7 mm thick slices

1 bunch Dutch carrots[3], scrubbed clean (10–12 carrots)

2 tbsp extra-virgin olive oil

1 tsp sumac powder[4]

1 tsp salt*

½ tsp black pepper

CHICKEN SPICE PASTE

1 tsp paprika*

1 large garlic clove*, crushed using a garlic crusher

½ tsp dried thyme

½ tsp ground cumin

1 tsp sumac powder[4]

½ tsp white sesame seeds

1 tsp salt*

½ tsp black pepper

3 tbsp plain yoghurt (substitute sour cream)

1 tbsp extra-virgin olive oil

TO SERVE

Handful of coriander leaves or parsley (optional)

Preheat the oven to 200°C (180°C fan). Line a large baking tray with foil, then baking paper.

Toss vegetables – Place the potato and carrots in a large bowl. Drizzle with the olive oil, then sprinkle with the sumac, salt and pepper. Toss well, separating the potato slices to coat the surface of each piece. Pile onto the tray, overlapping the potato slices slightly, as pictured, leaving space for the chicken.

Coat chicken – In the same bowl, add all the chicken spice paste ingredients. Mix to combine, then add the chicken and use your hands to rub the mixture into all the cracks and crevices. Nestle the chicken among the vegetables on the tray. Scrape out all the remaining paste in the bowl and dab it onto the chicken skin. Spray with the extra-virgin olive oil spray.

Bake – Bake for 45–50 minutes, rotating the tray at the halfway mark, until the chicken is deep golden.

Serve – Rest for 5 minutes on the tray, then divide the chicken, carrots and potato among plates. Use the tray juices as the sauce – don't waste a drop! Sprinkle with coriander or parsley (if using). Dig in!

NOTES

1 Bone-in, skin-on thighs are best as they will stay juicy with the bake time required to cook the potato and carrots. Drumsticks work well too – use 6–8. However, to use boneless, skinless breast and thighs, roast the vegetables alone for 20 minutes, then add the chicken breast or thighs and roast for a further 20 minutes. Finish with a 5-minute blast under the oven grill to get some colour on the chicken.

2 Any potatoes will work for this recipe, large or small, waxy or floury. Just be sure to cut them fairly thinly so they cook through. My default are all-rounders like sebago* potatoes – the dirty, brushed ones you see 'everywhere' in Australia. (Maris Pipers would be good UK alternatives.)

3 Or regular carrots, peeled, then cut into 10 cm long batons about 1.5 cm wide.

4 Sumac is a wonderful Middle Eastern spice with a lemony flavour and vibrant red colour. Find it in large grocery stores, priced the same as other spices. It's a key ingredient in this recipe so it's worth getting! Substitute with paprika and finish the dish with a good squeeze of fresh lemon just before serving.

LEFTOVERS Fridge 3 days, freezer 3 months.

BAKED BEEF KOFTAS

Yes, koftas done in the oven! The trick is to bake them in sauce ...

SERVES: 4 | PREP: 15 MINUTES | COOK: 25 MINUTES

I once tried baking koftas in the oven, hoping for browned and juicy, fuss-free kebabs. Instead I got pale strips of mealy beef that looked more like Dozer's* treats than a kofta. Bake the koftas in a little tomato sauce, though, and we're talking deliciously succulent and tender mince that almost looks like it's glazed! It's a technique I picked up from a recipe in Turkish chef Özlem Warren's book, *Özlem's Turkish Table*. I've added in some courgettes, as well as thick slices of tomato, which break down and sort of become part of the tray sauce. Stuff it all into warm flatbreads with yoghurt for killer home Turkish comfort food (and so little effort!).

8 wooden skewers (no need to soak)

1 tbsp extra-virgin olive oil

KOFTAS

500 g beef mince[1] (or lamb)

2 tsp ground cumin

1 tsp dried chilli flakes* (reduce or omit)

1 tsp salt*

1/2 tsp black pepper

1 brown onion, grated using a box grater

45 g (3/4 cup) panko breadcrumbs*

10 g (1/4 cup) finely minced parsley

1 egg

VEGETABLES[2]

2 large tomatoes, cut into 1 cm thick slices

2 tbsp extra-virgin olive oil

1/2 tsp salt*

1/2 tsp black pepper

1 large red onion, halved and cut into 1 cm wedges

2 courgettes, cut into 7 mm thick slices

KOFTA TOMATO SAUCE

2 tsp tomato paste

1 tbsp lemon juice

2 tbsp water

1/4 tsp salt*

1/4 tsp black pepper

TO SERVE

2 tbsp finely chopped parsley

4 Lebanese breads (or other flatbread – see Easy Flatbread on page 325), slightly warmed[3]

Lemon Yoghurt Sauce (page 228)

Preheat the oven to 240°C (220°C fan).

Koftas – Mix together the kofta ingredients in a bowl using your hands. Divide equally among the skewers, shaping the meat into 2.5 cm wide cylinders. (Feel free to skip the skewers and just make free-form koftas!) Place the skewers in the middle of a large baking tray – close but not touching each other.

Vegetables – Place the tomato on one side of the tray, with the slices overlapping slightly. Drizzle with half the olive oil and sprinkle with half the salt and pepper. On the other side of the tray, toss the red onion and courgettes with the remaining olive oil, salt and pepper, then spread them out.

Sauce – Mix the sauce ingredients in a small bowl.[4] Pour the sauce over the koftas, aiming for even coverage. Drizzle the koftas with the extra-virgin olive oil.

Bake – Bake for 20 minutes. Rest for 3 minutes. Toss the vegetables with the pan juices, then sprinkle with parsley. Serve with Lebanese breads and Lemon Yoghurt Sauce on the side so everyone can make their own mini kofta kebabs! PS: Don't waste the tray juices!

NOTES

1 Either beef or lamb works equally well here. Which do you feel like today?

2 Feel free to substitute with other vegetables that will cook quickly, such as tenderstem broccoli, asparagus, green beans or bell pepper.

3 Use any flatbreads or pita pockets that can be used for stuffing or wrapping. Otherwise, serve over rice (see pages 318–21) or couscous (see Slow-roasted Middle Eastern Lamb Shoulder on page 251 for instructions on preparing couscous).

4 Loosen the sauce with a touch of extra water if needed to make it pourable, but keep it thick enough to blanket the koftas. PS: If you're thinking the sauce sounds really plain, have faith! It gets flavour from the beef and vegetable pan juices. It really works.

LEFTOVERS Fridge 3 days. Not suitable for freezing.

VEGETABLE CASHEW BIRYANI

A big bowl of rich, curried vegetables and fragrant rice.

SERVES: 4–5 | **PREP: 15 MINUTES** | **COOK: 35 MINUTES**

To most people, biryani is a dish of alternating layers of perfumed white rice and curried meat with patches of bright yellow saffron rice. But there are other kinds (1.4 billion people live in India, remember!). This recipe follows a home-style biryani that is just as delicious, but dispenses with the fiddly assembly and meat – closer to a spiced rice mixed with vegetables. You will love the juicy, fragrant rice and stewy curried vegetables, punctuated by the crunch of cashews and pops of fresh coriander in this biryani. I've fallen hard for this!

2 tbsp (30 g) ghee* or unsalted butter

120 g (1 cup) unsalted cashews

1 brown onion, diced

4 garlic cloves*, finely minced

1 tbsp finely grated ginger*

1 small courgette[1], cut into 1.5 cm thick half-moons

280 g (2 cups) peeled, cubed pumpkin[1] (1.5 cm cubes)

180 g (2 cups) small cauliflower florets[1]

BIRYANI VEGETABLE SPICES

½ tsp cayenne pepper (optional, for slight spiciness)

¾ tsp ground turmeric

1 tsp ground coriander

2 tsp garam masala*

¾ tsp salt*

RICE

180 g (1 cup) basmati rice, uncooked[2]

400 g can chickpeas, drained

500 ml (2 cups) low-salt vegetable stock*

¾ tsp salt*

1 cinnamon stick

2 bay leaves*

¾ tsp ground cardamom

2 star anise

70 g (½ cup) frozen peas

MINTED YOGHURT

185 g (¾ cup) plain yoghurt

¼ tsp salt*

2 tsp lemon juice

15 g (½ tightly packed cup) mint leaves

TO FINISH AND GARNISH

10 g (½ cup) chopped coriander leaves

35 g (½ cup) crispy fried shallots*

2 tbsp (30 g) ghee* or butter, melted

Cashews – Melt the ghee in a large heavy-based pot* over high heat. Add the cashews and stir for 2 minutes or until they have brown spots. Scoop them out using a slotted spoon, transfer to a bowl and set aside.

Curried vegetables – Cook the onion in the same pot for 2 minutes. Add the garlic and ginger and cook for a further 2 minutes until the edges of the onion are tinged with gold. Add the courgette, pumpkin and cauliflower and stir to coat them in the onion-y ghee. Add the biryani vegetable spices and stir for 1 minute to toast the spices.

Rice – Add the rice and chickpeas and stir well to coat in the tasty flavours. Add the stock, salt, cinnamon, bay leaves, cardamom and star anise. Stir, then let it come to a simmer. Sprinkle the peas across the surface, cover with a lid and reduce the heat to low. Cook for 15 minutes or until all the liquid is absorbed. Remove the pot from the stove and leave to rest, uncovered, for 10 minutes.

Minted yoghurt – Set aside 130 g (½ cup) of the yoghurt, then place the remaining yoghurt, salt, lemon juice and mint in a jug large enough to fit the head of a stick blender. Blitz until the mint is very finely chopped. Gently stir in the reserved yoghurt, then transfer to a small serving bowl.

Assemble – Use a rubber spatula to gently toss the rice. (It will be a little juicy rather than dry and fluffy because the vegetable curry is essentially jumbled throughout.) Tumble half onto a serving platter. Sprinkle with half the coriander and half the crispy fried shallots and drizzle over half the ghee. Then repeat with the remaining rice, coriander, crispy fried shallots and ghee. Sprinkle with the cashews. Serve with the minted yoghurt on the side!

NOTES

1. I chose these vegetables because they are a good combination of curried stewiness (courgette and pumpkin) while the cauliflower holds its form nicely. However, feel free to substitute with other vegetables.
2. No need to rinse the rice if purchased in packets at the grocery store. But if you're concerned about rice cleanliness, rinse the rice and drain well, then reduce the stock in the recipe by 2 tablespoons. Long-grain and medium-grain rice can be substituted. Other types of rice are not suitable for this recipe as written.

LEFTOVERS Fridge 3 days, freezer 3 months.

BAKED FISH WITH GOLDEN COCONUT SAUCE

Almost any fish will work beautifully with this coconut sauce.

SERVES: 4 | PREP: 10 MINUTES | COOK: 40 MINUTES

You don't need an armload of ingredients to make a fragrant and full-bodied curry. In fact, many great curries around the world feature just a handful of carefully chosen spices and flavourings. In this creamy coconut sauce, a good amount of fresh ginger and garlic does a lot of the heavy lifting. Just a pinch of turmeric follows – it's all you need to perfume and stain the curry sauce a lovely earthy yellow. But it's the fish cooking juices that really bring the flavours home, underlined by a dash of fish sauce for extra umami oomph.

GOLDEN COCONUT SAUCE

¾ tsp ground turmeric

1 tsp freshly grated garlic*

1 tbsp freshly grated ginger*

400 ml can coconut cream*[1]

185 ml (¾ cup) low-salt chicken stock*

2 tsp fish sauce

2 tbsp lime juice

ADD-INS

400 g can chickpeas, drained

2 bird's eye* or Thai red chillies, cut in half lengthways and deseeded (optional)

FISH

1 tsp olive oil

4 x 180 g white fish fillets*[2] at least 1 cm thick

½ tsp salt*

¼ tsp black pepper

TO SERVE

2 tbsp roughly chopped coriander[3]

Extra lime wedges (optional)

Rice (see pages 318–21)

Preheat the oven to 200°C (180°C fan).

Bake sauce – Whisk the sauce ingredients in a 23 x 33 cm pan, at least 4 cm deep. Add the chickpeas and chilli (if using). Bake for 25 minutes, then remove from the oven.

Top with fish – Use your fingers to spread the oil on both sides of the fish, then sprinkle with the salt and pepper. Place the fish into the sauce on top of the chickpeas.[4]

Bake – Bake for 15 minutes or until the fish is cooked.[5] The flesh should flake and the internal temperature of the fish should be 55°C or a little higher, measured using a cooking thermometer*.

Serve – Remove from the oven and rest for 3 minutes. Serve over rice sprinkled with coriander, and extra lime wedges, if desired.

NOTES

1 Coconut cream gives the sauce the right thickness. Coconut milk* is thinner, but it does work just fine.

2 Use any white fish fillets that are at least 1 cm thick, such as cod, pollock, haddock, John Dory, basa or hake. Salmon and trout also work. Avoid lean fish such as tuna, and oily fish* like sardines and mackerel.

3 Substitute with parsley or omit.

4 Don't bother attempting to squidge the fish between the chickpeas. First, it's difficult with so many chickpeas. Second, the surface of the fish needs to lightly oven-roast, which adds to the flavour.

5 Thicker and larger fillets will take longer, but be mindful that fish cooks faster than meat.

LEFTOVERS Fridge 3 days, freezer 3 months.

ONE-POT PIZZA MAC

Equal parts pizza and pasta, this cheeky mashup isn't just a fun dish but is ridiculously delicious!

SERVES: 4 | **PREP: 15 MINUTES** | **COOK: 30 MINUTES**

Is it crustless pizza with macaroni? Or macaroni topped with a pizza? I don't even know, but I do know you're going to love it! I've taken the flavours of classic pizza sauce to make a rich tomato sauce for macaroni. The crowning glory (literally!) is stretchy melted mozzarella blanketing the top, dotted with sliced salami. Plonk that pot in the middle of the table and spoon out big, stringy helpings. Watch eyes and smiles grow wide! PS: Don't shortcut sautéing the salami properly at the beginning – it will ooze tasty red oil that flavours the whole dish!

---

1 tbsp extra-virgin olive oil

125 g salami slices[1], chopped into 1 cm squares

1 brown onion, finely chopped

1 red bell pepper, deseeded and chopped into 1 cm squares

2 garlic cloves*, finely minced

1 tsp dried oregano

1 tsp dried basil

500 ml (2 cups) low-salt beef stock*

800 g can chopped tomatoes

1 tsp salt*

½ tsp black pepper

250 g (2½ cups) elbow macaroni (or other small pasta)

PIZZA TOPPING

200 g (2 tightly packed cups) grated* mozzarella

50 g pepperoni slices (or more chopped salami)

12 kalamata olives, pitted (or olive slices)

Preheat the oven grill to high with the shelf 25 cm from the heat source.

Sauté – Heat the oil in a large ovenproof pot* over high heat. Cook the salami for 3 minutes or until the edges are tinged with light gold. Add the onion, bell pepper, garlic, oregano and basil. Stir for 2 minutes or until the onion is translucent.

Cook pasta – Add the stock, tomatoes, salt and pepper. Stir, bring to a simmer, then add the pasta. Give it another stir and once it comes back up to a simmer, lower the heat slightly to medium–high so it's bubbling energetically but not boiling rapidly. Cook for 10 minutes, stirring every minute so the base doesn't catch, until the macaroni is just about cooked. The mixture should still be quite liquid at this stage.

Pizza toppings – Turn the stove off and wait for the bubbles to subside. Smooth the surface. Sprinkle with the cheese, then top with the pepperoni and olives.

Melt and serve – Place under the oven grill for 5 minutes, just until the cheese is melted and the pepperoni is sizzling. Serve immediately!

NOTES

1 I like to use the pre-sliced large salami sold at deli counters in grocery stores.

LEFTOVERS Fridge 3 days, freezer 3 months.

PROSCIUTTO-WRAPPED PORK WITH GREEK LEMON POTATOES

A rustic and fabulous pork tenderloin dinner.

SERVES: 5 | PREP: 15 MINUTES | COOK: 1 HOUR 10 MINUTES

The problem with roasted pork tenderloin is it's hard to get enough colour on the meat before the inside is cooked, leaving it looking pale and sad. Enter prosciutto! Wrapping the pork in thin slices of the ham hides this problem and provides a much classier presentation. The prosciutto also adds bags of flavour and creates a tasty pan sauce for serving. Garlicky Greek potatoes with bright lemon flavours, cooked underneath the roast, couldn't be a more perfect match.

LEMON GARLIC POTATOES

1 kg sebago* potatoes[1], washed, cut into 2.25 cm thick wedges

3 tbsp extra-virgin olive oil

2 large garlic cloves*, finely minced using a garlic crusher or knife

1 tsp salt*

¼ tsp black pepper

1½ tsp dried oregano

3 tbsp lemon juice

PORK

750 g pork tenderloin[2], cut into 5 x 150 g even-sized pieces

½ tsp salt*

¼ tsp black pepper

5 slices prosciutto[3] (70 g)

250 g cherry tomatoes (I used vine tomatoes)

1 tbsp extra-virgin olive oil

Preheat the oven to 200°C (180°C fan).

Bake potatoes – Toss all the lemon garlic potato ingredients in a 23 x 33 cm roasting pan. Bake for 40 minutes.

Wrap pork – Sprinkle the pork with the salt and pepper. Wrap each pork tenderloin in a slice of prosciutto, finishing with the seam-side down. Leave on a work surface while the potatoes are in the oven to bring it slightly to room temperature.

Roast pork – Remove the pan from the oven. Place the pork on top of the potato, seam-side down, and surround with the cherry tomatoes. Drizzle everything with the 1 tablespoon of extra-virgin olive oil. Bake for 25–30 minutes or until the centre of the pork registers 60°C, for medium[4], measured using a cooking thermometer*.

Rest and serve – Rest for 5 minutes, then serve, being sure to use all the pan juices as the sauce!

NOTES

1 Or other all-purpose or starchy potatoes. See 'Sebago potatoes' in the Glossary for more information.

2 I buy two pork tenderloins, then cut even-sized pieces from only the thick ends. (The pieces need to be the same size so they take the same time to cook.) If you want to use the thin ends (which will cook much faster), you'll need to stack two pieces on top of each other so they are the same thickness as the other pieces. Any left-over pieces of pork are perfect for tossing into a stir-fry (see the Charlie chapter) or Stir-fried Noodles (page 141).

3 Look for prosciutto slices large enough to fully wrap the pork pieces. If you can only find small ones, use two slices per piece of pork.

4 Medium is the recommended level of doneness for optimum juiciness. It will have the faintest hint of blush. See the Internal Cooked Temperatures chart on page 335 for other levels of doneness.

LEFTOVERS Fridge 3 days, freezer 3 months.

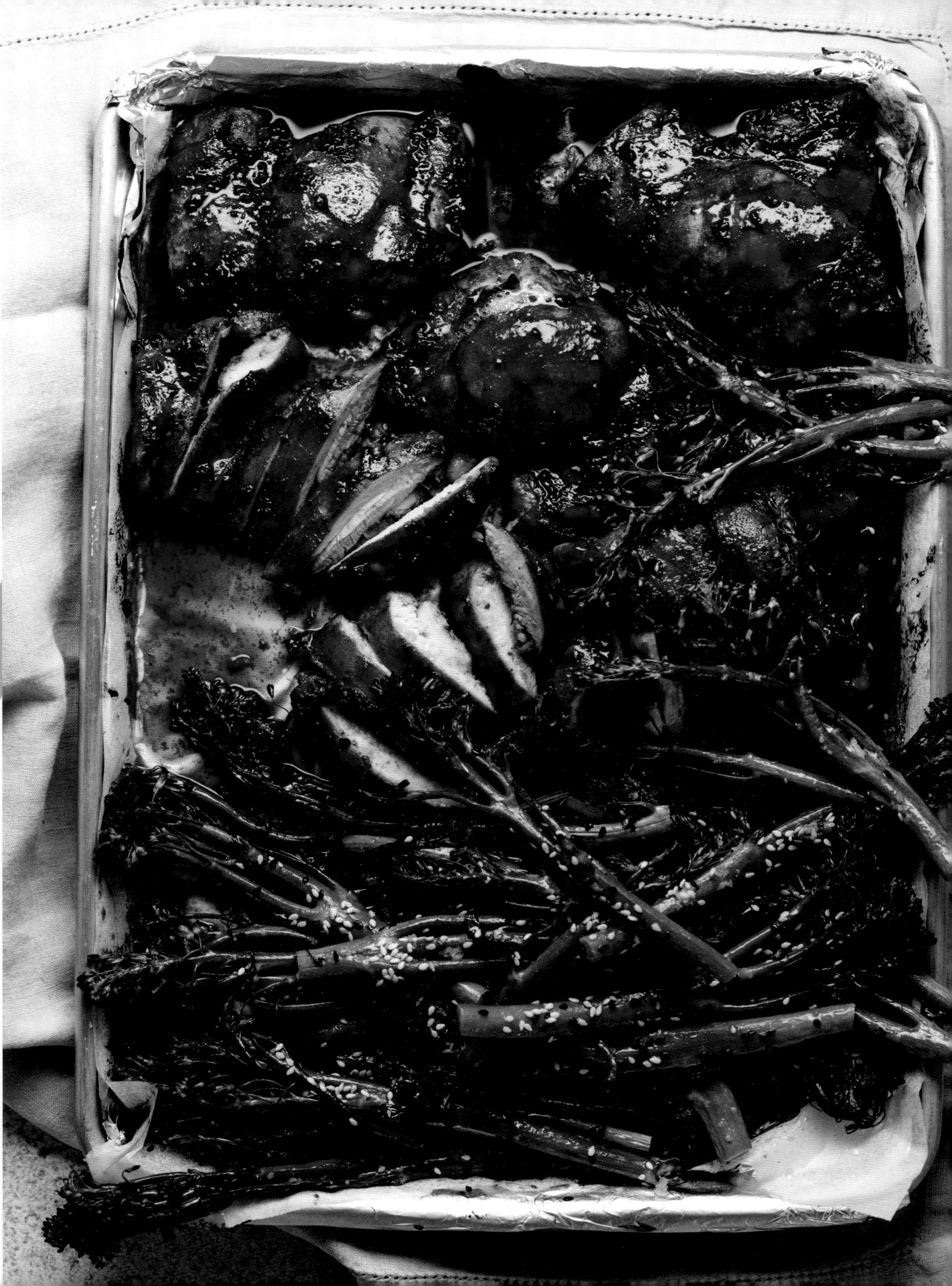

STICKY SOY CHICKEN WITH SESAME BROCCOLI

Everybody loves this sticky honey-soy glaze!

SERVES: 5 | **PREP: 15 MINUTES** | **COOK: 25 MINUTES**

Getting a dark, glossy soy glaze on baked chicken requires a few things. First, a nice and dark, sticky sauce painted multiple times onto the chicken. Next, quick cooking in the oven is the key to setting the glaze without drying out the chicken. And last, the trick is to use the oven grill so the surface of the meat develops a beautifully deep, caramelly flavour. Tenderstem broccoli is the ideal vegetable to team with the chicken – the florets get nice charry bits as they roast, which go brilliantly with the rich, Chinese barbecue-like flavours of the glazed soy chicken.

---

600 g boneless, skinless chicken thighs[1]

ASIAN SAUCE

3 tbsp hoisin sauce

2 tbsp honey

1 tbsp oyster sauce

1 tbsp dark soy sauce*

2 garlic cloves*, finely minced or grated

1 tsp Chinese five spice*

ASIAN GLAZE

2 tsp dark soy sauce*

1 tbsp honey

SESAME BROCCOLI

3 bunches tenderstem broccoli[2], trimmed, thicker stems cut in half lengthways

1½ tbsp sesame oil*

2 tsp finely grated ginger*

¼ tsp salt*

¼ tsp black pepper

TO SERVE

1½ tsp white sesame seeds, to garnish

¼ tsp black sesame seeds, to garnish (optional)

Rice (see pages 318–21) (optional)

Preheat the oven to 240°C (220°C fan). Line a large baking tray with foil (not paper as it will burn under the oven grill).

Marinate chicken – Mix the sauce ingredients in a bowl. Add the chicken and toss to coat. Place the chicken on the tray and dab the surface with the residual sauce left in the bowl. Set the bowl aside for later use.

Bake – Bake for 10 minutes. Remove the tray from the oven. Switch the oven grill to high and position the shelf 15 cm from the heat source.

Make glaze – While the chicken is in the oven, make the glaze by mixing the dark soy and honey in the used bowl.

Tenderstem broccoli – In a separate bowl, toss together the sesame tenderstem broccoli ingredients, using your hands to massage the oil and ginger into the florets. Spread the tenderstem broccoli on the tray around the chicken.

Glaze – Dab half the glaze onto the chicken surface. Place under the grill for 5 minutes. Remove from the oven and dab with more glaze, then grill again until the surface is nicely caramelised and the tenderstem broccoli florets are charred and crispy, about 2–3 minutes.

Rest and serve – Remove the tray from the oven. Sprinkle the tenderstem broccoli with sesame seeds. Transfer the chicken and tenderstem broccoli to serving plates and serve with rice, if desired, drizzled with the tray juices.

NOTES

1 Boneless, skinless chicken breast will work but, because it's leaner, it won't caramelise as nicely as pictured.

2 Make the tenderstem broccoli stems approximately the same thickness so they cook evenly. Asparagus and green beans also work well in this recipe.

LEFTOVERS Fridge 3 days, freezer 3 months.

TAPAS-Y CHORIZO TRAY BAKE

Try this Spanish-inspired spin on an all-in-one tray bake.

SERVES: 4 | PREP: 10 MINUTES | COOK: 1 HOUR

I know plenty of people will cry foul that this is nothing like tapas! And they'd be right. It's not intended as a snacky small plate. But it is inspired by classic tapas dishes you get in a Spanish tavern – sizzling chorizo, patatas bravas and sweet plancha red peppers. As good as these things are alone, the flavours and textures work fantastically together as a homey, all-in-one, Spanish-inspired tray bake. A liberal squeeze or two of fresh lemon lifts and freshens the whole dish. Serve with plenty of crusty bread for mopping up those super tasty tray juices!

---

500 g baby potatoes, halved

2 tbsp extra-virgin olive oil

1/2 tsp smoked paprika* (substitute regular paprika)

3/4 tsp salt*

1/4 tsp black pepper

4 garlic cloves*, unpeeled, smashed to release flavour

VEGETABLES AND CHORIZO

350 g chorizo[1] (3 pieces), sliced diagonally into 1.5 cm thick slices

1 red bell pepper, cut into 2.5 cm squares

1 red onion, cut into wedges

2 tsp smoked paprika*

1/2 tsp salt*

1/4 tsp black pepper*

2 tbsp extra-virgin olive oil

TO FINISH

2–3 tbsp fresh lemon juice

20 g (1 lightly packed cup) parsley leaves

Easy Crusty Artisan Bread (page 326) or other bread, for mopping

Preheat the oven to 200°C (180°C fan).

Roast potatoes – Pile the potatoes onto a large baking tray and toss with the olive oil, paprika, salt, pepper and garlic cloves. Spread out on the tray and bake for 30 minutes.

Toss vegetables and chorizo – In a large bowl, toss together all the vegetable and chorizo ingredients.

Bake – Remove the tray from the oven. Add all the vegetables and chorizo, scraping out all the oil in the bowl, and spread the ingredients in a single layer. Bake for 30 minutes until the chorizo is golden.

Finish and serve – Drizzle the lemon juice all over the tray and sprinkle with parsley leaves. Divide among bowls, scraping out every drop of the tasty tray juices! Serve with crusty bread for mopping the bowls clean.

NOTE

1 Other types of smoked sausages, like kranskies, work really well in this dish too. I don't recommend using raw sausages for this recipe as you can't slice them.

LEFTOVERS Fridge 3 days, freezer 3 months.

ONE-POT CAJUN CHICKEN & RICE

Hearty and spicy rice, Cajun-style.

SERVES: 5 | PREP: 15 MINUTES | COOK: 30 MINUTES

I love food from the South! Hearty dishes with bold, spice-flecked flavours drawn from different cultures, this sort of food is 100% me. Here's a recipe inspired by the many great rice dishes in Cajun cuisine. It's really a kind of jambalaya, pared back a little for easy midweek cooking. But it checks all the authentic spice and flavour boxes, including a kick of chilli! If you aren't big on spicy food, reduce the cayenne pepper to $\frac{1}{4}$ teaspoon or omit completely. Also, make sure you cut the chicken into nice big pieces. This will ensure they stay juicy and don't overcook.

---

750 g boneless, skinless chicken thighs[1]

$\frac{3}{4}$ tsp salt*

2 tbsp olive oil

CAJUN SEASONING

5 tsp smoked paprika* (substitute regular paprika)

$2\frac{1}{2}$ tsp garlic powder

$1\frac{1}{2}$ tsp dried thyme

$1\frac{1}{2}$ tsp dried oregano

$1\frac{1}{2}$ tsp black pepper

$\frac{1}{2}$ tsp cayenne pepper (omit or reduce)

CAJUN RICE

1 brown onion, chopped

2 garlic cloves*, minced

1 celery stalk, cut into 1 cm cubes

1 red bell pepper, deseeded and cut into 1 cm squares

300 g ($1\frac{1}{2}$ cups) long-grain white rice[2], uncooked

625 ml ($2\frac{1}{2}$ cups) low-salt chicken stock*

$\frac{3}{4}$ tsp salt*

TO GARNISH (OPTIONAL)

1 tbsp finely chopped parsley

Chicken – Cut small chicken thighs into two pieces and larger ones into three. Keeping them in large pieces means they stay juicier.

Cajun seasoning – Mix the seasoning ingredients in a small bowl.

Season chicken – Sprinkle the chicken with the $\frac{3}{4}$ teaspoon of salt and 5 teaspoons of the Cajun seasoning, coating both sides. Reserve the remaining spice mix.

Sear chicken – Heat the oil in a large heavy-based pot* over medium–high heat. Place the chicken in the pot, smooth-side down, and cook for 2 minutes until golden. Turn and cook the other side for just 30 seconds, then transfer to a plate.

Cook rice – Add the onion, garlic, celery and bell pepper and cook for 3 minutes until the onion is translucent. Add the remaining Cajun seasoning and the rice and stir for 30 seconds to coat the rice in the tasty flavours. Add the stock and salt and stir. Gently place the chicken on top – it will partially submerge, that's okay. Tip in all the chicken juices pooled on the plate too – free flavour! Bring to a simmer, then put the lid on and reduce the heat to low. Cook for 15 minutes – do not stir, do not lift the lid – or until all the liquid is absorbed (lift the lid quickly and tilt to check).

Rest and serve – Remove the pot from the stove. Rest for 10 minutes with the lid on. Fluff the rice, sprinkle with parsley (if using) and serve!

NOTES

1 Thighs work best because they stay juicy with the time required to cook with the rice. However, you can substitute with boneless, skinless chicken breast, cut into pieces.

2 Basmati and medium-grain rice can also be used. Short-grain rice will also work but the rice will be a little more sticky and less fluffy than pictured. Jasmine rice, brown rice, risotto rice and wild rice are not suitable for this recipe as written.

LEFTOVERS Fridge 3 days, freezer 3 months.

SALADS I LOVE

No boring salads in my world!

COWBOY CHICKEN SALAD WITH SMOKY CHIPOTLE DRESSING

A big and juicy Southwest-style chicken salad, fully loaded!

SERVES: 4 | PREP: 25 MINUTES | COOK: 10 MINUTES

This is the sort of hearty and satisfying Tex-Mex American salad that gets everybody excited! We're talking grilled, seasoned chicken, marinated with lime and spices. We're talking crisp lettuce, pops of sweetcorn, silky avocado and earthy black beans (the world's most underrated legume!) for extra heft. And we're talking a smoky and rich chipotle mayo with just the right tickle of heat to bring it all together. Getting your fresh veggie quota doesn't get any tastier than this, believe me!

---

1 batch Texas Cowboy Chicken (page 51)

SMOKY CHIPOTLE DRESSING

2 tbsp chipotle in adobo*[1] (2 chillies + sauce from the jar)

1 garlic clove, peeled

260 g (1 cup) plain yoghurt

70 g (1/3 cup) whole-egg mayonnaise*

1 tbsp lime juice

2 tbsp extra-virgin olive oil

1/4 tsp ground cumin

3/4 tsp onion powder

3/4 tsp salt*

1/4 tsp black pepper

9 g (1/4 tightly packed cup) coriander leaves

SALAD

350 g (7 lightly packed cups) chopped cos lettuce[2] (large bite-sized pieces)

1/4 red onion, finely sliced

400 g can black beans, drained and rinsed

400 g can sweetcorn, drained

200g grape or cherry tomatoes, halved

1 large avocado, cut into 8 wedges

2 tbsp finely chopped coriander leaves

Dressing – Put all the dressing ingredients, except the coriander, in a jug just large enough to fit the head of a stick blender. Blitz until smooth, then add the coriander and blitz until it's finely chopped. Keep the dressing in the fridge until required.

Chicken – Cook the chicken and rest as per the Texas Cowboy Chicken recipe. Cut into 1 cm thick slices.

Assemble – Either assemble the salad in individual bowls or one big bowl for sharing, as pictured. Place the lettuce in the bowl and sprinkle with the red onion. Top with the chicken, black beans, corn, tomato and avocado, then sprinkle everything with coriander leaves. Serve with the dressing on the side so people can help themselves. Just pour the dressing over the salad, then dig in – it's not the tossing sort!

NOTES

1 Take 2 chillies and squish them into a tablespoon measure, then add sauce until you have 2 tablespoons combined. If you can only find chipotle sauce (which is pureed chipotle in adobo), just measure out 2 tablespoons.

2 I use 2 large baby cos lettuces. Iceberg lettuce is also great here, or other crispy lettuce. Soft lettuce doesn't work as well because of the weight of the toppings and the creamy dressing.

LEFTOVERS The dressing will keep for 3 days in the fridge. The salad components can be prepared up to 3 days ahead. But once you put the dressing on, the salad is best eaten straight away.

THAI BEEF NOODLE SALAD

Not your garden-variety Thai beef noodle salad!

SERVES: 2 | PREP: 25 MINUTES + 24 HOURS MARINATING | COOK: 3 MINUTES

I know, the ingredients list in this Thai beef noodle salad may look a little long. You *could* skip the beef marinade and sear plain meat. And you *could* forgo the lime peanut crumble for plain nuts. It'd be quicker and still taste fantastic. But if you want to pass 'fantastic' and go for 'un-freaking-believable', it's worth the effort, I promise! The marinade not only injects bags of sweet and savoury flavour into the beef, but also tenderises the meat. And the zesty lime crumble brings a special finishing touch. This ain't no ordinary Thai beef salad anymore!

---

250 g beef rump steak[1], cut into 5 mm strips, 5 cm long

1 tbsp vegetable oil

MARINADE

1 tsp dark soy sauce*

2 tsp oyster sauce

1 garlic clove*, minced

¼ tsp bicarbonate of soda*[2]

½ tsp white sugar

DRESSING

1 tbsp finely chopped coriander

¼ tsp finely grated garlic* (or ½ tsp finely minced with a knife)

2 tbsp sweet chilli sauce

1 bird's eye chilli*[3] or red Thai chilli, deseeded and finely minced

5 tsp fish sauce

1 tsp white sugar

3 tbsp lime juice

2 tbsp grapeseed oil

LIME PEANUT CRUMBLE

40 g (¼ cup) unsalted roasted peanuts

1½ tsp lime zest

½ tsp salt*

¼ tsp white sugar

1 tsp lime juice

SALAD

75 g dried rice vermicelli noodles

160 g (2 tightly packed cups) finely shredded wombok cabbage*

1 baby cucumber*, cut in half lengthways, watery seeds removed, then into 5 mm thick slices

10 grape or cherry tomatoes, halved

6 g (¼ cup) roughly chopped mint leaves

2 tbsp finely chopped coriander leaves

Marinate beef – Mix the marinade ingredients in a bowl. Add the beef and toss well to evenly coat. Cover with plastic wrap, then refrigerate for 24 hours.

Dressing – Place the dressing ingredients in a jar and shake well until combined.

Lime peanut crumble – Heat a cast-iron frying pan* over medium heat (no oil). Toast the peanuts until they have golden spots. Tip onto a cutting board, then roughly chop. Transfer to a bowl and add the remaining crumble ingredients. Toss to coat, then set aside to cool.

Prepare salad – Prepare the noodles according to the packet directions. Drain, rinse under cold water, then set aside to thoroughly drain any excess water. Transfer to a bowl and add the remaining salad ingredients – but don't toss yet, just set the bowl aside.

Cook beef – Heat the oil in the same cast-iron pan over high heat until smoking. Spread the beef in the pan in a single layer, then leave to cook for 30 seconds. Use two spatulas to toss for a further 2 minutes (so 2½ minutes in total – no longer!), aiming to get as much caramelisation as possible, then immediately transfer to a plate.

Assemble – Pour the dressing over the salad ingredients. Toss well, then divide between bowls. Top with the beef, then sprinkle with a mound of the lime peanut crumble. DEVOUR!

NOTES

1. Rib-eye steak or porterhouse/sirloin are also ideal for this recipe. Other steak cuts listed on page 170 can also be used, though quick-cooking steak cuts generally have better beef flavour so are more suitable for this recipe.
2. This is used to tenderise the beef so even an economical piece of beef will be beautifully tender.
3. One chilli makes the sauce mild. Feel free to dial it up to 2 chillies!

LEFTOVERS The undressed salad, dressing and beef will keep in the fridge for 3 days. Once dressed, it is best to serve the salad immediately!

KALE & APPLE SALAD WITH MAPLE BACON PECAN CRUMBLE

This one's all about the crunchy, salty, sweet bacon pecan crumble!

SERVES: 3 AS A MAIN, 5 AS A SIDE | PREP: 15 MINUTES | COOK: 30 MINUTES

The crumble steals the show in this salad! You can serve whatever leafy greens and vegetables you want with it, and it's still going to be the best salad you have all week. I've headed in an autumnal direction here – chewy kale leaves with apple batons and cranberries. I also crumble over some soft goat's cheese, which works beautifully with the sweet and sour elements of the salad. All together it's a great combination of textures, colours and flavours. It's substantial enough as a standalone meal or as a statement side dish (official term!). The cranberry-plumping step (another official term) is optional. But once you've plumped, you'll never go back!

MAPLE BACON PECAN CRUMBLE

100 g streaky bacon

60 g (½ cup) pecans[1], half roughly chopped, half finely chopped

2 tbsp maple syrup

SALAD

70 g (½ cup) dried cranberries

250 ml (1 cup) boiling water

180 g (4 tightly packed cups) kale leaves*, torn into 3 cm pieces

1 granny smith apple

1 tsp lemon juice

70 g (⅓ cup) crumbled goat's cheese or Danish feta

DRESSING

3 tbsp apple cider vinegar

6 tbsp (90 ml) extra-virgin olive oil

2 tsp dijon mustard

1½ tsp white sugar

½ tsp salt*

¼ tsp black pepper

Crisp bacon – Put the bacon in a cold non-stick frying pan on the stovetop, then turn the heat to medium–high. Cook the bacon until golden, about 2 minutes on each side. Drain on a paper towel–lined tray. Cool for 5 minutes until crisp, then finely chop.

Crumble – Pour off and discard the bacon fat in the pan, but don't wipe the pan clean. Put it on the stove over medium heat and add the pecans and maple syrup. Stir, then once the maple syrup starts simmering, reduce the heat to low and stir constantly for 2 minutes. Return the bacon to the pan and stir constantly for another 2 minutes. Don't walk away – it will burn if you stop stirring! Tip the bacon onto a plate and spread it out. Set aside for 10 minutes to cool and become crisp.

Plump cranberries – Put the cranberries in a bowl and cover with the boiling water. Leave for 10 minutes to plump up, then drain well. Set aside to cool and dry for about 10 minutes.

Dressing – Add all the dressing ingredients to a jar and shake to combine.

Soften kale – Put the kale in a large bowl. Drizzle with 1 tablespoon of dressing, then scrunch the kale with your hands for 15 seconds, ensuring every piece of kale gets coated with a little dressing. Set aside for 20 minutes to soften and flavour the kale.

Apple – Just before serving, slice the apple into 4 mm batons. Toss in a bowl with the lemon juice[2].

Assemble – Add the apple to the bowl with the kale. Drizzle with most of the remaining dressing and toss. Place half the kale and apple in a serving bowl. Sprinkle with half of the crumble, cranberries and goat's cheese. Top with the remaining kale and apple, crumble, cranberries and goat's cheese. Drizzle with the remaining dressing and serve immediately!

NOTES

1 Almonds and walnuts also work great here.

2 Prevents the apple from going brown.

3 Make ahead: The dressing, plumped cranberries and crumble will keep for 5 days in the fridge. If the crumble gets sticky, toast it in the oven for 5 minutes at 180°C (160°C fan), then cool and allow to crisp. Bring everything to room temperature before serving.

LEFTOVERS The dressed salad is still good the next day, as kale is so much more robust than other leafy greens! Store it in the fridge. Not suitable for freezing.

GINGER SALMON QUINOA SALAD

I love salads you can eat with a spoon!

SERVES: 2 AS A MAIN, 4 AS A SIDE | PREP: 15 MINUTES | COOK: 25 MINUTES

This is a big salmon salad bowl inspired by the textures of tabbouleh, but with Asian flavours. Nutty quinoa is tossed with finely chopped kale and little bits of radish for some contrasting sharpness, then topped with pan-seared salmon. The salmon needs nothing more than a pinch of salt because the whole bowl is generously doused with not one, but two dressings: a Japanese-style ginger dressing, plus a little drizzle of a spicy creamy dressing for a touch of richness. It's filling, interesting, good for you and I love that it can be eaten with a spoon! PS: Don't skip toasting the quinoa for free nutty flavour!

PAN-SEARED SALMON

250 g skinless salmon fillets, cut lengthways into 1.5 cm thick pieces

¼ tsp salt*

1 tbsp vegetable oil

QUINOA

90 g (½ cup) white quinoa (or other colour of choice)

250 ml (1 cup) water

¼ tsp salt*

GINGER DRESSING

2 tbsp rice vinegar

2 tbsp sesame oil*

2 tbsp grapeseed oil or other neutral-flavoured oil

1½ tbsp light soy sauce* or all-purpose soy sauce*[1]

2 tsp finely grated ginger*

½ tsp white sugar

Pinch of white pepper (substitute black pepper)

CREAMY SPICY SAUCE

2 tsp Ginger Dressing (above)

1 tbsp Kewpie mayonnaise* or whole-egg mayonnaise*

1 tsp sriracha*, adjust amount to your taste (optional)

SALAD

75 g (1½ tightly packed cups) finely chopped curly kale leaves*[2]

4 red radishes, finely sliced, then cut into batons

2 heaped tbsp crispy fried shallots*

Toast quinoa – Preheat the oven to 200°C (180°C fan). Spread the quinoa on a baking tray. Toast in the oven for 15 minutes until it smells nutty, shaking the tray once halfway through. Rinse under running tap water for 10 seconds using a fine-mesh sieve and thoroughly shake off any excess water.

Cook quinoa – Tip the quinoa into a medium saucepan*. Add the water and salt. Bring to the boil over high heat, then turn the heat down to medium, put the lid on and simmer for 8 minutes or until the water is absorbed. Remove the saucepan from the stove and set aside to rest for 10 minutes. Remove the lid and fluff the quinoa with a fork. Transfer to a bowl and let the quinoa cool to room temperature before assembling the salad, about 20 minutes.

Ginger dressing and creamy spicy sauce – Put all the dressing ingredients in a jar and shake to combine. Place the creamy sauce ingredients in a small bowl and add 2 teaspoons of the ginger dressing. Mix to combine.

Cook salmon – Sprinkle both sides of the salmon pieces with the salt. Heat the oil in a large non-stick frying pan* over medium–high heat. Cook the first side of the salmon for 1½ minutes. Turn and cook the other side for 1 minute, then transfer the salmon to a plate. Set aside for 5 minutes to rest.

Assemble – Add the kale and radish to the bowl with the quinoa. Pour most of the dressing over and toss well. Divide between two serving bowls. Top with the salmon, breaking it gently into large chunks with your fingers. Pour over the remaining dressing, then drizzle with the creamy sauce. Sprinkle with crispy fried shallots, then dig in immediately!

NOTES

1 Do not use dark soy sauce*. It's too intense and will ruin your dish!

2 Curly kale is easier to chop into little pieces – the natural curly shape of the leaves lends itself to crumbling into small pieces with less chopping effort. You can also use cavolo nero (Tuscan kale), baby spinach or even raw bok choy would be on-point here.

3 Make ahead: Just keep the dressings in separate jars and the salmon separate from the rest of the salad. Store in the fridge for 3 days.

LEFTOVERS Dressed leftovers will keep for 2 days in the fridge. Not suitable for freezing.

LOADED WEDGE

The highest and best use for iceberg lettuce?

SERVES: 2 AS A MAIN, 4 AS A SIDE | PREP: 15 MINUTES | COOK: 7 MINUTES

Wedge salad is all about the toppings. It's definitely not about the iceberg lettuce! That's just the delivery vehicle for the toppings to get from the plate to my mouth. So, when I make a wedge salad, I do not hold back on toppings. Mandatory creamy blue cheese, bacon and a sprinkle of chives. Plus my extras – crunchy, golden, bacon-flavoured mini croutons, juicy little pops of tomato and chopped-up bits of egg. It's a celebration of colours, textures and also how I turn this nostalgic appetiser into a main meal!

BACON-Y MINI CROUTONS

125 g streaky bacon

30 g (1 cup) cubed sourdough, ciabatta or similar bread[1], crusts removed (5 mm cubes)

1/8 tsp salt*

BLUE CHEESE DRESSING

90 g (1 lightly packed cup) crumbly blue cheese like Roquefort[2], at room temperature

70 g (1/3 cup) whole-egg mayonnaise*

80 g (1/3 cup) sour cream

80 ml (1/3 cup) buttermilk*[3]

1/2 tsp garlic powder

2 tsp apple cider vinegar

1/4 tsp salt*, plus more as needed

1/4 tsp black pepper

SALAD

1 iceberg lettuce, cut into quarters with the core intact (so the wedges hold together)

1 hard-boiled egg*, chopped into 5 mm cubes (the yolk will crumble, that's okay)

10 cherry tomatoes, cut into 8 mm dice

2 tbsp finely chopped red onion

1 tbsp finely grated parmesan*

2 tsp finely chopped chives

Cook bacon – Put the bacon in a cold non-stick frying pan on the stovetop, then turn the heat to medium–high. Cook the bacon until the underside is golden, about 2 minutes. Turn, then cook the other side until golden. Transfer to paper towels, leaving the bacon fat in the pan. Once cool and crisp, finely chop the bacon, then set aside.

Bacon-y mini croutons – Cool the pan slightly, then return it to medium heat. Add the bread cubes and cook for 3–4 minutes, stirring regularly, until golden. Transfer to a bowl. Add the salt and toss, then set aside to cool.

Blue cheese dressing – Put the blue cheese in a bowl and mash with a fork. Add the remaining dressing ingredients and whisk well to combine. The thickness and smoothness will depend on the creaminess of your blue cheese. I personally like small lumps of blue cheese in my dressing!

Assemble – Place the lettuce wedges on a large platter. Spoon the dressing over each wedge. Sprinkle with the bacon, mini croutons, egg, tomato, red onion, parmesan and chives. Serve immediately with any left-over toppings and dressing on the side!

NOTES

1. Best to use a chewy bread like sourdough for extra crunchy croutons. I wouldn't make a trip to the store just for the bread – regular sandwich bread will work fine too, but it won't have the same crunch. Bread is easier to cut into small pieces if it's a bit stale. But don't worry, it will still become crispy once fried up even if yours is fresh.
2. Roquefort is my favourite cheese to use because of its assertive, complex flavour. So you can actually taste the blue cheese in this blue cheese dressing! I also like using Gorgonzola Piccante and stilton, both of which are slightly milder, but Danish blue is a good value option. If you're after something more mild, use a soft, creamy blue cheese like Gorgonzola Dolce or Blue Castello.
3. Buttermilk gives this dressing a bit of tang and a silky consistency that clings to the lettuce. Substitute with a mix of plain yoghurt and milk (equal portions).

LEFTOVERS The blue cheese sauce and toasted bread will keep for a week in the fridge. The cooked bacon will keep for 3 days. Once assembled, the salad is best served immediately.

CRISPY HALLOUMI PEARL COUSCOUS SALAD

My pick of the chapter.

SERVES: 4 AS A MAIN, 6–8 AS A SIDE | PREP: 20 MINUTES + 30 MINUTES COOLING | COOK: 20 MINUTES

I have a lot to say about this salad. The pearl couscous salad part itself is already great – with the slippery pearl couscous beads cooked in a garlicky broth, rather than just water, so it gets infused with flavour from the outset. Then we add a load of salad-y goodness: chopped baby spinach, a medley of fresh herbs, juicy bits of tomato, crunchy cubes of cucumber and creamy bits of avocado, before tossing it all in a bright lemon dressing. But the crowning glory here is the golden, crispy, honey-glazed halloumi bites that we pile on top. Chopping the halloumi into cubes rather than the usual slices is a game changer – more golden surfaces! This is a brilliant one for taking to gatherings and for work lunches. Not only is it excellent for making ahead, but it's a salad that will attract envy from everyone who sees it. So sharpen your knives and get chopping!

PEARL COUSCOUS

1 tbsp extra-virgin olive oil

1 large garlic clove*, finely minced

165 g (1 cup) pearl couscous[1]

375 ml (1½ cups) low-salt vegetable stock*

¼ tsp salt*

LEMON DRESSING

3 tbsp lemon juice

80 ml (⅓ cup) extra-virgin olive oil

1 garlic clove*, very finely minced

1 tsp salt*

¼ tsp black pepper

CRISPY HONEY-GLAZED HALLOUMI

1 tbsp olive oil

400 g halloumi[2], cut into 1.5 cm cubes

2 tsp honey (or maple syrup)

SALAD

100 g (2 tightly packed cups) baby spinach, roughly chopped into 7 mm pieces

3 tomatoes*, watery seeds removed, cut into 1 cm squares

2 cucumbers*, cut into quarters lengthways, then into 5 mm thick slices

2 spring onion* stems, finely sliced

1 avocado, cut into 1 cm cubes

6 g (¼ cup) roughly chopped mint leaves[3]

5 g (¼ cup) roughly chopped coriander leaves[3] (substitute parsley)

2 tbsp roughly chopped dill[3], plus extra for garnish

Pearl couscous – Heat the oil in a large saucepan* over medium heat. Add the garlic and cook for 20 seconds or until light golden. Turn the heat up to high, add the couscous and stir for 1 minute. Add the stock and salt. Once it comes to the boil, reduce the heat to medium and place the lid on. Cook for 10 minutes or until the liquid is absorbed.[4] Transfer the couscous to a large bowl and set aside to cool to room temperature, around 30 minutes. It will solidify into a block, which is normal. It will separate when we toss it with the dressing.

Dressing – Put all the dressing ingredients in a jar and shake well to combine.

Crispy honey-glazed halloumi – Heat the oil in a large non-stick frying pan* over medium–high heat. Add the halloumi and use two spatulas to toss regularly to make the cubes light golden on as many sides as possible (it's hard to make *all* sides perfect!). Turn the heat down if they are browning too quickly. Once light golden, drizzle the honey over, then continue tossing for another 1 minute until they are golden. Tumble into a bowl – they will clatter because they're crispy! Set aside while you toss the salad.

Salad – Pour half the dressing over the couscous and toss to separate the beads. Add all the salad ingredients and the remaining dressing. Toss well, then divide among bowls. Top with the crispy halloumi, sprinkle with a pinch of the extra dill, then dig in with a spoon!

NOTES

1 Pearl couscous is the larger variety of couscous that looks like beads, sometimes sold labelled as Israeli couscous. Larger than African couscous (the tiny grains used in the One-pan Chorizo Couscous on page 77) and smaller than Lebanese Moghrabieh couscous. When cooked it has a slippery texture and tastes like pasta. Excellent for salads that you can eat with a spoon!

2 Halloumi is the salty, firm cheese that looks like Greek feta that holds its form when fried so you get a gorgeous golden crust without the inside oozing everywhere.

3 Use the left-over dill as an excuse to make Green Goddess Dressing (page 224) – it's so good! – and the left-over mint and coriander for Thai Beef Noodle Salad (page 202).

4 There will be a layer of thickened liquid on the surface of the couscous, which is totally normal. Don't worry about it, it will get mixed up and absorbed by the couscous as it rests.

5 To make ahead or to take to a gathering: Store the components separately in the fridge, then toss together when you're ready to serve. Cool the halloumi and pearl couscous before placing them in separate containers. The halloumi will stay quite crispy for a couple of days! Toss the chopped avocado in a little lemon juice to keep it from going brown. I store all the vegetables and herbs in separate piles in one large container, rather than tossing together.

LEFTOVERS This recipe is best served freshly made. Not suitable for freezing. See note 5 for how to make ahead.

THE AUSSIE CHOP

Turn a takeaway roast chicken into this belly-filling, healthy, Aussie-style chopped salad!

SERVES: 4 | **PREP: 15 MINUTES** | **COOK: NIL**

Here's a filling, meal-ready salad to make all summer long when it's too hot to sweat away in front of the stove! Just pick up a roast chook on the way home and you'll have this on the table in a jiffy. The vegetables in this recipe channel Greek salad – an ode to that staple you'll see offered in the glass cabinets of many charcoal chicken shops. But feel free to throw together whatever vegetables you've got. The Greek dressing goes with anything! And so does the cheese. (Wait, you've never put grated cheese in a salad before? You're about to have an epiphany!)

DRESSING

7 tbsp (105 ml) extra-virgin olive oil

2½ tbsp red wine vinegar

¾ tsp dijon mustard

¾ tsp salt*

¼ tsp black pepper

2 tsp dried oregano

¾ tsp white sugar

½ tsp finely minced garlic*

2 tbsp finely minced red onion (or eschalot*)

SALAD[1]

600 g (3 cups) cubed cooked chicken (1.5 cm cubes)

250 g (5 heaped cups) iceberg lettuce, cut into 3 cm pieces (or cos lettuce)

1 large baby cucumber*, halved lengthways, then cut into 5 mm thick slices

1 large avocado, quartered, then cut into 5 mm thick slices

100 g (1 cup) grated* tasty cheese (or other cheese of choice)

2 tomatoes, each cut into 8 wedges, then halved

130 g (¾ cup) pitted kalamata olives

Dressing – Put the dressing ingredients in a jar and shake well to combine. Set aside for 10 minutes to let the flavours meld.

Salad – Place all the salad ingredients in a (very!) big bowl and pour the dressing over. Toss, toss, toss! Transfer to a large serving bowl or divide among four individual bowls. Serve!

NOTES

1 Feel free to substitute the vegetables with what you've got and what you like. However, I really encourage you not to skip the grated cheese! It adds interest. Not just another boring salad!

LEFTOVERS Best consumed immediately once dressed as the lettuce will wilt.

CHICKEN SOBA SALAD WITH CREAMY MISO DRESSING

A Japanese-inspired noodle salad with cabbage – perfect for a light lunch in warmer months.

SERVES: 2 | PREP: 15 MINUTES | COOK: 5 MINUTES

Another Japanese salad that I've had on high rotation lately! Cold soba noodles are a favourite in Japan in the steamy summer months, mostly eaten plain with a dipping sauce. I also love them used in a salad like this, teamed with crunchy vegetables such as cabbage, carrot, radish and edamame. A creamy sauce flavoured with miso makes the perfect dressing. The miso adds rich umami flavour as well as thickening the dressing so it clings beautifully to the ingredients (coverage is everything!). In terms of noodle choice, soba has that special texture and lovely buckwheat taste, but any noodles will work fine.

MISO DRESSING

1½ tbsp red miso paste[1]

1 tbsp rice vinegar

1½ tbsp light soy sauce*

2 tbsp sesame oil*

¼ tsp finely grated garlic*

2 tsp finely grated ginger*

2 tsp white sugar

2 tbsp Kewpie mayonnaise*

SOBA SALAD

180 g (2 bundles) dried soba noodles[2]

240 g (1½ cups) shredded cooked chicken breast[3]

130 g (2 cups) finely shredded red cabbage

1 small carrot, peeled and finely julienned (or use a box grater)

1 spring onion*, finely sliced diagonally

70 g (½ cup) frozen edamame, cooked according to the packet directions

2 red radishes, finely sliced

1 tsp black sesame seeds

Miso dressing – Whisk all the dressing ingredients in a bowl until smooth. Set aside for at least 10 minutes to let the flavours meld.

Cook soba – Prepare the soba noodles according to the packet directions. They are usually boiled just for a few minutes. Drain in a colander, rinse under tap water, then set aside to cool and thoroughly drain any excess water, or your salad will be watery.

Toss salad – Toss the chicken with 2 tablespoons of the miso dressing in a large bowl. Pile on the soba, cabbage, carrot and spring onion. Pour the remaining dressing over, then toss.

Serve – Divide between bowls. Top with the edamame and radish, sprinkle with black sesame seeds, then serve.

NOTES

1 Shiro miso (white miso) is also suitable.

2 While other noodles will work here, the buckwheat flavour of soba works especially well!

3 Poach your own or use a store-bought roast chicken.

LEFTOVERS Will keep for 2 days in the fridge, though the salad is at its best freshly made.

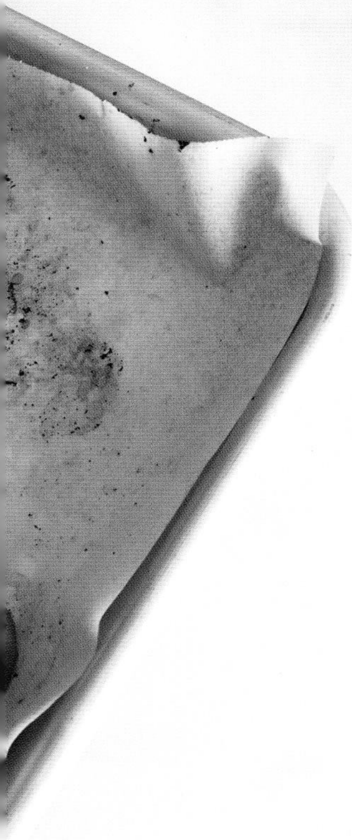

I LOVE ROASTED VEG

Proof – here's 699+ recipes!

HOW TO ROAST (ALMOST) ANY VEGETABLE

Roast hard and fast for better golden surfaces before the insides turn into a watery mush!

SERVES: 4–5 AS A SIDE, 2–3 AS A MAIN (USING SERVING OPTIONS IN THE RECIPES) | PREP: 2–10 MINUTES | COOK: 7–50 MINUTES

Roasting is hands-down the simplest way to coax out the natural sweetness and flavour of any vegetable to make it utterly delicious. Serve the vegetables just as they are, or go wild dressing them up using any of the recipes in this chapter.

GOLDEN RULE: However you cut the vegetables, make each piece roughly the same size so they cook in the same time.

Toss vegetables with olive oil (or other oil of choice), salt and pepper, then roast as per the table below, or until the vegetable is cooked through to your taste.

	ROASTING TIME	TEMPERATURE		CUT
		Standard	Fan	
ASPARAGUS	7 minutes	220°C	200°C	Whole
AUBERGINE^	30 minutes	240°C	220°C	3 cm cubes
AUBERGINE, ASIAN	20 minutes	220°C	200°C	Halved lengthways
BEANS, GREEN	10 minutes	220°C	200°C	Whole
BEETROOT	40 minutes+	200°C	180°C	Bake in foil packs[1]
BELL PEPPER	20 minutes	240°C	220°C	Quarters, deseeded
BROCCOLI	25 minutes	220°C	200°C	Florets, stems peeled, cut into batons
BROCCOLI (TENDERSTEM)	12 minutes	220°C	200°C	Whole[2]
BRUSSELS SPROUTS	15 minutes	240°C	220°C	Halved. Roast flat-side down, don't flip.
CARROTS	30 minutes	220°C	200°C	Diagonal 5 cm lengths, thicker end halved[2]
CAULIFLOWER	25 minutes	220°C	200°C	Florets
CELERIAC	35 minutes	220°C	200°C	Peeled, cut into 3 cm cubes
CORN COBS	30 minutes	200°C	180°C	Whole, each wrapped in foil[3]
COURGETTE	25 minutes	220°C	200°C	2 cm thick rounds or half-moons[5]
ESCHALOTS*	20 minutes	200°C	180°C	Peeled, halved lengthways
FENNEL	30 minutes	200°C	180°C	Cut into 2 cm thick wedges
LEEK	25 minutes	200°C	180°C	Halved lengthways[4], don't flip
MUSHROOMS, BUTTON	25 minutes	220°C	200°C	Small whole, large halved
MUSHROOMS, LARGE	35 minutes	220°C	200°C	Roast whole, gills-side up
ONIONS (ANY TYPE)	20 minutes	180°C	160°C	Peeled, wedges
PARSNIP	30 minutes	220°C	200°C	Peeled, cut into 4–6 long wedges
POTATO^	45 minutes	200°C	180°C	3 cm cubes or 6–8 wedges
POTATO, BABY/COCKTAIL	50 minutes	200°C	180°C	Halved
PUMPKIN^	25 minutes	220°C	200°C	3 cm cubes
SQUASH	25 minutes	220°C	200°C	Small halved, large quartered
SWEDE	45 minutes	200°C	180°C	3 cm cubes
SWEET POTATO	35 minutes	220°C	200°C	2.5 cm cubes
TOMATOES, CHERRY/GRAPE	15 minutes	200°C	180°C	Whole
TOMATOES, REGULAR	40 minutes	180°C	160°C	Halved, cut-face up
TURNIP	30 minutes	220°C	200°C	2 cm thick wedges

^ Baking paper–lined tray recommended

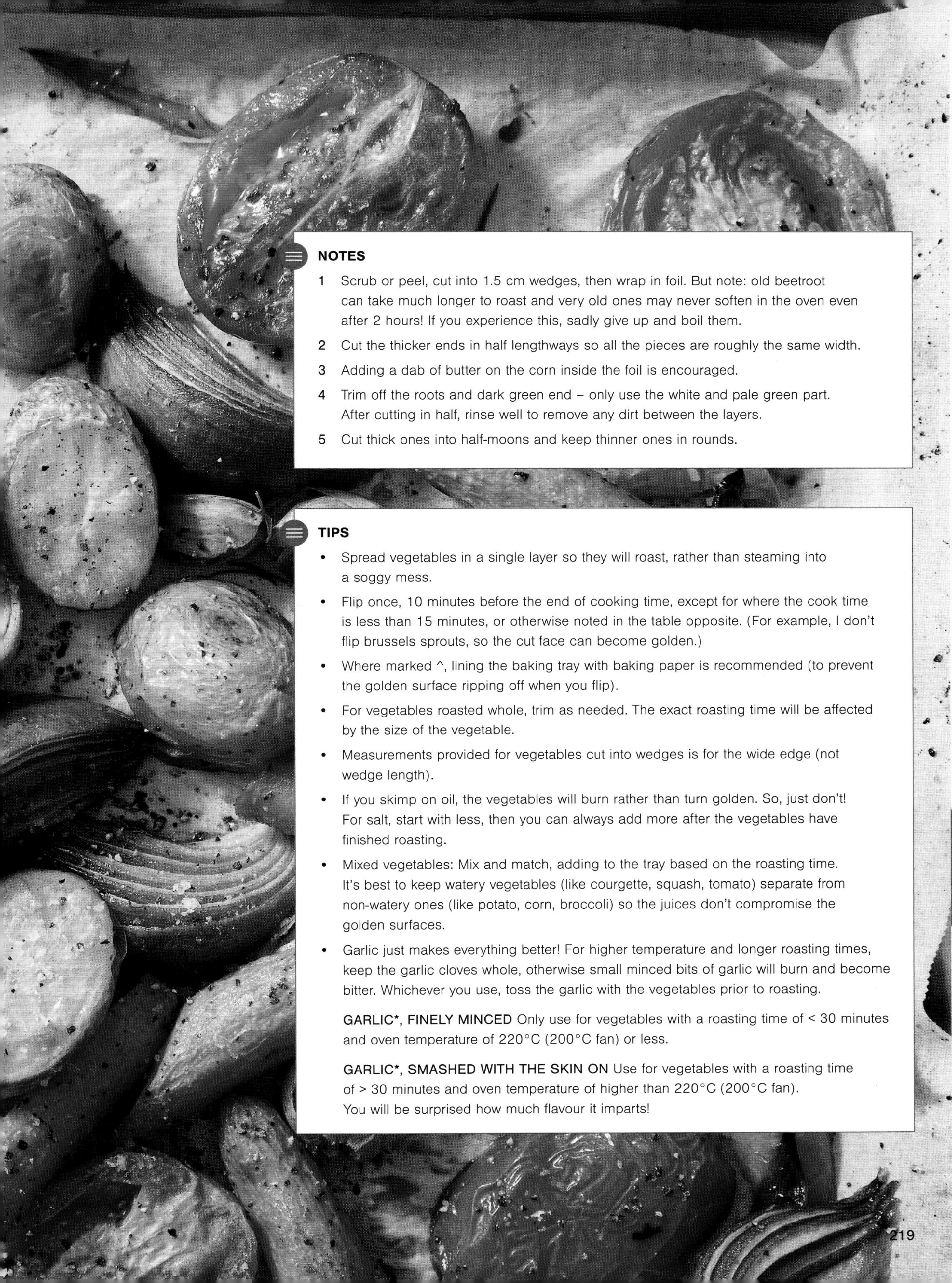

NOTES

1 Scrub or peel, cut into 1.5 cm wedges, then wrap in foil. But note: old beetroot can take much longer to roast and very old ones may never soften in the oven even after 2 hours! If you experience this, sadly give up and boil them.

2 Cut the thicker ends in half lengthways so all the pieces are roughly the same width.

3 Adding a dab of butter on the corn inside the foil is encouraged.

4 Trim off the roots and dark green end – only use the white and pale green part. After cutting in half, rinse well to remove any dirt between the layers.

5 Cut thick ones into half-moons and keep thinner ones in rounds.

TIPS

- Spread vegetables in a single layer so they will roast, rather than steaming into a soggy mess.
- Flip once, 10 minutes before the end of cooking time, except for where the cook time is less than 15 minutes, or otherwise noted in the table opposite. (For example, I don't flip brussels sprouts, so the cut face can become golden.)
- Where marked ^, lining the baking tray with baking paper is recommended (to prevent the golden surface ripping off when you flip).
- For vegetables roasted whole, trim as needed. The exact roasting time will be affected by the size of the vegetable.
- Measurements provided for vegetables cut into wedges is for the wide edge (not wedge length).
- If you skimp on oil, the vegetables will burn rather than turn golden. So, just don't! For salt, start with less, then you can always add more after the vegetables have finished roasting.
- Mixed vegetables: Mix and match, adding to the tray based on the roasting time. It's best to keep watery vegetables (like courgette, squash, tomato) separate from non-watery ones (like potato, corn, broccoli) so the juices don't compromise the golden surfaces.
- Garlic just makes everything better! For higher temperature and longer roasting times, keep the garlic cloves whole, otherwise small minced bits of garlic will burn and become bitter. Whichever you use, toss the garlic with the vegetables prior to roasting.

  GARLIC*, FINELY MINCED Only use for vegetables with a roasting time of < 30 minutes and oven temperature of 220°C (200°C fan) or less.

  GARLIC*, SMASHED WITH THE SKIN ON Use for vegetables with a roasting time of > 30 minutes and oven temperature of higher than 220°C (200°C fan). You will be surprised how much flavour it imparts!

QUICK WAYS TO DRESS UP ROASTED VEGETABLES

I'll happily devour a tray of sweet roasted vegetables unadorned. But sometimes I like to finish them with something extra when serving, to both bump up the flavour and give them a different character. Here are my 10 quick, go-to ways! See overleaf for more toppings and sauces for roasted vegetables.

---

1 **DRESSED**
Make any dressing on pages 312–13 but halve the salt. Drizzle over vegetables while hot (so they soak up the flavour). Serve warm or at room temperature.

2 **LEMON**
Grate lemon zest over vegetables, then drizzle with fresh lemon juice. Finish with a handful of chopped parsley.

3 **PARMESAN**
Spread vegetables on a platter and shower with finely grated parmesan*. Finish with shredded basil or chopped parsley. The addition of lemon zest and juice is also excellent, and I love adding toasted* pine nuts too!

4 **SPICY ASIAN**
Dollop/drizzle your favourite chilli crisp* all over the vegetables, or drizzle with sriracha*. Sprinkle with sliced spring onion*.

5 **ASIAN CRUNCH**
Shower vegetables with a good handful of crispy fried shallots* and sliced spring onion*.

6 **SESAME GARLIC**
Heat 1½ tablespoons of sesame oil* in a small frying pan* over medium heat. Add 2 finely minced garlic cloves* and 1 tablespoon of white sesame seeds. Stir for 30 seconds until both are golden, then immediately drizzle/scatter over the vegetables. Toss, then serve.

7 **MEDITERRANEAN**
Drizzle vegetables with lemon juice, crumble feta (Greek or Danish) over the top, then sprinkle with finely chopped red chilli and parsley.

8 **BALSAMIC GLAZE***
Drizzle vegetables with balsamic glaze – not too much as this stuff is intense!

9 **POMEGRANATE DRIZZLE**
For instant Middle Eastern flavour, drizzle vegetables sparingly with pomegranate molasses*. To elevate things further, sprinkle with pomegranate* seeds, chopped coriander and toasted* pistachios.

10 **SPICY PINK SAUCE**
Mix together 120 g (½ cup) of sour cream with 4 teaspoons of sriracha*. Drizzle the sauce over vegetables, then finish with chopped parsley, coriander or chives.

RECIPES

The recipes that follow provide versatile ways to turn a tray of roasted vegetables into an enticing and substantial side dish or even a main!

NOTES

- All these recipes make enough sauce or topping for a tray of roasted vegetables. However, the amount of each sauce or topping required will vary depending on which vegetable you use. For example, you will need far less for a tray of baked corn on the cob than a tray of broccoli florets. So use your judgement and taste, taste, taste!
- SALT* NOTE (IMPORTANT) – All these recipes assume the vegetables are already adequately seasoned. So the sauces and toppings have no or little salt in them, as that is how they are designed to be. Be sure to taste your dish before serving, and sprinkle with more salt if needed!

WHIPPED RICOTTA (WITH BURST TOMATOES)

Your new favourite sauce to create a statement veg side!

SERVES: 2 AS A MAIN, 4 AS A SIDE OR STARTER | PREP: 10 MINUTES + 20 MINUTES COOLING | COOK: 15 MINUTES

Whipping fresh ricotta with a little grated parmesan gives you the most gorgeously rich, smooth and umami-packed cream that's incredibly versatile – dip, smear, dollop! But I think it's especially stunning served with roasted vegetables. While it will go with just about any vegetable on page 218, it's particularly great with ripe cherry tomatoes, roasted quickly until tender and bursting with sweet juices. Finished with a handful of basil and a swish of extra-virgin olive oil, this pretty and sophisticated Italian plate makes a beautiful statement side or a summery lunch with Easy Crusty Artisan Bread (page 326).

WHIPPED RICOTTA

250 g (1 cup) full-fat, good-quality ricotta[1], at room temperature

50 g (½ tightly packed cup) finely grated parmesan*

2–3 tsp milk, if required

BURST TOMATOES

600 g cherry tomatoes or baby tomatoes (preferably a mix of yellow and red)

2 tbsp extra-virgin olive oil

½ tsp salt*

⅛ tsp black pepper

1½ tsp dried oregano

TO FINISH

1 tbsp good-quality extra-virgin olive oil

2 tsp lemon juice, plus extra to taste

12–15 small basil leaves

SERVING OPTIONS

Crostini (page 324) – to serve as a starter

Easy Crusty Artisan Bread (page 326) – to serve as a main

WHIPPED RICOTTA METHOD

Mix the ricotta and parmesan in a small food processor or a bowl using a hand-held electric beater or even a hand-held whisk![2] Beat until smooth. If the mix seems a bit too stiff and thick (which will depend on the ricotta you're using), dilute with 1 teaspoon of milk at a time until it's spreadable like whipped cream.

Use the sauce for any roasted vegetable. I think it's particularly great with asparagus, broccoli, brussels sprouts, carrots, cauliflower and mushrooms. And of course, tomatoes!

LEFTOVERS Will keep for 3 days in the fridge. Use as a dip, spread on toast, or use for more roasted veg!

RECIPE METHOD

Preheat the oven to 200°C (180°C fan).

Burst tomatoes – Toss the cherry tomatoes with the oil, salt, pepper and oregano on a baking tray. Spread out in a single layer and roast for 15 minutes until the skin starts to wrinkle slightly. Remove the tray from the oven. Leave the tomatoes on the tray to cool to room temperature, about 20 minutes.

Assemble – Dollop the whipped ricotta in the centre of a serving plate and smear it out into a 20 cm circle, pushing most of it to the outer edge of the circle. Scatter the tomatoes on top, then pour the juices from the tray over. Drizzle with olive oil and lemon juice, then scatter with basil leaves. Serve immediately!

Serving options – Serve as-is as a side salad. Add Crostini (page 324) for a starter, or Easy Crusty Artisan Bread (page 326) to serve it as a main.

LEFTOVERS Will keep for 2 days, though best served freshly made.

NOTES

1. The whipped ricotta will only be as good as the ricotta you buy. If you can't get it over the counter at a deli, then opt for the type sold in baskets that are vac-packed, rather than ricotta sold in plastic tubs, which is not as creamy.
2. In this step we want to make the ricotta smooth and creamy and there are multiple ways this can be done, so use the method that suits you best. Even a hand-held whisk works, as long as the ricotta is at room temperature.

GREEN GODDESS DRESSING (WITH ROASTED CAULIFLOWER)

Worth getting all the herbs for this!

SERVES: 4–5 AS A SIDE | PREP: 25 MINUTES + 5 MINUTES COOLING | COOK: 25 MINUTES

This well-known, vibrant green dressing is creamy yet so fresh thanks to the piles of herbs that go into it. Sometimes I hesitate because of the multiple herbs I need to buy, but I never regret the indulgence – this dressing always wows! While this is a sauce that will elevate any vegetable, one of my personal favourites is cauliflower. Besides adding a wonderful splash of colour, the natural sweetness and earthy flavour you get from roasting cauliflower is perfectly matched with the slightly creamy, refreshingly herbaceous dressing. Also – a dip: dunk your favourite crusty bread in it and prepare to swoon.

GREEN GODDESS DRESSING

50 g (1 tightly packed cup) baby spinach leaves

15 g (¾ lightly packed cup) parsley leaves

25 g (½ tightly packed cup) basil leaves

10 g (⅓ tightly packed cup) dill fronds

2 tbsp sliced spring onion* or chives

2 tsp lemon zest

2½ tbsp lemon juice

70 g (⅓ cup) whole-egg mayonnaise*

3 tbsp plain yoghurt

2 tbsp extra-virgin olive oil

3 small anchovies* (or 2 large)

1 small garlic clove, peeled

¼ tsp salt*

⅛ tsp black pepper

ROASTED CAULIFLOWER

1 large head cauliflower, broken into even-sized florets

3 tbsp olive oil

¾ tsp salt*

½ tsp black pepper

TO GARNISH (OPTIONAL)

Small basil and parsley leaves

Dill fronds

GREEN GODDESS DRESSING METHOD

Blitz all the ingredients in a bowl using a stick blender, or in a small food processor or blender, until smooth. Drizzle over roasted vegetables and serve.

Use for any roasted vegetables. Particularly great with broccoli, tenderstem broccoli and cauliflower.

LEFTOVERS Fridge 3 days (stays green!). Not suitable for freezing.

RECIPE METHOD

Preheat the oven to 220°C (200°C fan).

Roasted cauliflower – Pile the cauliflower on a large baking tray. Drizzle with the oil and sprinkle with the salt and pepper. Toss well, then spread the florets out on the tray in a single layer. Roast for 25 minutes, tossing at the 20-minute mark, until the edges are browned and the florets are almost fully softened in the middle of the stem (the cauliflower will cook a little more with residual heat). Cool on the tray for 5 minutes.

Assemble – Pile the cauliflower onto a serving platter and drizzle generously with the green goddess dressing. Scatter with fresh herbs (if using). Pour any remaining dressing into a jar and serve on the side, to let people help themselves to extra if they want (I want!).

LEFTOVERS Best served freshly made, though leftovers will keep in the fridge for 2 days.

CRUNCHY MAPLE BACON PECAN CRUMBLE & GOAT'S CHEESE (ON PUMPKIN)

Nutty, salty, creamy, bacon-y fabulousness.

SERVES: 2 AS A MAIN, 4 AS A SIDE | PREP: 15 MINUTES | COOK: 30 MINUTES

This is the crumble from the Kale & Apple Salad on page 205. It's so irresistibly good, I really wanted to show you how to put it to another use – just scatter over roasted vegetables to instantly make them impressive and substantial! The crumble is a match made in heaven with sweet potato and pumpkin, which I've used here, and brilliant with brussels sprouts. And that's just the tip of the iceberg – see below for more!

---

1 batch Maple Bacon Pecan Crumble from the Kale & Apple Salad on page 205

70 g (⅓ cup) goat's cheese (or Danish feta), crumbled

Roughly chopped parsley, to garnish (optional)

ROASTED PUMPKIN

1.25 kg pumpkin (any type), peeled, seeds removed, cut into 3 cm cubes

2½ tbsp olive oil

½ tsp salt*

¼ tsp black pepper

CRUNCHY MAPLE BACON PECAN CRUMBLE METHOD

Make the crunchy maple bacon pecan crumble as per the Kale & Apple Salad recipe on page 205 while the pumpkin is roasting.

Use for any vegetables except eschalots*, fennel, leek, onion and tomato. Especially good for brussels sprouts, cauliflower, pumpkin and sweet potato.

LEFTOVERS will keep for a week in an airtight container. Keep in the fridge to prevent it from becoming sticky.

RECIPE METHOD

Preheat the oven to 220°C (200°C fan).

Roasted pumpkin – Pile the pumpkin on a baking tray lined with baking paper. Drizzle with the oil and sprinkle with the salt and pepper. Toss well, then spread out so each piece is not touching. Roast for 25 minutes, tossing once at the 20-minute mark.

Assemble – Transfer the pumpkin to a serving plate, mostly in a single layer. Sprinkle with the maple bacon pecan crumble, goat's cheese and parsley (if using). Serve warm!

LEFTOVERS Will keep for 3 days, though best served freshly made.

LEMON YOGHURT SAUCE (WITH AUBERGINE)

I use this a LOT!

SERVES: 4 AS A SIDE | PREP: 15 MINUTES | COOK: 30 MINUTES

If you're like me and always have yoghurt in the fridge, this sauce is going to be on a permanent loop in your kitchen. Aside from drizzling over roast vegetables, I scoop it, spread it, dunk in it – you get the picture!

LEMON YOGHURT SAUCE

260 g (1 cup) Greek yoghurt, or other plain yoghurt

1 small garlic clove*, finely grated

1 tbsp lemon juice

1 tbsp extra-virgin olive oil

¼ tsp salt*

¼ tsp black pepper

ROASTED AUBERGINE

2 large aubergines (800 g total), cut into 3 cm cubes[1]

3 tbsp olive oil

¾ tsp salt*

¼ tsp black pepper

TO SERVE

2 tsp extra-virgin olive oil

2 tbsp toasted* pine nuts or roughly chopped roasted almonds (or other nuts of choice)

1 tsp chopped coriander leaves

Pinch of sumac or paprika*

LEMON YOGHURT SAUCE METHOD

Mix all the sauce ingredients together. Set aside for 10 minutes to let the flavours develop.

Use the sauce for any vegetable. Especially great with asparagus, green beans, broccoli, tenderstem broccoli, carrots, cauliflower, pumpkin, sweet potato and courgettes.

LEFTOVERS Fridge 3 days. Not suitable for freezing.

RECIPE METHOD

Preheat the oven to 240°C (220°C fan).

Roasted aubergine – Line a large baking tray with baking paper. In a large bowl, toss the aubergine with the oil. Sprinkle with the salt and pepper and toss again. Spread the aubergine on the tray and roast for 30 minutes, tossing once at the 20-minute mark. Cool for 5 minutes on the tray.

Serve – Smear 125 g (½ cup) of the lemon yoghurt sauce on a plate, then pile the aubergine on top. Dollop another 60 g (¼ cup) of the lemon yoghurt sauce over the top. Drizzle with the extra-virgin olive oil, sprinkle with pine nuts, coriander leaves and sumac and serve!

LEFTOVERS Best eaten immediately, though it will keep in the fridge for 2 days.

NOTE

1 I leave the skin on as I have never experienced bitterness in aubergine skin – a characteristic from the past that has now largely been bred out. The skin also makes the pieces hold together better for roasting. However, feel free to cut the skin off if you prefer.

AVOCADO CREMA (WITH ROASTED SWEET POTATO)

A creamy avocado sauce that works wonders with vegetables.

SERVES: 4–5 AS A SIDE | PREP: 15 MINUTES + 10 MINUTES COOLING | COOK: 35 MINUTES

This limey sauce gets most of its creamy goodness from avocado. It's naturally great with all things Mexican/Tex-Mex but also delicious on so many vegetables – raw (think crudités!) or roasted. Here, I'm using it with roasted sweet potato cubes finished with a crumble of feta – and toasty pepitas (pumpkin seeds), which is on theme, being commonly used in Mexican cooking. With sweet from the potato, salty from the feta, nutty from the pepitas and creamy from the avocado crema, this dish is a terrific combination of flavours that just works.

AVOCADO CREMA

115 g (½ cup) avocado flesh[1]

50 g (¼ cup) sour cream

50 g (¼ cup) mayonnaise*

2½ tbsp lime juice

6 g (½ lightly packed cup) coriander leaves

¼ tsp finely grated garlic*

¼ tsp salt*

¼ tsp black pepper

ROASTED SWEET POTATO

1 kg sweet potato (2 large), peeled and cut into 2.5 cm cubes

3 tbsp olive oil

¾ tsp salt*

½ tsp black pepper

TO FINISH AND GARNISH

75 g feta, crumbled

30 g (¼ cup) pepitas (pumpkin seeds), toasted*

Coriander leaves (optional)

AVOCADO CREMA METHOD

Combine the avocado crema ingredients in a bowl and blitz with a stick blender until smooth. Ready for use!

Use the sauce for any vegetable other than celeriac, eschalot*, fennel, leeks, onion, parsnip, swede and turnip. Particularly great with green beans, pumpkin and sweet potato. Also use for dipping with vegetable sticks, smearing on toast or dolloping on tacos (its natural home!).

LEFTOVERS Will keep for 3 days in the fridge and won't go brown! Not suitable for freezing.

RECIPE METHOD

Preheat the oven to 220°C (200°C fan).

Roasted sweet potato – Line a large baking tray with baking paper. Pile the sweet potato on the tray, drizzle with the oil, then sprinkle with the salt and pepper. Toss well, then spread out so each piece is not touching. Roast for 35 minutes, tossing once at the 20-minute mark. Cool for 10 minutes on the tray.

Serve – Smear 100 g (½ cup) of avocado crema on a serving plate and pile the sweet potato on top. Drizzle with more avocado crema – you mightn't use it all. Crumble the feta over, sprinkle with the pepitas and coriander leaves (if using), then serve.

LEFTOVERS Best served freshly made, though leftovers will keep for 2 days in the fridge.

NOTE

1 1 small or ½ large avocado. Cut in half, scoop out the flesh and smoosh into a 85 g (½ cup) measure.

SALSA VERDE (WITH ROASTED BABY POTATOES)

The punchier pesto.

SERVES: 4 AS A SIDE | PREP: 15 MINUTES + 10 MINUTES COOLING | COOK: 50 MINUTES

This impressively fresh Italian herb sauce is amazingly versatile. It pairs as well with grilled meats and seafood as it does roasted vegetables! It's particularly great with roast potatoes, which is one of the more classic ways to serve it, and never fails to impress. Dollop or toss, or even add it to your favourite dressing. Just remember a little goes a long way (think of it like a pesto).

SALSA VERDE

20 g (1 lightly packed cup) parsley leaves

20 g (1 lightly packed cup) basil leaves, plus extra for garnish

6 g (½ lightly packed cup) mint leaves

½ garlic clove, roughly chopped

1 tbsp chopped gherkins

½ tbsp capers

1 anchovy*, around 6 cm long

1½ tsp dijon mustard

4 tbsp extra-virgin olive oil

2½ tsp red wine vinegar

Pinch of salt*

Pinch of black pepper

ROAST BABY POTATOES

1 kg baby potatoes (any colour is fine), skin on, halved (larger ones quartered)

¾ tsp salt*

½ tsp black pepper

2½ tbsp olive oil

SALSA VERDE METHOD

Blitz all the ingredients to a fine puree in a food processor or in a bowl using a stick blender.

Use the sauce for any roasted vegetable. Particularly great with starchy and firm vegetables like potatoes, carrots and celeriac. And I personally think everyone should experience roasted mushrooms with salsa verde at least once in their life!

LEFTOVERS Freeze in ziplock bags*, flattened, so it's easy to snap off what you need. Or store in the fridge for 3 days with a thin layer of olive oil on the surface to prevent it from going brown.

RECIPE METHOD

Preheat the oven to 200°C (180°C fan).

Roast potatoes – Toss the potatoes with the salt, pepper and olive oil. Spread them out on a large baking tray and roast for 50 minutes, tossing once at the 30-minute mark, until golden and soft all the way through. Allow to cool on the tray for 10 minutes, or even to room temperature.[1]

Toss – Tumble the potatoes into a bowl. Add 60 g (¼ cup) of salsa verde. Toss gently, then taste and add more salt if desired. Serve warm or at room temperature.

LEFTOVERS Once the potatoes are tossed in the salsa verde, the vibrant green colour will dull a bit with time but it won't turn brown. Store in the fridge for 2 days.

NOTE

1 If the potatoes are piping hot it will make the salsa verde go brown, so toss when warm or even fully cool. This is the sort of salad that's ideal for taking to gatherings and serving at room temperature!

WHIPPED TAHINI WITH A MOUNTAIN OF PANKO (ON ASPARAGUS)

This combination of flavour and texture is to die for!

SERVES: 4–5 AS A SIDE | PREP: 20 MINUTES | COOK: 15 MINUTES

A shower of crunchy golden breadcrumbs over this creamy-yet-bright tahini turns any roast vegetable into a texture-filled statement side! I particularly like using this topping with stringy vegetables like beans and asparagus so I can pick them up with my fingers and eat them like a snack. It's addictive! Try it once and you'll understand!

GOLDEN PARMESAN PANKO

45 g (¾ cup) panko breadcrumbs*

3 tbsp extra-virgin olive oil

⅛ tsp salt*

25 g (¼ tightly packed cup) finely grated parmesan*

WHIPPED TAHINI

260 g (1 cup) plain yoghurt

2½ tbsp tahini*

1½ tbsp lemon juice (substitute 1 tbsp apple cider vinegar or white wine vinegar)

1 garlic clove*, finely grated

¼ tsp salt*

ROASTED ASPARAGUS

4 bunches asparagus (30–40 stems), woody ends trimmed[1]

2 tbsp olive oil

½ tsp salt*

¼ tsp black pepper

TO GARNISH (OPTIONAL)

Finely chopped parsley

PANKO AND WHIPPED TAHINI METHOD

Panko – Mix the parmesan panko ingredients in a bowl. Preheat a large non-stick frying pan* over medium–high heat. Add the panko and stir for 3–5 minutes or until golden. Transfer to a bowl and cool before using.

Whipped tahini preparation – Place the ingredients in a heatproof bowl and whisk briefly to combine. Set aside.

Whip tahini – Once the roasted vegetables are done, microwave the tahini yoghurt mixture in the bowl for 20 seconds on High, then whisk vigorously for 10 seconds until it resembles softly whipped cream. Use immediately.

Use for any vegetable. Especially great with asparagus, green beans, broccoli, tenderstem broccoli, carrots, cauliflower, pumpkin, sweet potato and courgettes.

LEFTOVERS Whipped tahini will keep for 3 days in the fridge. Microwave for 20 seconds to warm gently then re-whip. Not suitable for freezing. The golden panko can be kept in the fridge for a week, or frozen for 3 months.

RECIPE METHOD

Preheat the oven to 220°C (200°C fan).

Roasted asparagus – Pile the asparagus on a large baking tray. Drizzle with the oil and sprinkle with the salt and pepper. Toss well, then spread out on the tray in a single layer. Roast for 7 minutes or until just about tender – the asparagus will continue softening in the residual heat. Immediately transfer the asparagus to a serving platter – either piled up on a smaller one (as pictured) or in a single layer on a larger plate. Cool for 3 minutes.

Serve – Pour the warm whipped tahini over the asparagus, then pile a mountain of panko on top. Sprinkle with parsley (if using) and serve!

LEFTOVERS Best served freshly made as the panko breadcrumbs will go soggy.

NOTE

1 Cut with a knife or just snap the ends off using your hands – they will naturally break at the right point!

TAHINI DRIZZLE SAUCE (WITH CHARRED BROCCOLI)

Nutty and rich tahini sauce adds instant pizzazz to just about any vegetable!

SERVES: 4–5 AS A SIDE | PREP: 15 MINUTES | COOK: 12 MINUTES

Tahini is a brilliant way to make a quick sauce that's beautifully creamy with a lovely sesame flavour and a thick texture that clings to anything lucky enough to be drizzled with it. It's especially great for adding a modern Middle Eastern spin to a side dish for a themed menu. While tahini sauce works with almost any vegetable, hands-down my favourites are broccoli because the florets act like a sponge for the sauce!

TAHINI DRIZZLE SAUCE

55 g (1/4 cup) tahini*

2 1/2 tbsp water

1 1/2 tsp honey

1 tbsp lemon juice

1/2 garlic clove*, finely grated

1/4 tsp salt*

1/4 tsp black pepper

ROASTED TENDERSTEM BROCCOLI

3 bunches tenderstem broccoli (18–25 stalks)

2 tbsp olive oil

1/2 tsp salt*

1/4 tsp black pepper

TO SERVE

25 g (1/4 cup) flaked almonds, toasted* (or 2 tbsp toasted* pine nuts)

TAHINI DRIZZLE SAUCE METHOD

Mix the sauce ingredients together until smooth.

Use for any vegetable. Fantastic with broccoli and tenderstem broccoli. Green beans, cauliflower and carrots are a close second – I just particularly enjoy these vegetables with tahini flavour.

LEFTOVERS Fridge 3 days. Bring to room temperature, then mix well until smooth. Not suitable for freezing.

RECIPE METHOD

Preheat the oven to 220°C (200°C fan).

Even size – Cut the stalk of thicker tenderstem broccoli in half lengthways so they are all roughly the same thickness.

Roasted tenderstem broccoli – Pile the tenderstem broccoli on a large baking tray. Drizzle with the oil, then sprinkle with the salt and pepper. Toss well, rubbing the oil into the florets. Spread the tenderstem broccoli out on the tray in a single layer. Roast for 12 minutes until the stems are crisp-tender (they will cook more from the residual heat) and some of the florets are a little charred and crisp (my favourite part!). Transfer to a plate.

Assemble – Drizzle the tenderstem broccoli with the tahini sauce. Use it all! Sprinkle with toasted almonds and serve immediately.

LEFTOVERS Best served freshly made, though leftovers will keep in the fridge for 2 days. Not suitable for freezing.

SMOKY CHIPOTLE DRESSING (WITH ROASTED CORN)

Beautiful earthy, smoky flavour with a subtle tang.

SERVES: 5 AS A SIDE | PREP: 15 MINUTES | COOK: 30 MINUTES

The Smoky Chipotle Dressing in the Cowboy Chicken Salad on page 200 is a terrifically versatile sauce that I use on many things, from tacos to rice bowls, grilled salmon to roast chicken. It's just an instant pick-me-up! It's not that spicy and is all about the earthy flavour, and I love how it's so quick to make but delivers big on the flavour department. More to the point, it will make immediate friends with pretty much any vegetable you choose, though it's particularly good friends with corn. This has very strong Mexican street corn vibes. Side-worthy, snack-worthy, starter-worthy!

---

1 batch Smoky Chipotle Dressing from the Cowboy Chicken Salad on page 200

50 g (½ tightly packed cup) finely grated parmesan*

2 tsp finely chopped coriander leaves

1 lime, cut into wedges (optional)

ROASTED CORN

5 corn cobs

30 g unsalted butter, melted

½ tsp salt*

SMOKY CHIPOTLE DRESSING METHOD

Make the dressing as per the Cowboy Chicken Salad on page 200.

Use for any roasted vegetable. Drizzle or spoon over, then serve! Also excellent for dipping things like asparagus, green beans and broccoli florets. Use your hands or spear with a fork, then dip!

LEFTOVERS 3 days in the fridge, 3 months in the freezer.

RECIPE METHOD

Preheat the oven to 200°C (180°C fan).

Roasted corn – Drizzle and rub the corn with the butter, then sprinkle all over with the salt. Wrap each corn cob in a sheet of foil. Bake for 30 minutes. Unwrap and allow to cool for 5 minutes.

Assemble – Place the corn on a plate. Spoon the dressing generously over each cob, turning the corn as you go to coat it all over. Sprinkle each piece of corn with the parmesan, again rotating for coverage all over. Sprinkle with coriander, then serve immediately with lime wedges on the side, if desired.

LEFTOVERS Best served immediately but it will keep in the fridge for 3 days. Not suitable for freezing.

CURRY OIL (WITH CABBAGE WEDGES)

Just a little drizzle makes everything more interesting (and exotic!).

SERVES: 4 AS A SIDE | PREP: 20 MINUTES | COOK: 30 MINUTES

Four ingredients, one incredibly fragrant oil! Use it over any roasted vegetables or even as the oil for roasting the vegetables. A spoonful of this spiced oil over scrambled eggs or an omelette, as well as barbecued seafood and grilled chicken, is also brilliant. Here, I'm using it for cabbage. The oil drips between the leaves so you get some in every mouthful! I've also added a bed of yoghurt here for an extra element but it's entirely optional.

CURRY OIL

125 ml (1/2 cup) olive oil

2 tbsp curry powder*

2 large garlic cloves, finely sliced

1/2 tsp white sugar

Salt*, if needed

ROASTED CABBAGE

1/2 green cabbage, cut into 4 x 4 cm wedges[1]

2 tbsp olive oil

3/4 tsp salt*

1/2 tsp black pepper

TO SERVE

1 quantity Lemon Yoghurt Sauce (page 228)

2 tbsp roughly chopped cashews, toasted*

2 tbsp roughly chopped coriander leaves

CURRY OIL METHOD

Place the ingredients in a small saucepan on the stovetop, then turn the heat to medium. Once the garlic starts gently sizzling, remove the pan from the heat. Leave to infuse and cool for 20 minutes, then transfer to a jar and blitz with a stick blender until the garlic is pureed. Give it a good stir, then drizzle it over vegetables. Taste and add salt if needed – this recipe assumes the vegetables are already adequately seasoned.

Goes with all vegetables. Especially great drizzled in the caps of large roasted mushrooms, and on broccoli and tenderstem broccoli.

LEFTOVERS Fridge 1 month, freezer 3 months.

RECIPE METHOD

Preheat the oven to 220°C (200°C fan).

Lemon Yoghurt Sauce – Make the Lemon Yoghurt Sauce as per the instructions on page 228, then set aside to give the flavours time to meld.

Roasted cabbage – Lay the cabbage wedges on their side on a baking tray. Drizzle with half the oil and use your fingers to rub it across the surface. Sprinkle with half the salt and pepper. Turn and repeat with the remaining oil, salt and pepper. Roast for 25 minutes until the edges of the cabbage are browned (the most delicious part!). Leave on the tray to cool for 5 minutes.

Assemble – Spread the yoghurt sauce on a plate, then arrange the cabbage on top. Give the curry oil a good mix to stir the curry powder through the oil, then drizzle about 3 tablespoons of the curry oil over the cabbage. Sprinkle with cashews and coriander and serve immediately.

LEFTOVERS Best eaten immediately once assembled, though it will keep in the fridge for 2 days.

NOTE

1 Handle the wedges carefully so they stay together as a wedge when roasting.

KOREAN CHILLI SAUCE (WITH ROASTED MUSHROOMS)

A savoury-sweet-slightly-spicy Korean flavour rocket!

SERVES: 4 AS A SIDE | PREP: 20 MINUTES | COOK: 25 MINUTES

This is actually the chilli sauce I use for classic Korean bibimbap. I'm always telling people this flavour-packed sauce makes anything taste amazing – so I'm committing that statement to the pages of this cookbook! In this recipe, I'm using it to toss with roasted mushrooms. Serve as a side (think – Korean banchan!) or over rice as a meal.

KOREAN CHILLI SAUCE

4 tbsp gochujang*

2 tbsp mirin*

2 tbsp rice vinegar (substitute apple cider vinegar)

1½ tsp light soy sauce*

3 tsp white sugar*

1 garlic clove*, finely grated

2½ tsp sesame oil*

ROASTED MUSHROOMS

500 g white button mushrooms, halved[1]

3 tbsp olive oil

½ tsp salt*

¼ tsp black pepper

TO SERVE

2 tbsp finely sliced spring onion*

2 tsp white sesame seeds*, toasted

KOREAN CHILLI SAUCE METHOD

Mix the sauce ingredients together in a bowl. Dollop over roasted vegetables. Sprinkle with spring onion and sesame seeds and serve!

Use for absolutely any vegetable. This is a sauce that works with everything! Tip: Some vegetables, like mushrooms, need less of this sauce, whereas vegetables like tenderstem broccoli and onion, which have sponge-like characteristics, will take more.

LEFTOVERS Fridge 5 days, freezer 3 months.

RECIPE METHOD

Preheat the oven to 220°C (200°C fan).

Roasted mushrooms – Pile the mushrooms on a baking tray. Drizzle with oil, then sprinkle with salt and pepper. Toss well and spread out on the tray in a single layer. Roast for 25 minutes or until the mushrooms are lightly browned and soft all the way through.

Toss – Transfer the hot mushrooms to a bowl, along with any juices on the tray. Pour over half the chilli sauce (or more, if you want!) and toss. Transfer the mushrooms and all the sauce into a serving dish. Sprinkle with the spring onion and sesame seeds. Serve warm (my preference) or at room temperature.

LEFTOVERS Fridge 3 days. Not suitable for freezing.

NOTE

1 Smaller mushrooms can be kept whole. Remember, mushrooms shrink a fair bit when they cook!

SIZZLING GARLIC, CUMIN & CORIANDER (GREEN BEANS)

Make this for the flavour. Enjoy it for the sizzle!

SERVES: 4–5 AS A SIDE | PREP: 15 MINUTES | COOK: 15 MINUTES

Sizzling spices in oil to release their flavour, before pouring them warm over food, is a technique I've borrowed from Indian cuisine. However this fragrant oil is equally at home in a Middle Eastern–style spread too. I love the crunch of the seeds – such great texture and bursts of flavour. While this sort of topping works exceptionally well with seed-catching and seed-sticking vegetables like cauliflower florets and onion, I have a particular fondness for using this with beans. Very Ottolenghi vibes!

SIZZLING GARLIC, CUMIN AND CORIANDER

2 tbsp extra-virgin olive oil

2 tsp coriander seeds

1 tsp cumin seeds

1 tbsp finely minced garlic* (about 3 cloves)

Salt*, if needed

ROASTED GREEN BEANS

500 g green beans, ends trimmed

2 tbsp olive oil

3/4 tsp salt*

1/2 tsp black pepper

SIZZLING GARLIC, CUMIN AND CORIANDER METHOD

Heat the oil in a small frying pan* over medium–low heat. Add the coriander and cumin seeds and gently sizzle for 1 minute. Add the garlic and stir for 30 seconds or until very light golden – don't let it burn as it will become bitter. Pour over roasted vegetables immediately. Taste and add salt if needed – this recipe assumes the vegetables are already adequately seasoned.

Use for any vegetables. Especially good for asparagus, green beans, broccoli, tenderstem broccoli, bell pepper, cauliflower, eschalot*, leek, onion, tomato (any) and courgettes.

LEFTOVERS Fridge 5 days, freezer 3 months. Bring to room temperature before using.

RECIPE METHOD

Preheat the oven to 220°C (200°C fan).

Roasted beans – Pile the beans on a baking tray. Drizzle with oil, then sprinkle with salt and pepper. Toss well, then spread the beans out in a single layer. Roast for 10 minutes or until the beans are just barely softened – they will continue cooking with the residual heat. Hopefully the beans around the edges of the tray get a little browned!

Assemble – Transfer the hot beans into a bowl. Pour the sizzling sauce over and toss. Transfer to a serving bowl. My preference is to serve this warm but it's also excellent at room temperature.

LEFTOVERS Fridge 3 days. Bring to room temperature or warm gently before serving. Not suitable for freezing.

SUNDAY SUPPERS

For leisurely meals with your favourite people

ROAST CHICKEN FOR COMPANY

Delicate herbs in a classic French sauce elevate roast chook and spuds to dinner-party status!

SERVES: 4–5 | PREP: 15 MINUTES | COOK: 1½ HOURS

Here's a beautiful roast chicken served French-style with an elegant, herb-flecked white wine and cream sauce. Chervil and tarragon are key to giving the sauce its distinctly French character. If you can't find chervil you can replace it with more parsley. But please don't skip the tarragon. Its gentle aniseed flavour is the magic ingredient that makes people sit up and exclaim: 'Ohhh it's just like the sauce at that restaurant!'

1.8 kg whole chicken, patted dry

75 g unsalted butter, softened

1½ tsp salt*

¾ tsp black pepper

250 ml (1 cup) chardonnay wine*[1]

POTATOES

600 g kipfler potatoes[2], scrubbed clean and halved lengthways

25 g unsalted butter, melted

½ tsp salt*

¼ tsp black pepper

HERB CREAM SAUCE

1½ tsp cornflour

250 ml (1 cup) double cream*

3 tsp finely minced chervil[3]

3 tsp finely minced tarragon[3]

1 tsp finely minced parsley[3], plus extra to garnish

Pinch of black pepper

Salt*, if needed

Preheat the oven to 220°C (200°C fan).

Butter chicken – Place the chicken in a roasting pan and slather it all over with the butter. Sprinkle the underside with ½ teaspoon of the salt and ¼ teaspoon of the black pepper. Sprinkle the top and sides with the remaining salt and pepper. Tie the drumsticks together with kitchen string and tuck the wing tips under the chicken.

Prepare for roasting – Toss the potatoes in the melted butter, salt and pepper in a bowl (not in the pan[4]). Pour the wine into the pan around the chicken, then place the potatoes in the wine.

Roast[5] – Place the pan in the oven. Roast for 20 minutes, then turn the oven down to 180°C (160°C fan). Roast for a further 50–60 minutes, basting with the pan juices at the 30-minute mark, or until the internal temperature in the joint between the thigh and leg is 72°C, measured using a cooking thermometer*.

Rest – Tilt the pan so the juices inside the cavity of the chicken flow into the pan. Transfer the chicken and potatoes to a serving platter and rest for 15 minutes.

Herb cream sauce – Pour all the juices, including all the golden bits stuck to the base of the pan (use a rubber spatula), into a medium saucepan*. Reduce to 125 ml (½ cup) over high heat – measure with a jug to check.[6] In a jug, mix the cornflour with 1 tablespoon of the cream until lump-free, then mix in the remaining cream. Pour the cream into the saucepan. Bring to a simmer, then reduce the heat to medium and simmer for 2 minutes or until the sauce thickens into a thin syrup consistency. Remove from the stove. Stir in the chervil, tarragon, parsley and pepper. Taste and add more salt if required (I find there's enough residual salt from the chicken so I don't add more). Pour into a serving jug.

Serve – Serve the chicken and potatoes with a sprinkle of parsley, with the jug of herb cream sauce on the side so everybody can help themselves – but keep an eye out for Sauce Monsters (like myself) who may try to take more than their fair share. (Can't blame them! That sauce is special!)

See Notes overleaf.

NOTES

1. Substitute with any other dry white wine that's not too sweet or woody. For non-alcoholic, it is best to use non-alcoholic white wine, otherwise, use low-salt chicken stock* and reduce the salt on the chicken by ½ teaspoon.
2. Also known as fingerling potatoes, these are small, long, waxy potatoes that become buttery and creamy inside when roasted. Substitute with baby potatoes (halve any large ones).
3. Fresh herbs are required for this recipe. Dried herbs can be used but won't have the same flavour, I'm sorry to say!
4. I know it's tempting to toss the potatoes in the pan rather than dirtying an extra bowl. But if you do, most of the salt ends up on the base of the pan instead of sticking to the potatoes, which makes the roasting juices a little too salty.
5. Starting off the roasting at a higher temperature kick starts the browning of the skin before lowering the oven heat so the flesh cooks evenly.
6. If you have less than 125 ml (½ cup) of pan juices, top up with water and proceed to make the sauce. Measure to ensure the juices have been reduced to 125 ml (½ cup). If you have more, the flavour will be diluted. Too little, and they will be too concentrated!

LEFTOVERS Fridge 3 days, freezer 3 months.

SLOW-ROASTED MIDDLE EASTERN LAMB SHOULDER

Fall-apart lamb crusted in heady spices. This is as special as it gets!

SERVES: 6–8 PEOPLE | PREP: 20 MINUTES | COOK: 4½ HOURS

The vision for this recipe is magnificent – a Middle Eastern-inspired roasted lamb feast with all the trimmings. This is food made for sharing! Plonk the platter in the middle of the table and let your guests tear into it with glee. The lamb is smeared with a homemade ras el hanout mix (forget store-bought stuff!) before slowly cooking in the oven, half roasting and half braising. Cooking this way results in a gorgeous caramelised skin with the juiciest flesh imaginable. It's the little details though that I think really make the dish. A handful of dried figs that impart natural sweetness into the broth. A light honey glaze here, a sprinkle of cumin seeds there, a fresh pistachio herb garnish to finish. Served with a lemony couscous and yoghurt sauce, I think it truly nails the brief: magnificent!

---

3 tbsp tomato paste

375 ml (1½ cups) low-salt chicken stock*

1 brown onion, peeled and cut into 8 wedges

1 garlic bulb, whole, unpeeled, cut in half horizontally

2 cinnamon sticks

1.8–2.2 kg lamb shoulder, bone-in[1]

8 dried figs, halved (160 g) or 16 dried apricots

400 g can chickpeas, drained

15 g (½ cup) finely chopped mint leaves

20 g (½ cup) finely chopped coriander leaves

60 g (½ cup) toasted* pistachio kernels, roughly chopped

RAS EL HANOUT

1½ tbsp ground coriander

1½ tbsp ground cumin

3 tsp ground cardamom

3 tsp ground turmeric

2 tsp ground fennel

¾ tsp cayenne pepper[2]

¼ tsp ground cloves

½ tsp ground ginger

LAMB RUB

2 tbsp olive oil

2 tbsp lemon juice

1½ tsp salt*

FINISHING HONEY GLAZE

4 tbsp honey, very slightly warmed[3]

1 tsp cumin seeds

LEMON HERB COUSCOUS

380 g (2 cups) couscous

435 ml (1¾ cups) low-salt vegetable stock*

¼ tsp salt*

1 tbsp lemon zest (1 large lemon)

60 ml (¼ cup) fresh lemon juice (2 lemons)

TO SERVE

1 batch Lemon Yoghurt Sauce (page 228)

Preheat the oven to 140°C (both standard and fan).[4]

Ras el hanout – Mix the spices in a small bowl.

Braising liquid – Measure out 3 tablespoons of the ras el hanout and put it in a roasting pan. Add the tomato paste and stock and mix until combined. Place the onion wedges, garlic bulb halves and cinnamon sticks into the liquid.

Rub lamb – Add the lamb rub ingredients into the remaining ras el hanout and stir to combine. Slather the rub all over the lamb using your hands.

Prepare to roast – Set the lamb on top of the onion and garlic, fat-side up. Place a sheet of baking paper on top, then cover tightly with foil.

Slow roast – Roast for 3½ hours. Add the figs and chickpeas, then cover again with the paper and foil. Roast for another 30 minutes. The meat should be very tender by now – check in a discreet spot with a fork.

Honey glaze – Remove the pan from the oven. Turn the oven up to 180°C (160°C fan). Remove the foil and spoon the pan juices over the lamb. Drizzle the surface all over with the honey without touching the spice crust. Sprinkle the cumin seeds all over the surface.

Roast uncovered – Roast for 30 minutes, uncovered, until the surface is beautifully caramelised. Rest for 15 minutes in the pan while you prepare the couscous.

continued – – ►

Couscous – Place the couscous in a 20 cm square pan (or other dish of similar size).[5] Heat the stock and salt in a saucepan to just before boiling over high heat. Pour over the couscous, then quickly shake the pan to spread the couscous out evenly. Cover with a plate or baking tray, then leave for 5 minutes. Fluff the couscous with a fork. Stir through the lemon zest and juice. Set aside 1 tablespoon each of the mint, coriander and pistachios (for garnish), then toss the rest through the couscous.

Plating up – Transfer the lamb to a serving platter. Tilt the roasting pan so you can skim off and discard any excess fat. Spoon all the pan juices and chickpeas around the lamb. Garnish with a sprinkle of the reserved herbs and pistachios. Serve with the couscous and Lemon Yoghurt Sauce on the side! The meat will be so tender you can pull it off with tongs. No carving required!

NOTES

1 Lamb shoulder has a layer of fat on the surface. I know it's tempting to trim it, but don't! The fat makes the lamb beautifully succulent as it melts and bastes the meat. We will skim the excess fat out of the sauce at the end.

2 This amount of cayenne pepper gives the lamb a warm hum – I'd hardly call it spicy! But feel free to reduce or omit.

3 You will get the best coverage when drizzling if the honey is very lightly warmed so it's fairly thin. Don't try to dab it on using a brush or you'll remove the spice crust.

4 Ordinarily, the fan temperature is 20°C lower than the standard oven temperature. But this does not always apply for slow-roasted recipes, like this lamb.

5 Spread the couscous out fairly thinly to soak. This will make it fluffy rather than mushy (we've all been there!).

LEFTOVERS Fridge 3 days, freezer 3 months.

ITALIAN STUFFED PORK TENDERLOIN

A pork roast stuffed with a bold Italian-inspired filling!

SERVES: 3–4 | PREP: 30 MINUTES | COOK: 35 MINUTES

Tenderloin is great for stuffing as its uniform shape makes the job much easier and tidier, and also ensures even cooking. This pork tenderloin gets an Italian-inspired filling that includes rosemary, spinach and sun-dried tomato. The colourful spirals of meat that you carve off look almost Christmassy (there's an idea)! To finish, a quick homemade balsamic glaze is just the thing to tie it all together. This is definitely the sort of dish that will have people eagerly leaning in when you plonk it down in the centre of the table!

500–600 g pork tenderloin[1]

1 tsp paprika*

½ tsp salt*

¼ tsp black pepper

1 tbsp extra-virgin olive oil

STUFFING

1 tbsp extra-virgin olive oil

¼ small brown onion, finely chopped

150 g button mushrooms, finely chopped into 5 mm pieces

¼ tsp salt*

¼ tsp black pepper

¾ tsp finely minced rosemary[2]

1 garlic clove*, finely minced

75 g (½ cup) no-added-oil sun-dried or semi-dried tomatoes[3], chopped into 1 cm squares

100 g (2 tightly packed cups) baby spinach, chopped into 1 cm squares

2 tbsp grated parmesan*

BALSAMIC GLAZE[4]

125 ml (½ cup) balsamic vinegar

85 g (¼ cup) honey

TO GARNISH (OPTIONAL)

1 tbsp toasted* pine nuts

Rosemary sprigs

Butterfly pork – Cut a long slit down the middle of the pork lengthways, taking care not to cut all the way through. Open up the pork like a book. Cover with a plastic sheet. Use a meat mallet, rolling pin or heavy frying pan to pound the pork to an even 7 mm thickness. Set aside.

Stuffing – Heat the oil in a large non-stick, ovenproof frying pan* over high heat. Add the onion, mushrooms, half the salt and pepper and all the rosemary. Cook for 2 minutes until the mushrooms start to release water. Add the garlic and tomatoes, then continue cooking until the mushrooms are softened and the water evaporates, about 5 minutes. Add the spinach and toss until wilted. Transfer the mixture into a bowl and stir in the remaining salt and pepper, plus the parmesan. Leave to cool for 15 minutes or so. Wipe the pan clean with paper towels.

Preheat the oven to 180°C (160°C fan).

Stuff – Place the stuffing in the middle of the tenderloin. Use as much as you can but ensure you can still roll up the tenderloin with the stuffing fully enclosed. Secure with four or five toothpicks. Sprinkle the pork with the paprika, salt and pepper.

Sear and bake – Heat the oil in the same pan over medium–high. Put the pork in the pan and brown the top and sides until golden, about 1½ minutes on each side. Set the pork seam-side down, then transfer to the oven to bake for 15–20 minutes or until the internal temperature of the meat registers 60°C using a cooking thermometer*.

Rest – Remove the pork from the pan and rest it on a carving board for 5 minutes.

Glaze – Scrape out and discard any loose burnt bits in the pan. Put the pan back on the stove and add the balsamic vinegar and honey for the glaze. Turn the heat to medium–high and rapidly simmer the mixture until it reduces down to a syrupy glaze. Remove from the stove.

Serve – Remove the toothpicks from the pork. Slice the meat into 1.5 cm thick slices, holding it as needed to stay together as you cut. Lay the pork on a serving plate, drizzle with the balsamic glaze, sprinkle with the pine nuts, and tuck in some rosemary sprigs for garnish, if desired. Serve.

NOTES

1 The larger the pork, the better as it's easier to roll. However, this recipe can also be made with a smaller pork tenderloin.

2 Substitute with ½ teaspoon of dried rosemary.

3 These types of sun-dried tomato are a little softer and more red than the sun-dried tomatoes sold in jars in oil, though they can be used in a pinch.

4 You could skip making the glaze and use store-bought balsamic glaze* instead.

LEFTOVERS Fridge 3 days, freezer 3 months.

A MAGNIFICENT SEAFOOD PIE WITH CREAMY TARRAGON SAUCE

Truly restaurant-worthy and easier than you ever imagined.

SERVES: 4–5 | PREP: 30 MINUTES | COOK: 1 HOUR

This recipe is loosely based on the legendary seafood pie by English chef and seafood master Rick Stein. Rather than the usual béchamel sauce, his pie uses a velouté – a fancy French term for a roux-thickened stock. A homemade fish stock (never carton stuff – it's just horrible!) would usually be the go here, but I've got a secret trick instead. I simply steam mussels and use the beautiful salty juices, which are full of seafood flavour, as the stock. Of course the mussel meat then goes into the pie, along with fish, prawns and scallops. The result is a luxurious seafood pie worthy of any restaurant, which anybody can make at home!

---

3 x 100 g kipfler potatoes[1], scrubbed

1/4 tsp salt*

1/8 tsp white pepper

350 g boneless, skinless cod or other firm white fish fillets*[2], around 1 cm thick, cut into 4 cm pieces

1 tbsp plain flour

1 tbsp vegetable oil

EASY SEAFOOD STOCK

125 ml (1/2 cup) chardonnay or other dry white wine*[3]

1 kg fresh mussels*[4, 5]

Up to 300 ml low-salt chicken stock*, only if needed

PARMESAN TOPPING

30 g unsalted butter

45 g (3/4 cup) panko breadcrumbs*

25 g (1/4 cup) finely grated* parmesan

1/8 tsp salt*

CREAMY TARRAGON SAUCE

60 g unsalted butter

1 eschalot*, finely chopped (substitute 1/4 brown onion)

4 1/2 tbsp plain flour

250 ml (1 cup) double cream*, warmed

2 bay leaves*

1/8 tsp white pepper

Pinch of ground nutmeg

30 g (1/3 cup) finely grated parmesan*

2 tsp lemon juice

1 1/2 tbsp finely chopped tarragon

PIE ADD-INS

8 medium to large raw prawns*[6], peeled and deveined (20 g each, 8 cm long excluding tail)

8 scallops[6], roe removed (20 g each)

70 g (1/2 cup) frozen peas (not thawed)

TO GARNISH (OPTIONAL)

Finely chopped chives

Cook potatoes – Place the potatoes in a large saucepan* of cold water. Bring to the boil over high heat, then reduce the heat to medium–high and cook for 15 minutes or until soft. Drain, then cool for 10 minutes until they can be handled. Peel off and discard the skin, then slice the potatoes into 1 cm thick rounds. Set aside.

Seafood stock – Pour the wine into a large pot* over high heat and bring to a simmer. Add the mussels, put the lid on, and cook for 3 minutes or until the mussels open, shaking the pot once. Drain the mussels into a colander set over a bowl to catch the liquid. Pour the juices into a measuring jug. If you don't have 400 ml, top up with the chicken stock. If you have more, lucky you! Use it all for the sauce. Set aside.

Mussel meat – Remove the mussel meat from the shells.[7] Reserve the mussel meat and discard the shells.

Topping[8] – Melt the butter in a large non-stick frying pan* over medium heat. Add the breadcrumbs and cook, stirring constantly, until the breadcrumbs change from white to light golden. Transfer to a bowl and cool for 5 minutes. Stir in the parmesan and salt, then set aside. Wipe the pan clean with a paper towel.

Preheat the oven to 200°C (180°C fan).

Cook fish – Sprinkle the salt and pepper on both sides of the fish. Coat the fish with the flour, thoroughly shaking off any excess. Heat the vegetable oil in the same pan over medium–high heat. Cook the fish pieces for just 45 seconds on each side. Transfer the fish to a plate and set aside. The inside should still be raw.

continued - - ►

Creamy tarragon sauce – Reduce the heat to medium and add the butter to the same pan. Once melted, add the eschalot and cook for 3 minutes until softened. Add the flour and cook for 1 minute. While stirring, slowly pour in the cream. Once the cream is incorporated, stir in the mussel stock – use a whisk if needed to remove any flour lumps. Add the bay leaves, then sprinkle the white pepper and nutmeg across the surface. Stir, then turn the heat up to medium–high. Let the sauce simmer energetically for 10 minutes, stirring frequently to ensure the base doesn't catch, until it thickens enough to coat the back of a wooden spoon very thickly.[9] Lower the heat as it thickens, if the base starts to catch. Remove from the heat and stir in the parmesan until it melts. Mix in the lemon juice and tarragon. Taste and add salt if needed (I don't add more, but read note 5).

Assemble and bake – Remove the bay leaves from the sauce. Pour 250 ml (1 cup) of the still-warm sauce into the base of a 24 cm (1.5 litre) round pie dish. Place the fish, mussels, potatoes, prawns and scallops in the dish, then sprinkle the peas on top. Pour the remaining sauce over and smooth the surface. Sprinkle with the crumb topping. Bake for 35 minutes until the panko topping is deep golden.

Serve – Rest for 5 minutes before serving, sprinkled with chives, if desired.

NOTES

1 Kipfler potatoes, also known as fingerling potatoes, are a variety of small potatoes that are long and narrow. They have a great creamy texture that is perfect for this pie – 100 g per potato is a good size for this pie but don't fret if yours are larger. Just cut them into half-moons instead of coins. You can also substitute with baby potatoes.

2 This recipe will work with most white fish fillets that are at least 1 cm thick, such as ling, cod, monkfish, cod, snapper, tilapia, pollock, hake, haddock, John Dory, basa, hoki, perch, sea bass, turbot or flathead. Avoid lean fish, such as tuna and kingfish, and oily fish* like sardines and mackerel.

3 Substitute with low-salt chicken stock.

4 See page 340 of the Glossary for my guide to buying and cleaning mussels.

5 Not all mussels are as juicy as they should be! If you have less than 400 ml liquid, top up with low-salt chicken stock (better than carton fish stock). I've had as little as 100 ml of mussel stock! I find the natural saltiness from mussel juices is sufficient for the sauce. However, the salt levels can vary between varieties, so add salt only if needed at the end of the sauce-making.

6 Prawns and scallops: It's best if they are on the larger side, around 20 g for each piece, to ensure they do not overcook in the oven (weight after peeling the prawns and removing the roe, the orange sac attached to the scallops). If scallops are out of reach, use more prawns or more fish. If using frozen, thaw thoroughly and pat dry. For prawns, I like to use tiger prawns for this pie because they become a vibrant orange-red colour once cooked.

7 Prise open any mussels that remain closed using a butter knife (it's a myth that these are off!).

8 I like to give the breadcrumbs some colour on the stove to give them a head start and a deeper, more dramatic golden colour than you can achieve in the oven alone.

9 The sauce will loosen slightly when the pie bakes due to the juices from the seafood. So you need to make the sauce slightly thicker than you want the sauce to be once it comes out of the oven. The parmesan thickens it slightly.

LEFTOVERS Fridge 3 days, freezer 3 months.

SLOW-BAKED ITALIAN MEATBALLS

For the softest, most succulent meatballs in tomato sauce EVER!

SERVES: 4–5 | PREP: 30 MINUTES | COOK: 2½ HOURS

This recipe is a bit of a sentimental favourite. I love it to bits and have been waiting for just the right occasion to share it! These meatballs are sort of the Rolls-Royce of my ever-popular Italian meatballs. What makes this version extra-special is baking them in a slow oven for 1½ hours. The tenderness of these meatballs surprises everyone! It also gives the meatballs time to suck up the sauce flavours while in turn enriching the sauce itself. Make these and I think they just might become your sentimental favourite too!

---

1 tbsp vegetable oil

50 g (½ cup) finely grated parmesan*

100 g (1 cup) grated* mozzarella

SILKY RICH TOMATO SAUCE

2 tbsp extra-virgin olive oil

½ brown onion, finely chopped

1 small carrot, peeled and finely diced

½ celery stalk, finely diced

2 garlic cloves*, finely minced

1 bay leaf* (preferably fresh)

1 thyme sprig[1]

3 tbsp tomato paste

185 ml (¾ cup) pinot noir wine*[2]

400 g can chopped tomatoes

500 ml (2 cups) low-salt chicken stock*

½ tsp salt*

¼ tsp black pepper

MEATBALLS

45 g (¾ cup) panko breadcrumbs*

1 small brown onion, grated using a standard box grater

500 g beef mince

1 egg

7 g (¼ cup) finely minced parsley

2 garlic cloves*, grated

25 g (¼ cup) finely grated parmesan*

¾ tsp salt*

¼ tsp black pepper

TO SERVE

400 g spaghetti, cooked according to packet directions

1 tsp finely chopped parsley (optional)

Tomato sauce – Heat the oil in a small pot* over medium heat. Add the onion, carrot, celery, garlic, bay leaf and thyme and cook for 8 minutes or until the onion is translucent and the carrot is sweet. Don't rush this step – this is the key to an extra flavourful sauce! Add the tomato paste and stir for 2 minutes or until the colour deepens from bright red to crimson. Add the wine, then increase the heat to high and simmer rapidly until the sauce reduces by half, about 2 minutes. Add the tomatoes, stock, salt and pepper. Stir, let it come to a simmer, then reduce the heat to medium–low. Simmer gently without a lid for 20 minutes.

Blitz – Remove the bay leaf and thyme sprig. Blitz the sauce until smooth using a stick blender. Simmer for 1 minute, then remove from the stove. Cover with a lid and keep warm.

Meatballs – Place all the meatball ingredients in a bowl (including all the grated onion juice) and mix well with your hands. Roll 2 tablespoon (35 g) portions of the mixture into 3.5 cm balls. Refrigerate for 30 minutes if you want your meatballs to stay nice and round.[3]

Preheat the oven to 140°C (both standard and fan[4]).

Brown meatballs – Heat the vegetable oil in a large ovenproof cast-iron pan*[5] over medium–high heat. Place the meatballs in the pan and brown them all over lightly, using tongs or two dessert spoons to turn them, around 5 minutes.

Slow-bake – Turn the stove off. Gently pour the sauce into the pan around the meatballs. Use as much sauce as you can fit into the pan but keep a bit of the meatballs showing. You might not need all the sauce – it will depend on the size of your pan.[6] Cover the pan with foil, a lid or a baking tray[7] and transfer to the oven. Bake for 1½ hours. Remove the foil, sprinkle the parmesan and mozzarella over, then bake, uncovered, for a further 20 minutes until the cheese is melted.

Serve – Rest for 10 minutes, then serve over spaghetti, garnished with parsley, if desired!

See Notes overleaf.

NOTES

1. Or ½ teaspoon of dried thyme.
2. Or other dry red wine. If you can't consume alcohol, use non-alcoholic red wine or just omit.
3. Refrigerating will firm up the meatballs so they hold their shape better when browning.
4. Ordinarily, the fan temperature is 20°C lower than the standard oven temperature. But this rule does not always apply for slow-baked recipes, such as these meatballs.
5. You will need a cast-iron or other ovenproof frying pan at least 26 cm wide and 4 cm deep to hold the meatballs and sauce. If you don't have one, transfer the browned meatballs to a baking dish. Simmer the sauce in the pan before pouring into the baking dish so all the golden bits stuck to the pan from browning the meatballs dissolve into the sauce – free flavour!
6. Left-over sauce will keep in the fridge for 5 days or freezer for 3 months.
7. You don't need to tightly cover the pan, just something to protect the meatballs from browning too fast. I just use a rectangular baking tray or the lid of a large pot*.

LEFTOVERS Fridge 3 days, freezer 3 months.

SUMMER SALMON WITH MANGO SALSA

A stunning, summery side of salmon that's super easy!

SERVES: 6–8 PEOPLE | PREP: 25 MINUTES + 30 MINUTES COOLING AND RESTING | COOK: 25 MINUTES

Here's a dazzling whole side of salmon that will be the talk of your next summer lunch party! This oven-baked beauty is all about layering flavours, starting with a smoky spice rub that's slathered on all surfaces. A drizzle of hot honey (it's all the rage, dontcha know!) while the salmon bakes is next for some sweet and spicy zip. Finally, it's topped with a mango and avocado salsa tossed with zesty lime dressing to freshen everything and add eye-popping colour. It's a rainbow of flavours, colours and textures with a properly festive summer vibe!

Olive oil spray

1.25 kg whole salmon side,[1] skin-on, pin-boned

1 tbsp extra-virgin olive oil

HOT HONEY

345 g (1 cup) honey

60 ml (1/4 cup) sriracha*[2]

1 tsp dried chilli flakes* (omit for not spicy)

2 garlic cloves*, crushed with a garlic crusher or very finely minced with a knife

SMOKY SALMON RUB

1 tsp salt*

1/2 tsp black pepper

2 tsp smoked paprika*

1 tsp onion powder

2 tsp garlic powder

1 tsp dried thyme, crushed with fingers

MANGO AVOCADO SALSA

460 g (2 1/2 cups) cubed (1 cm) mango (2 large mangoes)

250 g (1 1/2 cups) cubed (1 cm) avocado (2 avocados)

80 g (1/2 cup) chopped (5 mm squares) red bell pepper

55 g (1/3 cup) finely diced red onion

15 g (1/3 cup) roughly chopped coriander, plus extra for garnish

80 ml (1/3 cup) lime juice

2 tbsp extra-virgin olive oil

1/2 tsp salt*

1/4 tsp black pepper

Hot honey – Place the hot honey ingredients in a small saucepan* over medium–low heat. Bring to a simmer, then allow to cook gently for 1 minute. Remove from the heat and allow to fully cool before using, about 20 minutes. We will be using some to glaze the salmon, and some for serving.

Seasoning – Mix the smoky salmon rub ingredients in a bowl.

Preheat the oven to 200°C (180°C fan).

Bake salmon – Line a baking tray with foil and spray lightly with the oil. Place the salmon on the foil, skin-side down. Rub the salmon flesh with the oil, then sprinkle the whole surface evenly with the rub. Bake for 10 minutes. Remove from the oven and use a spoon to drizzle about 125 ml (1/2 cup) of the hot honey all over the salmon. Some of it will slide off down the side and that's okay. Bake for a further 10 minutes until the surface is glazed and the salmon is cooked with an internal temperature of 50°C.[3] Remove from the oven and rest for 10 minutes.

Salsa – Just before serving, place all the salsa ingredients in a bowl and gently toss.

Serve – Serve the salmon on a platter topped with some of the salsa for presentation purposes. Serve the rest of the salsa and remaining hot honey on the side for everybody to help themselves!

NOTES

1 It's best to use a salmon with the skin on for ease of handling. Make sure the salmon is pin-boned and trimmed (to make the shape even and tidy).

2 Substitute with 2 tablespoons of apple cider vinegar for a non-spicy option to make a honey-garlic glaze instead. It's so good!

3 The salmon is cooked when the internal temperature is 50°C for medium–rare, which will rise to 53°C after resting. This is the level of doneness served at restaurants because it is the optimum juiciness for salmon. For medium, target 60°C – it will rise to 63°C once rested. If you don't have a thermometer*, check to ensure the flesh flakes.

4 Make ahead: The hot honey can be made up to 3 days before. The salsa ingredients can be chopped ahead except for the avocado, which is best cut fresh. Do not mix the olive oil, salt and pepper through until just before serving.

LEFTOVERS Fridge 3 days. Not suitable for freezing.

DUCK RAGU PAPPARDELLE

An indulgently rich and meaty sauce with shredded braised duck and porcini, ideal for a special occasion.

SERVES: 5 | PREP: 30 MINUTES + 30 MINUTES SOAKING | COOK: 2½ HOURS

The best duck ragu pastas I've enjoyed in Italian restaurants are never tomatoey and red, unlike the majority of recipes you'll see in books and online. Instead, the chunky sauce is a rich brown colour and has an incredibly robust meatiness that comes from braising bone-in duck in a good strong stock. I've recreated that intensity here partly by reducing the chicken stock first to concentrate it. Porcini mushrooms also pack oodles of woody flavour, deepening the taste even further for a truly restaurant-quality duck ragu! Wide ribbons of pappardelle are the classic pasta for a duck ragu, but feel free to use any shapes that will hug that meaty sauce.

---

20 g dried porcini mushrooms[1], pieces or slices

1.5 litres low-salt chicken stock* (be sure to use low-salt)[2]

1 tbsp olive oil

1 kg duck marylands[3] (about 4)

1 brown onion, roughly chopped

1 celery stalk, grated using a box grater[4]

1 small carrot, peeled and grated using a box grater[4]

6 garlic cloves*, finely minced

375 ml (1½ cups) pinot noir wine*[5]

195 g (¾ cup) tomato passata*

½ cinnamon stick

2 star anise

2 bay leaves*, crushed in your hand

½ tsp black pepper

1½ tbsp roughly chopped fresh rosemary leaves

1 tbsp plain flour

15 g unsalted butter, softened

¼ tsp salt*, if needed

PASTA

1 tbsp salt*, for cooking the pasta

400 g pappardelle pasta (or other pasta of your choice)[6]

Freshly grated parmesan*, to serve

Soak porcini and reduce stock – Place the porcini in a bowl. Pour the stock into a large frying pan* over high heat (it will reduce faster than in a pot). Bring to the boil. Scoop out 125 ml (½ cup) of the hot stock and pour it over the porcini. Leave to soak for 30 minutes until softened. Lower the heat to medium–high, so the remaining stock is simmering rapidly, and reduce to 750 ml (3 cups), about 8–10 minutes. Pour into a measuring jug to ensure you have the right amount.

Porcini – Squeeze the excess liquid out of the porcini with your hands, reserving all the soaking liquid. Chop the porcini into 5 mm pieces, then set aside. Add the soaking liquid to the reduced chicken stock.

Brown duck – Heat the oil in a large pot* over high heat. Place the duck in, skin-side down, and cook until golden brown, about 4 minutes. Turn and brown the flesh side for 2 minutes until light golden, then brown the skin on the edges as best you can, about 2–3 minutes. Transfer the duck to a bowl and set aside.

Sauce – In the same pot, still over high heat, remove all but 3 tablespoons of the duck fat.[7] Add the onion, celery, carrot and garlic and cook for 8 minutes until they halve in volume, reducing the heat if necessary so the vegetables don't brown. Add the wine and simmer for 5 minutes until reduced by 50%. Add the passata, cinnamon, star anise, bay leaves, pepper and the reserved stock, pouring the stock in carefully to leave behind the last bit if there is dirt and grit from the porcini.[8] Stir to combine.

Slow cook – Arrange the duck so it is submerged under the liquid.[9] Once the liquid comes to a simmer, reduce the heat to low. Simmer very gently for 1½ hours, uncovered, checking every now and then to ensure the duck remains submerged. At the 1-hour mark, add the rosemary and chopped porcini.

Shred duck – Transfer the duck to a bowl and cover loosely with foil. Once cool enough to handle, remove the skin and shred the flesh off the bone with your hands. Shred fairly finely. Discard the bones. Finely chop half the skin.[7]

continued - - ►

Thicken sauce – In a small bowl, mix together the flour and butter until a smooth paste forms.[10] Stir the mixture into the pot, then simmer for 3 minutes. Add the shredded duck and chopped skin. Taste and add the salt only if needed (the reduced chicken stock provides plenty of salt). The duck ragu pasta sauce is now ready to use. Keep warm until ready to toss with the pasta. Don't forget to remove the bay leaf, cinnamon stick and star anise!

Toss ragu with pasta – Bring a large pot* of water to the boil with the salt. Boil the pasta according to the packet directions. Just before draining, scoop out a big mugful of the pasta cooking water and set aside. Drain the pasta, then add the pasta to the warm ragu with 125 ml (½ cup) of the pasta cooking water. With the stove on medium heat, toss the pasta using two spatulas until the sauce thickens and is mostly clinging to the pasta, and the pappardelle is stained red. Use the reserved pasta cooking water to loosen if it gets too thick.

Serve – Divide among bowls and serve immediately, topped with parmesan!

NOTES

1 Porcini really add a beautiful, earthy depth of flavour into the sauce, so they're worth getting. If you really can't find them, use 1½ teaspoons finely minced anchovies* in oil or anchovy paste and sauté with the onion.

2 Be sure to use low-salt chicken stock or the sauce will be too salty as the liquid is reduced significantly to concentrate the flavour.

3 Fairly widely available these days at grocery stores, poultry shops and butchers, this is the duck leg attached to the thigh. Using duck breast or just duck leg is not recommended for this recipe – they are quite lean.

4 A box grater is a nifty way to make the carrot and celery fine enough so they almost disappear into the sauce. Aim to make the strands shorter rather than longer. Nobody wants carrot spaghetti in their duck ragu! You could also use a food processor. Blitz until very fine. For the grated celery, you'll end up with stringy celery bits. Discard this.

5 Or other dry red wine. If you can't consume alcohol, use non-alcoholic red wine or just omit.

6 If you do not want to use all the ragu in one go, use 80 g of dried pasta and one-fifth of the ragu per serving.

7 I don't use all the skin because the sauce gets a little too rich. The remaining skin and duck fat can be used to roast vegetables. While the skin won't become crisp – so you mightn't want to eat it – the fat will impart great flavour into the vegetables.

8 Sometimes porcini will release grit into the stock. It will settle on the bottom of the stock jug so it's easy to avoid pouring it into the pot.

9 If you're struggling to fit all the duck, just arrange them as best you can to keep the meaty parts in the liquid. The duck marylands will shrink as they cook, so you can rearrange them during the cooking time.

10 This is called a beurre manié*. It will thicken the sauce slightly so it will coat the pasta better. Refer to the Glossary (page 337) for how to convert to gluten-free.

LEFTOVERS The sauce will keep in the fridge for 3 days or freezer for 3 months. However, once the sauce and pasta are tossed together, it is best eaten straight away.

SPINACH & FETA BÖREK

These spinach-filled flaky pastries are so much more straightforward to make than you imagine!

SERVES: 3–4 | PREP: 40 MINUTES + 20 MINUTES COOLING | COOK: 55 MINUTES

It's hard to find a great börek here in my hometown of Sydney. Many miss the mark with what I think are the essentials. For one, the pastry needs to be light and shatteringly crispy. The filling should also be flavourful and well seasoned, juicy and not dry – but not make the base soggy! To this end, I've taken to making my own ideal spinach börek. And because I am the first to admit that sometimes dealing with a large mound of fresh spinach is all too much, I'm providing a simple frozen spinach version too. It's really, really good!

This recipe makes six individual böreks – enough for four people as a main (perhaps only three if I'm there!).

CHOOSE ONE FILLING:

FRESH SPINACH FETA FILLING[1] (TRADITIONAL)

½ tbsp extra-virgin olive oil

½ brown onion, finely chopped

3 garlic cloves*, finely minced

400 g fresh spinach leaves[2], washed well, dried, chopped into 2.5 cm squares (from 2 bunches weighing 800 g)

¼ tsp salt*

¼ tsp black pepper

250 g Danish feta[3]

FROZEN SPINACH OPTION[1] (EASIER OPTION)

750 g frozen chopped spinach

1 spring onion*, finely sliced

1 large garlic clove*, finely grated

150 g Danish feta[3]

200 g ricotta[4]

½ tsp salt*

¼ tsp black pepper

TO MAKE THE BÖREK:

YOGHURT WASH FOR FILO[5]

1 large egg*

2 tbsp plain yoghurt

30 g unsalted butter, melted

PASTRY

12 sheets (43 x 28 cm) filo pastry, refrigerated[6]

30 g unsalted butter, melted and cooled

Olive oil spray[7]

½ tsp white sesame seeds

¼ tsp (heaped) black sesame seeds

Fresh spinach filling option – Line a baking tray with a tea towel (to absorb excess liquid from the cooked spinach). Heat the oil in a large non-stick frying pan* over medium heat. Add the onion and garlic and cook for 2 minutes until the onion is translucent but not browned. Add the spinach and toss until wilted. Transfer onto the tea towel–lined tray and let it cool to room temperature, about 20 minutes. Transfer the spinach to a bowl. Add the salt, pepper and feta. Mix gently (to avoid squeezing liquid out of the spinach), then set aside.

Frozen spinach filling option – Thaw the spinach, then use a tea towel to squeeze out as much water as you can. You should end up with around 250 g of spinach. Place it in a bowl and add the remaining filling ingredients. Mix well, then set aside. (Optional: transfer the filling to a piping bag, then pipe the filling onto the pastry. Efficient!)

Whichever above option you used (fresh or frozen spinach filling), proceed with the following steps.

Yoghurt wash – Whisk the yoghurt wash ingredients together in a small bowl – it will look a little curdled, but that's okay.

Preheat the oven to 210°C (190°C fan).

Make coils – Each pastry will have four sheets of filo. Place a sheet of filo on a work surface. Use a brush to flick or drizzle the yoghurt wash across the surface, then brush a light coating across the pastry. Cover with another sheet of filo, brush with yoghurt wash, then repeat again twice more but do not brush the fourth sheet with yoghurt. Cut the pastry in half diagonally. Place a slightly heaped 100 g (½ cup) of filling on the long edge. Roll it up, finishing with the seam-side down. Roll into a coil. Repeat to make six in total.

Bake – Place the coils on a baking tray lined with baking paper, with the end of each coil pressed up against the edge of the tray to hold it in place. Brush with butter, spray generously with olive oil, then sprinkle with sesame seeds. Bake for 35–40 minutes until golden. Dig in!

See Notes overleaf.

NOTES

1 Traditional börek is made using fresh spinach. You need two large bunches weighing around 800 g to yield 400 g of leaves. But when short on time or spinach is out of season, use my frozen spinach alternative. For this version, I add ricotta because once you wring out the enormous amount of water from the frozen spinach, it becomes quite dry and crumbly (which fresh spinach does not). So the ricotta adds desirable creaminess back into the filling. The frozen spinach version tastes more like ricotta, but it's equally delicious.

2 Cavolo nero (Tuscan kale) also works. Use the same quantity, sliced 1 cm thick. I don't recommend baby spinach, it's too delicate so it goes mushy.

3 Danish feta is creamier than Greek feta so I prefer it. But you can absolutely use Greek feta if you like!

4 Not all ricotta is created equal! If you can't get it over the counter at a deli, then opt for the type sold in baskets that are vac-packed, rather than ricotta sold in plastic tubs, which are not as creamy and sometimes unpleasantly powdery.

5 This prevents the filo pastry from cracking as you roll it into a coil.

6 I use the refrigerated type, not frozen, because I find it less prone to breaking. If using frozen, thaw overnight in the fridge.

7 This ensures the börek bakes up beautifully golden! Butter alone doesn't cut it, I find – but I can't give up the butter flavour.

LEFTOVERS Best served fresh but leftovers will keep in the fridge for 3 days, or freezer for 3 months. Bake at 180°C (160°C fan) for 10 minutes to reheat and re-crisp!

FRENCH ONION BRIE MUSHROOM PIE

A vegetarian masterpiece designed to wow!

SERVES: 5–6 | PREP: 1 HOUR + 3 HOURS COOLING | COOK: 1½ HOURS

Mushroom ragu + caramelised onion + brie + potato gratin, enclosed in an incredible buttery, brioche pastry that's brioche-bread-like on the inside and crispy-pastry-golden on the outside. This pie is a spectacular flavour combination – and something that money can't buy! It's an original invention, one of those 'hmm, I wonder if ...' ideas that came out even better than in my wildest dreams. A recipe intended to draw applause and gasps of amazement when you serve it, this is a vegetarian centrepiece that looks incredible – and tastes phenomenal. The river of brie that pours out when you cut into the pie is a heart-stopping moment that your friends and family will be talking about for months on end ... Honestly, when was the last time you were served something where melted brie was the sauce??

MUSHROOM RAGU

20 g dried porcini mushrooms[1]

250 ml (1 cup) boiling water

2 tbsp extra-virgin olive oil

400 g portobello mushrooms[2], stems removed, sliced 5 mm thick

½ tsp salt*

¼ tsp black pepper

2 garlic cloves*, finely minced

1 tsp finely chopped rosemary leaves[3]

60 ml (¼ cup) chardonnay or other dry white wine* (optional)

2½ tsp plain flour

POTATO GRATIN

500 g (2 large) sebago* potatoes, scrubbed clean (skin on)

20 g unsalted butter

1 leek, white part only, cut in half lengthways, then finely sliced

2 garlic cloves*, finely minced

80 ml (⅓ cup) double cream*

½ tsp salt*

⅛ tsp black pepper

1 tsp finely chopped fresh thyme leaves[3]

CARAMELISED ONION

30 g unsalted butter

2 brown onions, peeled, halved and finely sliced

¼ tsp salt*

BRIOCHE PASTRY (OR PUFF PASTRY![4])

2 tsp (7 g) active dry yeast[5]

60 ml (¼ cup) full-fat milk, warm

1 tbsp white sugar

400 g (2⅔ cups) plain flour, plus extra for dusting

1 tsp salt*

3 large eggs*, whisked

150 g unsalted butter*, cut into 1 cm pieces, at room temperature

PIE

200 g brie[6], whole, 30% fat or less

1 large egg*, white and yolk separated, each whisked

TO SERVE

Dijon mustard

Thyme leaves for decorating (optional)

MUSHROOM RAGU

Rehydrate porcini – Soak the porcini mushrooms in the boiling water for 20 minutes or until soft. Drain, reserving the soaking water. Squeeze out any excess water from the mushrooms using your hands (reserve this too, it has the most intense flavour!), then finely chop the porcini into 2 mm pieces.

Make ragu – Heat the oil in a large pot* over high heat. Add the portobello mushroom slices, salt and pepper. Cook for 5 minutes or until the water released by the mushrooms has mostly evaporated – the mushrooms will be quite soft by this stage. Add the garlic, rosemary and porcini and cook for a further 3 minutes until the portobello mushrooms are softened. Add the wine (if using) and let it simmer rapidly until evaporated. Turn the heat down to medium–low.

Sauce – Sprinkle the flour across the surface of the ragu (don't dump it in one place) and stir to mix it through. Pour all the porcini soaking liquid in, leaving behind any gritty residue that will have settled at the bottom of the bowl or jug. Then cook, stirring regularly, for 5 minutes or until the liquid thickens and reduces enough so you can draw a path through the ragu across the base of the pan.[7] Scrape the mixture into a bowl. Cool to room temperature.

continued – – ➤

POTATO GRATIN LAYER

Cook potato – Place the potatoes in a large saucepan* and fill with enough cold tap water so it is 5 cm higher than the potatoes. Turn the stove to high heat and bring to the boil. Cook the potatoes for 20 minutes or until fully soft all the way through.

Slice – Remove the potatoes from the water and let them cool for 20 minutes or until they can be handled. Peel the skin off, then cut the potatoes into 1 cm thick slices.

Toss – Melt the butter in a large non-stick frying pan* over medium heat. Once foaming, add the leek and garlic. Sauté for 5 minutes or until the leek has softened – but don't let it become golden. Add the potatoes, cream, salt, pepper and thyme. Gently toss together (expect some potato breakage; it's totally fine), then scrape into a bowl. Cool to room temperature, then refrigerate for at least 30 minutes.

CARAMELISED ONION

Caramelise onion – Melt the butter in a large non-stick frying pan* over medium heat. Once foaming, add the onion and salt. Cook for 20–25 minutes or until the onion turns a deep golden brown and becomes sweet. Stir every now and then at the beginning, then more regularly as the onion starts to colour. Cool to room temperature.

FILLING

Shape filling – Line an 18 cm bowl (at least 6.7 cm deep) with plastic wrap.[8] Scrape the mushroom ragu into the bowl and make a well that is the width of the brie. Evenly spread the caramelised onion in the well, then place the brie on top and half 'bury' it in the mushroom ragu (so the ragu comes halfway up the side of the cheese). Place the potato on top and around the brie. Gently pack it in, then smooth the surface. Refrigerate for at least 2 hours (or overnight).

BRIOCHE PASTRY

Foam yeast – Mix the yeast, milk and sugar in a small bowl until lump-free. Cover with plastic wrap and leave for 10 minutes until foamy.[9]

Knead dough – Put the flour and salt in the bowl of a stand mixer fitted with a dough hook. Briefly mix to combine. Add the eggs and yeast mixture. Mix on medium speed until combined. With the stand mixer still running, add the butter gradually, over about 1 minute. Mix on medium–high for 5 minutes or until the dough is smooth (or knead with your hands). Shape the dough into a ball with your hands, then return it to the bowl. Cover with plastic wrap, then leave it in a warm place for 45 minutes or until it has doubled in size. Deflate the dough with your fist, give it a quick knead with your hands then bring it together into a ball.

Roll out – Cut off one-third of the dough for the base. Roll it out into a 24 cm round, 3–4 mm thick, on a lightly floured surface. Roll the remaining dough into a 34 cm round. Transfer each piece of pastry onto a separate sheet of baking paper and cover with plastic wrap. Chill in the fridge until required.

ASSEMBLE

Preheat the oven to 200°C (180°C fan).

Prepare pie – Keep the pastry base on the baking paper and transfer it onto an upside down baking tray.[10] Invert the bowl with the filling onto the base. Remove the bowl and plastic wrap. Brush the edge of the pastry with the egg white. Cover the dome with the pastry lid and press to firmly seal the edge around the base. Trim away the excess pastry using a small sharp knife, leaving a 1.5 cm edge. Press the edges firmly with a fork dipped in flour so the pastry is about 1 cm thick. Re-dip the fork in flour as needed to prevent the pastry from sticking to the fork. Brush the entire surface of the pastry with the egg yolk.

continued – – ➔

STEP 1: Mushroom ragu goal consistency

STEP 2: Bury brie (what an instruction!)

STEP 3: Cover with potato gratin

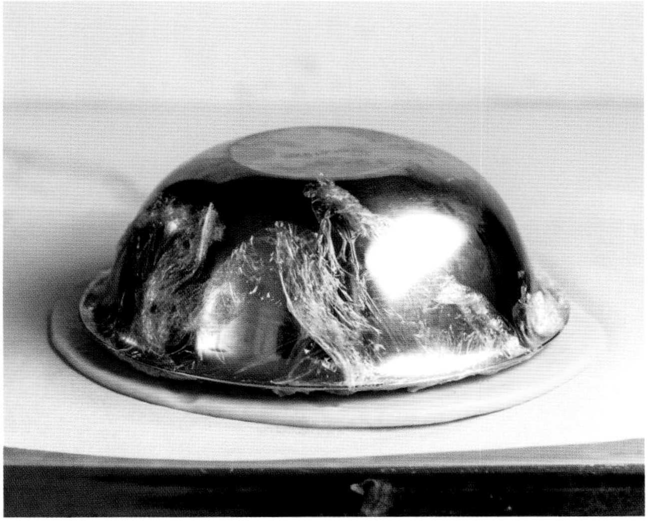

STEP 4: Invert

STEP 5: Filling holds its shape

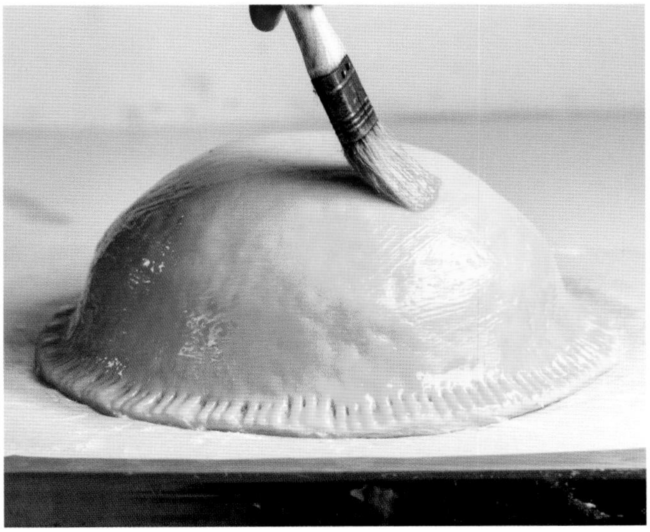

STEP 6: Ready to bake!

Bake – Bake for 20 minutes. Reduce the oven to 180°C (160°C fan) and rotate the tray. Bake for a further 20 minutes or until deep golden.

Serve – Rest the pie for 20 minutes.[11] To serve, gather everybody around to enjoy the spectacle (it's worth it!). First cut the pie in half and separate the pieces so everyone can see the dramatic vision of the lava of brie that oozes out. Cut thick slices like cake to serve, with a dab of dijon mustard on the side (it goes perfectly!).

NOTES

1 Dried porcini mushrooms come in small chopped pieces as well as larger slices. Either is fine as we chop them up once rehydrated.

2 Or other mushrooms of choice (sliceable sort, not mushrooms like enoki).

3 Substitute with dried thyme or dried rosemary.

4 Sure, this is extra-special when made with a buttery brioche pastry that is crispy on the outside and buttery-brioche-bread-like on the inside, which you can't pick up at any grocery store. But hand on heart, it is still excellent if made with store-bought butter puff pastry! You will need 500 g of puff pastry that is large enough to cut a 22 cm plus 32 cm circle. Stitch sheets together as needed, brushing the seam with egg white to firmly adhere them.

5 Use regular yeast, typically sold labelled as 'active dry yeast' in 7 g sachets. To make this with instant yeast (sometimes labelled 'rapid rise yeast'), follow the recipe as written, but after mixing the yeast into the milk, there is no need to wait 10 minutes to allow the mixture to foam. Just pour it straight into the flour and proceed with the recipe.

6 Look for brie with a fat percentage of 30% or less. Lower fat means the cheese will not be as runny when melted, so it will ooze slowly and thickly, as pictured, which is ideal. Higher-fat percentage brie still works but is often runnier when melted. To determine fat percentage of brie, look at the nutrition label. You want 30 g of fat or less per 100 g serving.

7 The mushroom ragu should be juicy but not watery. Nobody wants a dry mushroom filling, but it needs to be thick enough so it doesn't run out everywhere when you cut into the pie! Once you can draw a path across the base of the pan and it remains, then the mushroom ragu is done. It will firm up more in the fridge.

8 The exact shape and depth of the bowl isn't critical, as long as it is about 18 cm wide and will fit within the pastry base that you rolled out.

9 If it doesn't foam, sadly, your yeast is dead. Time to get another!

10 An upside-down tray makes it easier to assemble the pie without the edges getting in the way. We do not want to move the pie once assembled!

11 Resting the pie for 20 minutes is needed to let the inside firm up a bit so you can serve slices without the filling oozing out everywhere. Be warned, though – the brie will still ooze!

12 Make ahead: The pastry can be prepared up to the point just before rolling it out. Cover with plastic wrap, then refrigerate for up to 2 days. Let the dough soften enough so it can be rolled out, then proceed with the recipe. The mushroom ragu, caramelised onion and potato gratin mixtures can each be fully prepared up to 2 days ahead. Store them in the fridge. The pie is best assembled just prior to baking.

LEFTOVERS Definitely best served freshly made, though it will keep in the fridge for 4 days, or freezer for 3 months.

TORTA DI RIGATONI (RIGATONI CAKE!)

Upright pasta pie with bolognese sauce!

SERVES: 6–8 | PREP: 40 MINUTES + 30 MINUTES COOLING + 15 MINUTES RESTING | COOK: 2½ HOURS

I know it looks striking, but there's actually nothing too tricky about this torta! It's really just your favourite bolognese sauce stuffed into extra-large rigatoni tubes (called *paccheri* pasta) arranged upright in a cake tin. That doesn't stop people from oohing and aahing when it hits the table though! We really do eat with our eyes. Shocking absolutely nobody, I also love to cover the top with some cheese before baking. Oh and how does this torta not completely collapse at the touch of a fork, you ask? A little parmesan cheese is the trick. Like a cheesy glue, it sticks the pasta tubes together so you cut and serve the pie in lovely wedges just like a cake!

PASTA

300 g paccheri pasta[1] (or rigatoni)

50 g (½ tightly packed cup) finely grated parmesan*

BOLOGNESE SAUCE

2 tbsp olive oil

1 brown onion, finely chopped

3 garlic cloves*, finely minced

1½ tsp Italian herb mix[2]

750 g beef mince

2 tbsp tomato paste

125 ml (½ cup) pinot noir[3], or other dry red wine*

700 g tomato passata*

1 bay leaf*

1½ tsp salt*

¾ tsp black pepper

TO ASSEMBLE

Olive oil spray

100 g (1 cup) finely grated parmesan*, plus extra for serving

100 g (1 cup) freshly grated* mozzarella

1 tbsp finely chopped parsley, to garnish (optional)

Bolognese sauce – Heat the oil in a large heavy-based pot* over medium–high heat. Add the onion, garlic and Italian herbs and cook for 3 minutes until the onion is translucent. Turn the heat up to high. Add the beef and cook, breaking it up as you go, until you can no longer see raw beef, about 5 minutes. Add the tomato paste and cook for 1 minute, stirring constantly. Add the wine and simmer for 3 minutes, scraping the base of the pot until the liquid has mostly evaporated. Add the remaining sauce ingredients, stir and bring to a simmer.

Simmer[4] – Put a lid on the pot and transfer to your smallest burner on low heat. Slow-cook for 1½ hours, stirring every now and then to ensure the base doesn't catch. It should be fairly saucy as the extra sauce is needed to cook the par-boiled pasta in the oven.

Prepare tin and cool sauce – Generously spray the sides of a 20 cm springform cake tin with oil. Remove the bay leaf from the sauce, then spread 245 g (1 cup) of sauce on the base of the tin. Set the remaining meat sauce aside.

Cook pasta – Cook the pasta according to the packet directions minus 4 minutes so it is only partially cooked.[5] Drain the pasta in a colander, briefly rinse under tap water, then shake off any extra water. Return the pasta to the pasta cooking pot and toss with the parmesan while the pasta is still hot. Set aside.

Cool upright pasta – Arrange the pasta upright on top of the sauce, packing them so they stay in place. Let the pasta cool for 15 minutes, then refrigerate the tin with the pasta in it for 30 minutes – this makes the pasta stiffer so it's much easier to fill.

Preheat the oven to 200°C (180°C fan).

Fill pasta – Remove the tin from the refrigerator. Spread half the remaining meat sauce across the surface, then use a spatula to coax it into the pasta. (You could also use a piping bag.) Repeat with the remaining meat sauce, banging the cake tin lightly on the counter as needed to help the meat sauce fill the pasta tubes right to the base. Toss the parmesan with the mozzarella in a bowl, then sprinkle the cheeses over the top of the pasta.

Bake – Cover loosely with foil (so it's not touching the cheese) and bake for 25 minutes. Remove the foil and bake for a further 20 minutes. Remove from the oven and allow to rest for 15 minutes before removing the springform tin sides. Leave the base in place. Cut into generous wedges like cake! Serve sprinkled with extra parmesan and parsley, if desired.

See Notes overleaf.

NOTES

1 Paccheri is like rigatoni but wider, so it's easier to stuff just by pouring the meat sauce over. Rigatoni can be used in a pinch.

2 A mix of herbs labelled 'Italian herb mix' that you get from regular grocery stores.

3 If you can't consume alcohol, use non-alcoholic red wine or just omit.

4 Slow-cooking the beef makes the fibres fall apart so the meat pieces are smaller, which makes it easier to fill the pasta tubes. If you don't have the time for slow-cooking, simmer for 20 minutes without a lid over medium heat, then mash the beef using a potato masher to make it finer.

5 The par-cooked pasta will stand upright better (no floppage issues!) and the pasta will not be overcooked once baked.

LEFTOVERS Fridge 3 days, freezer 3 months.

ANDY'S WHOLE ROASTED CAULIFLOWER CHEESE

Be still my beating heart!

SERVES: 5–6 AS A MAIN, 8 AS A SIDE | PREP: 15 MINUTES + 15 MINUTES DRYING AND DRAINING | COOK: 50 MINUTES

With its commanding form, a whole roasted cauliflower makes a striking meat-free main dish. I've tried it all sorts of ways, but by far the stand-out has been a blanket of molten cheese sauce over the cauliflower. Think of it as a low-carb mac and cheese! This recipe is from my friend Andy Hearnden's debut cookbook, *Andy Cooks: The Cookbook*. Andy happens to be a social media sensation with tens of millions of followers (what do you mean, you haven't heard of Andy Cooks!?), but is one of the most down-to-earth guys you'll ever meet. And a chef at that! Serve this as a substantial side or as a main with a leafy green salad and crusty bread for mopping your plate clean. Don't waste a drop of that sauce!

---

1 kg cauliflower[1], 15–17 cm wide head after trimming

2 tsp salt* (for blanching)

ROASTING

1½ tbsp extra-virgin olive oil

½ tsp salt*

¼ tsp black pepper

CHEESE SAUCE AND TOPPING

60 g unsalted butter

50 g (⅓ cup) plain flour

625 ml (2½ cups) full-fat milk

150 g (1½ tightly packed cups) red Leicester cheese[2], freshly grated*

150 g (1½ tightly packed cups) gruyere cheese[2], freshly grated*

¼ tsp salt*

⅛ tsp black pepper

Trim cauliflower – Remove all the leaves and trim the core so the cauliflower sits flat. Cut a cross into the base about 2.5 cm deep. Take care to ensure the whole cauliflower stays together.

Preheat the oven to 180°C (160°C fan).

Blanch – Bring about 5 litres of water to the boil with the 2 teaspoons of salt in a large pot* over high heat. Place the cauliflower in gently, florets facing up – the top of the cauliflower will bob above the water, which is fine. Once the water comes back up to the boil, cook the cauliflower for 12 minutes or until you can insert a small knife into the core fairly easily.[3]

Dry – Transfer the cauliflower to a large colander.[3] Turn it upside down (florets down), which will help remove more water from the florets (nobody wants a watery cauliflower cheese!). Leave to drain for 5 minutes, then pat the surface dry with paper towels.

Roast – Transfer the cauliflower to a baking dish (I use my 26 cm cast-iron skillet*). Drizzle the surface with the oil and sprinkle with the salt and pepper (not the underside). Roast for 25 minutes.

Cheese sauce – Melt the butter in a large saucepan* over medium heat. Once the butter is foaming, add the flour and whisk for 1 minute. While whisking, pour the milk in slowly. Turn the heat up to high. Whisk every now and then, and more regularly as the milk starts to heat up and starts steaming – it will thicken into a creamy sauce. As soon as you see bubbles, reduce the heat to medium. Add about two-thirds of the cheese (reserve the rest for sprinkling), and all the salt and pepper. Whisk until the cheese is melted and you have a thick, molten cheese sauce with the consistency of a very thick honey.

Sauce it! – Remove the cauliflower from the oven. Set it aside for 10 minutes to let the surface dry (so the cheese sauce sticks). Switch the oven grill to high with the shelf 25 cm from the heat source. Use a ladle to pour the cheese sauce over the cauliflower, waiting 30 seconds between each coating to give it a chance to set before the next coating (this coats it more thickly!). Sprinkle the cauliflower with the remaining cheese.

Golden brown – Place the cauliflower under the grill for 10 minutes, rotating the baking dish at the halfway mark, until the surface is golden. Keep a close eye on it!

Serve – To serve, cut the cauliflower into wedges (like cake!) and serve with a big spoon. Be sure to take your fair share of the cheese sauce!

See Notes overleaf.

NOTES

1 Look for a firm cauliflower with tight florets. This recipe won't work with old, floppy cauliflower because it will fall apart!

2 Andy only uses gruyere cheese. I like to add red Leicester cheese because it gives the sauce a gorgeous amber glow and adds terrific sharp cheese flavour. It pairs beautifully with gruyere, which is a spectacular melting cheese that brings warm nutty tones to the flavour. I stick to these cheeses when making this for company, but feel free to use your favourite melting cheese instead, such as cheddar, tasty cheese, cheddar, manchego or Swiss cheese. Not mozzarella though, it's too mild. Whatever cheese you use, be sure to shred your own as pre-grated has anti-caking agents that can make your cheese sauce powdery.

3 Blanching tips: The easiest way to remove the cauliflower from the water is by using a slotted spoon and tongs. The cauliflower should be holding together firmly still, but partially cooked. Check by inserting a small sharp knife into the core.

4 Make ahead: Both the blanched cauliflower and cheese sauce can be made up to 2 days ahead. Fully cool, then refrigerate. Bring the cauliflower to room temperature, then roast it as per the recipe. Reheat the cheese sauce gently on the stove, then proceed with the recipe.

LEFTOVERS Fridge 3 days. Not suitable for freezing.

VIETNAMESE PULLED PORK FEAST!

My new signature recipe made for gatherings

VIETNAMESE COCONUT LEMONGRASS PULLED PORK

excluding bread

A master recipe for tender pulled pork with Vietnamese flavours, with loads of uses!

SERVES: 10–12 | PREP: 10 MINUTES | COOK: 3½ HOURS

This isn't authentic Vietnamese but takes its cue from the lemongrass-infused coconut sauces I've seen with seafood in Vietnam. Soaking up flavours after a long braise in the coconut milk, the pork is so tender it just falls apart. Delicious already, but the really special touch comes when we pan-fry the pork until golden. The flavour, texture and golden colour this adds to the pork strands is so incredible, so don't think about skipping this step! From here, there's a pile of DIY spread options: Noodle Bowls, Bánh Mi, Rice Paper Rolls (see pages 286–88). Even use the leftovers for Vietnamese Pizza (page 116). Meanwhile, the braising liquid goes in a killer Peanut Sauce to serve with the pork – free flavour bump! I like to also serve a zippy Chilli Lime Dipping Sauce to cut through all the richness. Both these recipes are on page 289.

2–2.25 kg boneless, skinless pork shoulder[1], cut into 3 equal pieces

4 lemongrass* stalks, white part only

3 tbsp vegetable oil

COCONUT BRAISING SAUCE

8 garlic cloves*, finely minced

50 g (¼ tightly packed cup) brown sugar

80 ml (⅓ cup) fish sauce

60 ml (¼ cup) white vinegar

1 tsp white pepper

2 bird's eye chillies*, deseeded and cut in half lengthways[2]

400 g full-fat coconut milk*

250 ml (1 cup) water

TO SERVE

Vietnamese Noodle Bowls, Rice Bowls, Rice Paper Rolls, Bánh Mi (see pages 286–89)

Preheat the oven to 160°C (both standard and fan).[3]

Prepare – Mix all the sauce ingredients in a heavy-based roasting pan, preferably metal not ceramic. Add the pork and turn to coat in the sauce, then arrange upside down (i.e. smooth-side down, flappy meat-side up).

Lemongrass – Bash the stalks with a meat mallet to make them burst open slightly. Bend them in half to release the flavour, then add them into the pan around the pork.

Slow cook – Cover the pork with foil and bake for 2 hours. Remove the foil and carefully turn the meat over. Bake for another 1 hour, uncovered, or until the meat shreds easily (the surface should be golden).

Shred – Transfer the pork into a separate pan for shredding. Use tongs plus a fork to shred the meat.

Reduce sauce – Transfer the lemongrass to a plate to cool so it can be handled. Pour all the sauce in the roasting pan into a medium to large saucepan*. Simmer rapidly over medium–high heat and reduce to 500 ml (2 cups), about 15 minutes. The reduction amount is important for the right salt and flavour concentration, so measure with a jug for accuracy. Squeeze as much juice as you can out of the lemongrass into the saucepan, then discard.[4]

Golden pork – Add 250 ml (1 cup) of the reduced pork juice into the shredded pork and toss through. Heat 1 tablespoon of the vegetable oil in a large non-stick frying pan* over high heat. Spread out one-third of the pork and pan-fry for 1–1½ minutes until golden. Turn the pork using tongs, then lightly pan-fry the other side for 30 seconds. Transfer to a serving platter. Add the remaining oil and repeat twice more to fry the remaining pork.

Serve – Now, it's up to you to decide how to serve this! Make: Noodle Bowls, Rice Bowls, Rice Paper Rolls or Bánh Mi – see pages 286–89 for the recipes, along with the sauce options. I like to lay everything out and then let everyone help themselves, which is especially great for gatherings!

continued – – ►

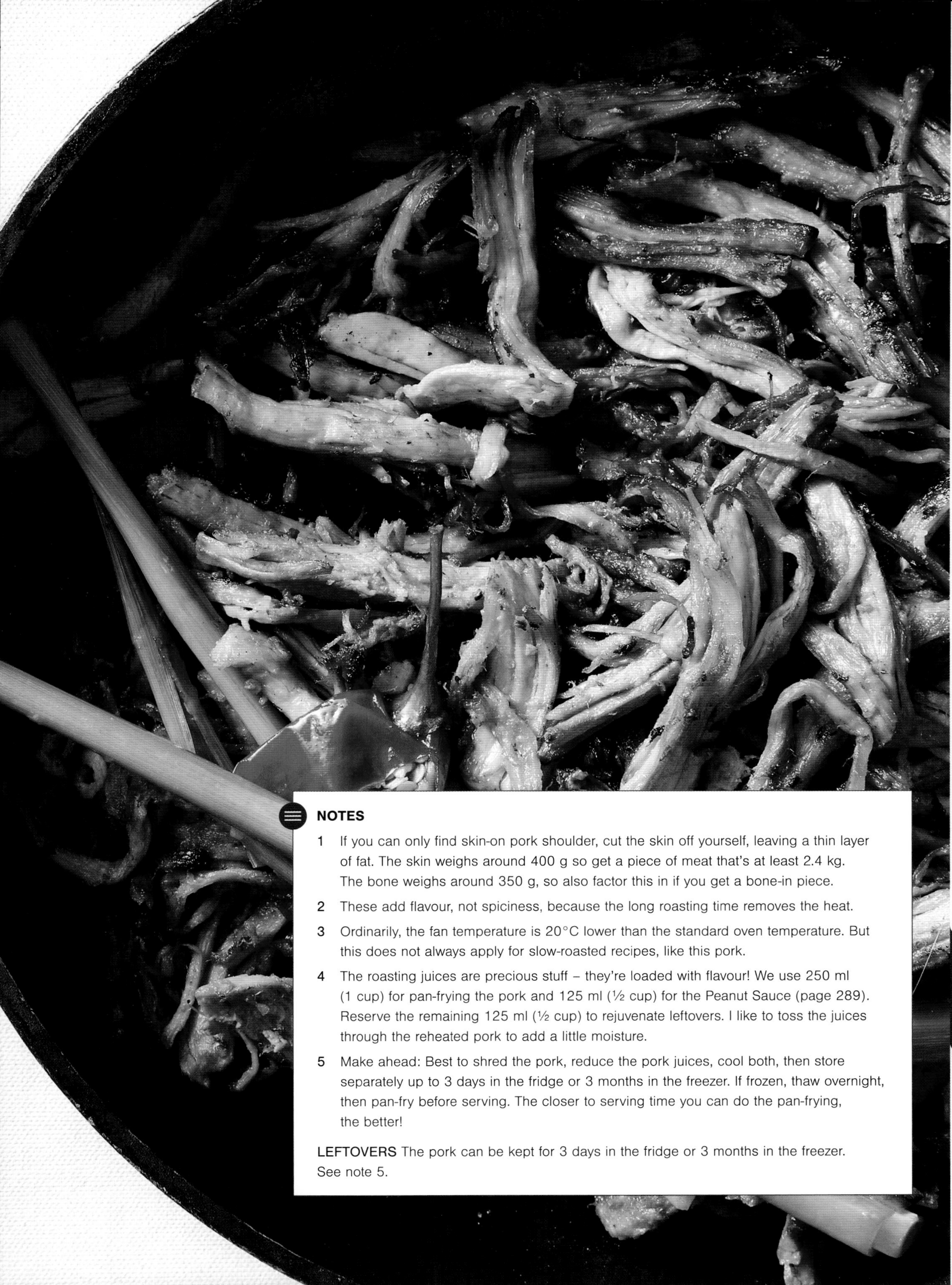

NOTES

1 If you can only find skin-on pork shoulder, cut the skin off yourself, leaving a thin layer of fat. The skin weighs around 400 g so get a piece of meat that's at least 2.4 kg. The bone weighs around 350 g, so also factor this in if you get a bone-in piece.

2 These add flavour, not spiciness, because the long roasting time removes the heat.

3 Ordinarily, the fan temperature is 20°C lower than the standard oven temperature. But this does not always apply for slow-roasted recipes, like this pork.

4 The roasting juices are precious stuff – they're loaded with flavour! We use 250 ml (1 cup) for pan-frying the pork and 125 ml (½ cup) for the Peanut Sauce (page 289). Reserve the remaining 125 ml (½ cup) to rejuvenate leftovers. I like to toss the juices through the reheated pork to add a little moisture.

5 Make ahead: Best to shred the pork, reduce the pork juices, cool both, then store separately up to 3 days in the fridge or 3 months in the freezer. If frozen, thaw overnight, then pan-fry before serving. The closer to serving time you can do the pan-frying, the better!

LEFTOVERS The pork can be kept for 3 days in the fridge or 3 months in the freezer. See note 5.

SERVING OPTIONS

All these options are a self-serve format for your guests. Everybody gets to pick and choose their own fillings or toppings (fussy eaters, sorted), plus it's less work for you!

NOODLE BOWLS

SERVES: 12

Classic Vietnamese rice noodle (bún) bowls with pork, crisp vegetables and herbs. Served at room temperature, this option is excellent for warmer weather or as a lighter meal.

---

600 g dried rice vermicelli, prepared according to packet directions

1 batch Vietnamese Coconut Lemongrass Pulled Pork (page 284)

1 iceberg lettuce, shredded

2 batches Quick Asian Pickles[1] (page 317)

3 baby cucumbers*, julienned

280 g (3½ cups) bean sprouts

70 g (6 lightly packed cups) coriander sprigs[2]

50 g (4 lightly packed cups) mint leaves[2] (smaller works better)

Double batch of Chilli Lime Dipping Sauce (page 289, primary sauce) plus one batch of Peanut Sauce (page 289, for accent, highly recommended)

130 g (1 cup) roasted peanuts, finely chopped

6 bird's eye chillies*, finely sliced (optional)

Place the noodles in a bowl. Top with the pork, lettuce, pickled vegetables, cucumber and bean sprouts. Add a generous amount of herbs – tear them by hand if needed and stuff them into your bowl! Douse with plenty of Chilli Lime Dipping Sauce (page 289), then drizzle with dollops of Peanut Sauce (page 289) (you don't need much). Sprinkle with plenty of peanuts and fresh chilli, if desired. Dig in with chopsticks!

RICE BOWLS

As above with the noodle bowls, except with steamed jasmine rice or other rice of choice instead of noodles – see pages 318–21.

BÁNH MI!

MAKES: 1

Pork finds its way into traditional bánh mi rolls in many forms, from the 'classic' pork roll with deli meats, to braised meatballs and barbecued pork patties. I think the pulled pork makes an excellent addition to the canon!

---

1 crusty roll, about 18 cm long

1½ tbsp chicken pâté

1½ tbsp whole-egg mayonnaise*

30 g (½ cup) shredded iceberg lettuce

20 cm piece of spring onion*, chopped into 5 cm lengths

2 cucumber* ribbons[3]

60 g (½ cup) Vietnamese Coconut Lemongrass Pulled Pork (page 284)

40 g (¼ cup) Quick Asian Pickles[1] (page 317)

3 g (¼ cup) coriander sprigs[2]

Drizzle of Chilli Lime Dipping Sauce (page 289)

Finely sliced red bird's eye chilli* – if you like the heat!

Split the bread roll but don't cut all the way through. Smear the base with pâté and the lid with the mayonnaise. Stuff with (in this order): the lettuce, spring onion, cucumber, pork, pickled vegetables, then the coriander sprigs. Drizzle with the Chilli Lime Dipping Sauce (page 289) and sprinkle with chilli, if desired. Close the lid and bite!

NOTES

1. I highly recommend using the pickled vegetables. They're quick and easy with big rewards for the tang they add to all these dishes!
2. It's hard to measure herb leaves. Just have plenty! One of the great things about Vietnamese food is the way richness is balanced with herby freshness. Tip: you can skip the coriander, if you must, but don't skip the mint!
3. Make cucumber ribbons by peeling thin strips from a baby cucumber* using a vegetable peeler.

continued - - ►

RICE PAPER ROLLS

MAKES: 40–50 (SERVES 12–15 PEOPLE AS A MEAL)

The rich flavour of the pork makes it ideal to use for rice paper rolls stuffed with plenty of fresh vegetables!

40–50 x 22 cm round, dried rice paper sheets[1]

1 batch Vietnamese Coconut Lemongrass Pulled Pork (page 284)

50 g dried rice vermicelli noodles, prepared according to the packet instructions

40–50 butter lettuce leaves (or other soft lettuce), crunchy core removed

320 g (4 cups) bean sprouts

3 baby cucumbers*, julienned

60 g (5 cups) coriander sprigs

50 g (4 cups) mint leaves

3 batches Peanut Sauce (opposite, recommended) or 2 batches Chilli Lime Dipping Sauce (opposite, if you prefer something lighter)

Fill a large bowl with warm water. Dip a rice paper sheet in the water for 2 seconds,[2] then place on a plate or work surface. Top with 25 g (¼ lightly packed cup) pork plus a bit of the noodles, lettuce, bean sprouts, cucumber, coriander and mint leaves. Pro tip: Bundle everything up in the lettuce leaf so it doesn't pierce the rice paper! Roll up (it will self-seal). Repeat to make more rice paper rolls. To serve, dip the roll into the peanut or chilli lime sauce and bite!

NOTES

1 Readily available these days in the Asian aisle of grocery stores and Asian stores.

2 If the bowl is not large enough to fit the rice paper, just rotate it and count 2 seconds for each section submerged in the water.

SAUCES

PEANUT SAUCE

MAKES 185 ML (¾ CUP)

60 g (¼ cup) natural unsweetened smooth peanut butter*

125 ml (½ cup) reduced roasting juices from the Vietnamese Coconut Lemongrass Pulled Pork (page 284)

2 tsp white sugar

2 tbsp rice vinegar

This peanut sauce is one of a kind thanks to the flavourful roasting juices from the Vietnamese pulled pork that go into it. It'd be a crying shame not to use those juices to make this, so don't skip it! This sauce is nutty and sweet with a deeply savoury taste from the meat drippings. Use it for dipping rice paper rolls, or drizzling over rice bowls, noodle bowls and in bánh mi.

Put all the ingredients in a bowl and whisk to combine. Serve at room temperature.

CHILLI LIME DIPPING SAUCE

MAKES 250 ML (1 CUP)

50 g (¼ tightly packed cup) brown sugar

60 ml (¼ cup) fish sauce

80 ml (⅓ cup) lime juice

1 tbsp water

3 tbsp finely minced coriander leaves

1 tbsp deseeded and finely minced long green (cayenne) chilli*

1 tsp deseeded and finely minced bird's eye chilli*

1 tsp very finely minced garlic*

A zesty and sharp sauce is the other essential condiment to accompany the rich Vietnamese pulled pork. Here I've adapted the universally useful Thai dipping sauce nam jim. Heavy on the lime and fresh coriander, it's not too sweet and works as a refreshing counterpoint.

Mix all the ingredients in a bowl and set aside for at least 10 minutes. Best made within a few hours of serving for the freshest flavour.

Make ahead: Keep the coriander, chilli and garlic in one container, and the rest of the sauce in another. Mix before serving.

MORE IDEAS FOR HOW TO USE THE PORK

- Make lettuce wraps with the pork and Quick Asian Pickles (page 317). Dunk them in the Peanut Sauce!
- Use as a topping for Vietnamese Pizza (page 116).
- Toss through fried rice.
- Add to Chinese Sweetcorn Soup (page 153) or Spicy Peanut Noodles (page 113).
- Make Vietnamese pork sliders by stuffing soft warm, buttered rolls with the pork, drizzled with the Peanut Sauce. What a way to feed a crowd!
- Vietnamese quesadilla – pan-fry the pork in folded tortillas* with melted cheese.
- Make the most amazing jaffle (also with cheese!).

SWEETS

Full from dinner, but still got room for dessert!

STRAWBERRY SWIRL SHORTCAKE

Finally, whipped cream on a cake that stays whipped.

SERVES: 16–24 | PREP: 30 MINUTES + COOLING | COOK: 55 MINUTES

Everybody adores anything piled high with whipped cream. Unfortunately, though, whipped cream can't be made very far in advance because it deflates and weeps. But I've got answers! The whipped cream in this swirly summer strawberry cake is stabilised with cream cheese. It keeps the cream fluffy for several days and adds a subtle tang that works perfectly with the sweet strawberry sauce. Make this cake today, serve it tomorrow and it will look as pristine as when freshly made!

STRAWBERRY SAUCE

1 kg strawberries, hulled and chopped into 1.5 cm pieces

100 g (½ cup) caster sugar

1 tbsp lemon juice

CAKE – DRY

450 g (3 cups) plain flour

6 tsp baking powder*[1]

⅛ tsp salt*

CAKE – WET

300 g (1½ cups) caster sugar

125 g unsalted butter, melted and cooled

60 ml (¼ cup) vegetable oil

60 ml (¼ cup) full-fat milk, at room temperature

3 large eggs*, at room temperature

390 g (1½ cups) full-fat Greek yoghurt, at room temperature

3 tsp vanilla extract

STABILISED WHIPPED CREAM

250 g block full-fat cream cheese[2] (not tub), taken out of fridge 20 minutes prior to using

600 ml (2⅓ cups) thick cream*, fridge-cold

3 tbsp caster sugar

1½ tsp vanilla extract

TO DECORATE

Extra fresh strawberries, whole or halved

Strawberry sauce – Place all the sauce ingredients in a large saucepan* over medium–high heat. Bring to a simmer, then reduce the heat to medium and simmer rapidly for 10 minutes. The strawberries will release a lot of juice! Mash the strawberries with a potato masher. Reduce the heat to low and simmer for a further 5 minutes, stirring regularly. Transfer to a bowl and allow to fully cool before using. (It will thicken into a loose jam consistency.)

Preheat the oven to 180°C (160°C fan). Grease a 23 x 33 cm metal pan[3] (at least 4 cm deep) with butter and line with baking paper.

Cake – Place the dry ingredients in a large bowl and whisk to combine. Place the wet ingredients in a separate bowl and whisk to combine. Pour the wet ingredients into the dry ingredients, then whisk just until lump-free.

Swirl and bake – Pour the cake batter into the pan and smooth the surface. Use 185 ml (¾ cup) of the strawberry sauce to make 10 dollops across the surface. Use a knife to swirl them into the mixture, leaving big streaks of strawberry (don't mix it in). Limit yourself to 15 seconds of swirling time – no more!

Bake – Bake for 40 minutes or until a skewer inserted into the centre comes out clean. Cool for 10 minutes in the pan, then cool completely on a wire rack.

Stabilised whipped cream – Place all the cream ingredients in a large bowl. Beat on high for 1½–2 minutes using hand-held electric beaters, or a stand mixer fitted with the whisk attachment until the cream is softly whipped.

Decorate – Spread 250 ml (1 cup) of strawberry sauce across the surface of the cake. Dollop the cream across the top, then spread it out. Dollop the remaining strawberry sauce over the cream, then swirl it through. Pile the fresh strawberries on top. Cut and serve!

NOTES

1 Dead baking powder is a common baking fail – expiry dates on jars are misleading! See Baking powder testing in the Glossary (page 337).

2 Low-fat cream cheese and spreadable soft cream cheese sold in tubs won't work as well to stabilise cream. To use spreadable cream cheese, use an extra 75 g.

3 The cake can also be made in 2 x 20 cm square cake tins, baked for 35 minutes.

4 Best way to make ahead: While the whipped cream already spread on the cake will stay fluffy for 2 days, if you are making this ahead intentionally, it is better to whip the cream the day before but spread it on the cake the day you are serving. Leave the whipped cream in a bowl overnight in the fridge. Make the cake ahead and refrigerate, covered. Refrigerate the strawberry sauce. On the day, take the cake out of the fridge 1 hour prior. Spread the cake with strawberry sauce. DO NOT stir the cream, it will deflate! Just scoop and spread straight onto the cake, then swirl the strawberry sauce through.

LEFTOVERS Fridge 4 days. Not suitable for freezing. Best served at room temperature.

BROWNIE COOKIE

Cookie, meet brownie.

MAKES: 18–20 COOKIES | PREP: 20 MINUTES + 1 HOUR DOUGH CHILLING | COOK: 13 MINUTES

Cross a brownie with a cookie and you ought to get the best of both worlds: chewy and fudgy inside, crackly and slightly crisp on the outside! It's a brainwave that struck me and I just had to try it out. I was so thrilled with the result that I proudly announced my epic cookie innovation to the world on Instagram ... only to be gently informed that in fact it's not a new thing at all and people have been making them forever. It's even got a name: a 'brookie' (of course!). There should be a word for the feeling you get when you believe you've thought of something amazingly original, only to realise you're the 16,277th person to think of it. Oh well, I take comfort in knowing it's an awesomely delicious cookie that's already widely appreciated!

---

200 g dark choc chips or melts[1]

50 g unsalted butter, melted

150 g (¾ tightly packed cup) brown sugar

2 large eggs*

1 tsp vanilla extract

100 g (⅔ cup) plain flour

25 g (⅓ cup) unsweetened cocoa powder[2], sifted

½ tsp baking powder*

⅛ tsp salt*

Pinch of sea salt flakes

Melted chocolate – Place the chocolate in a large heatproof bowl. Melt in 20 second bursts in the microwave on High, stirring between each burst, until melted and smooth. Add the butter, sugar, eggs and vanilla and whisk until smooth.

Finish batter – Sift the flour, cocoa and baking powder straight into the bowl. Add the salt. Switch to a wooden spoon and stir just until you can no longer see flour.

Refrigerate[3] – Place the bowl in the fridge for 1 hour so the cookie dough firms up enough to roll into balls.

Preheat the oven to 180°C (160°C fan). Lightly grease two large baking trays with butter and line with baking paper.

Bake – Scoop 1½ tablespoon portions of the dough (size 40 cookie scoop) and place them on the tray. Roll the portions into balls (wet your hands if they get tacky) and set them on the trays 5 cm apart – you should get 18 to 20 cookies[4]. Bake both trays at the same time for 13 minutes. The surface should be crackly (like brownies!) and they will be puffed up slightly (they will deflate as they cool).

Cool – Sprinkle each cookie with a pinch of sea salt. Leave to fully cool on the trays. Join gym.

NOTES

1 Be sure to use chocolate chips or melts from the baking aisle, which are specifically designed to melt smoothly for cooking purposes. Don't use eating chocolate, which usually does not melt very well.

2 Dutch processed cocoa powder is not recommended here. It will make the cookie drier than intended.

3 The refrigerating step is key for fudgy insides so don't skip it!

4 I scoop all the dough first and dollop onto the trays, then roll the balls.

LEFTOVERS 5 days in an airtight container in the pantry, though if it's warm where you are, the fridge is better. Not suitable for freezing.

COCONUT LIME BARS

A tangy citrus slice that's made to travel.

SERVES: 16 | PREP: 20 MINUTES + 3 HOURS REFRIGERATING | COOK: 40 MINUTES

When it comes to desserts that are perfect for sharing, there's a sort of holy grail ideal that lives in my head: quick to make, easy to transport, can be eaten with hands alone, doesn't require assembly to serve, and has a reasonable shelf life outside a fridge (hear that, whipped cream??). I'm always trying to think of new ones, and these delightful coconut lime bars are my latest creation. They consist of a tangy, not-too-sweet lime curd set on a lovely coconut shortbread base, topped with a showering of toasted coconut and fresh lime zest. Hello, summer! When lime is out of season (or hyper-inflated in price!), simply switch to lemon instead.

COCONUT SHORTBREAD BASE

110 g (3/4 cup) plain flour

45 g (1/2 cup) desiccated coconut, unsweetened[1]

60 g (1/2 cup) icing sugar, sifted

Pinch of salt*

110 g COLD unsalted butter, cut into 1 cm cubes

1/4 tsp coconut essence (optional)

LIME CURD FILLING

2 tbsp plain flour

150 g (3/4 cup) caster sugar

4 large eggs*

1 tbsp lime zest

170 ml (2/3 cups) lime juice

TOPPING

20 g (1/3 cup) toasted shredded coconut[1, 2]

1/2 tsp lime zest

Preheat the oven to 180°C (160°C fan). Grease a 20 cm square cake tin with butter and line with baking paper. Have plenty of overhang to lift the slice out at the end.

Base – Place all the base ingredients in a food processor. Pulse 10 times or until it becomes fine crumbs without large butter clumps. Tumble the mixture into the tin, then press it in with your hands, pushing it right up to the edges – I like to smooth the surface by pressing on it using a measuring cup with a flat base. Bake for 20 minutes until light golden. Remove from the oven. The base will be a little puffed up so use a spatula to lightly press down on the base to deflate it.

Filling – While the base is in the oven, make the filling. Whisk the flour and sugar in a bowl using a hand-held whisk. Add the remaining filling ingredients and whisk to combine.

Pour – Give the filling a quick whisk, then gently pour it on the still-warm base. Don't pour from a height or you might break the surface of the shortbread![3] (Note: Do not leave the base to cool as it will shrink and the filling will run down the sides.)

Bake – Bake for 15 minutes or until the edges are set but the centre is still jiggly.

Refrigerate – Cool on the counter for 1 hour, then refrigerate for 2 hours.

Serve – Cut into 16 squares. Sprinkle with the toasted coconut and lime zest, then serve!

NOTES

1 Desiccated coconut is the very fine, small flakes of coconut. I like to use the slightly larger shredded coconut for the topping for better texture and visuals, but if you'd prefer not to get a separate packet of coconut, just use desiccated coconut instead.

2 To toast shredded coconut, heat a small non-stick frying pan* over medium heat, then gently stir the coconut until some of it is lightly golden. Immediately transfer to a bowl, then set aside to cool before using.

3 Pour the curd onto the base with the edge of the bowl close to the surface of the shortbread base so the pour is gentle and doesn't break the surface. If you pour from a height (as I dramatically did once) it will destroy your shortbread!

LEFTOVERS Fridge 7 days, freezer 3 months.

HOMEMADE NUTELLA ICE CREAM CAKE – NO ICE CREAM MAKER!

A deliriously decadent ice cream cake that'll steal the show!

SERVES: 10–12 | PREP: 30 MINUTES + 11 HOURS FREEZING

This over-the-top Nutella ice cream cake would be a little ridiculous if it didn't taste so freaking good and wasn't so easy to make! Thanks to a magic freeze-and-forget recipe, there's no churner needed to make the ice cream – an instant game changer. I think of this ice cream cake as the ultimate celebration of chocolate and hazelnuts. Crushed Oreo cookies form the base, on which a slab of decadently rich and smooth Nutella ice cream sits. A layer of Nutella ganache is then smeared over the ice cream, and the cake is topped with a generous pile of hazelnuts and broken Ferrero Rocher chocolates. Like I said, a little bit ridiculous but guaranteed to turn heads and have people drooling!

BASE

256 g Oreo cookies[1] (2 standard packets)

60 g unsalted butter, melted

NO-CHURN NUTELLA ICE CREAM

320 g (1 cup) Nutella

395 g can condensed milk

500 ml (2 cups) thick cream*

105 g (¾ cup) skinless hazelnuts, toasted*, cooled and roughly chopped

NUTELLA GANACHE

110 g (⅓ cup) Nutella

1 tbsp vegetable oil[2]

TO DECORATE

10 Ferrero Rocher chocolates[3], 3 roughly chopped, 4 halved, 3 kept whole

45 g (⅓ cup) skinless hazelnuts, toasted*, cooled and roughly chopped

Grease a 23 cm springform tin with butter, then line the base and sides with baking paper.

Biscuit base – Roughly break up the Oreo cookies by hand. Blitz them into fine crumbs in a food processor. Pour in the butter and blitz to combine – it will look like wet sand. Pour the base into the tin and press down lightly (not firmly). Set aside.

Ice cream mixture – Using hand-held electric beaters, whip the Nutella and condensed milk with 125 ml (½ cup) of the cream on high speed for 1 minute. Stir in the hazelnuts. In a separate bowl, whip the remaining cream until stiff peaks form. Fold[4] approximately 250 ml (1 cup) of the whipped cream into the Nutella mixture. Pour all the Nutella mixture into the whipped cream and fold[4] it through until you no longer see streaks of cream.

Freeze cake – Pour the ice cream mixture onto the Oreo base. Smooth the surface. Cover with plastic wrap, then freeze for 10 hours (or longer).

Nutella ganache – Place the Nutella and oil in a heatproof bowl. Microwave for 20 seconds on High. Stir to combine, then cool for 5 minutes. Pour onto the surface of the cake and quickly spread before it sets. Freeze for 1 hour or until firm.

Serve – Pile the halved and whole Ferrero Rocher chocolates on the cake. Sprinkle over the chopped Ferrero Rochers, then sprinkle with the hazelnuts. Cut and serve like cake![5]

NOTES

1 256 g Oreos is two standard 128 g packets (28 cookies in total).

2 The oil prevents the Nutella from freezing rock-solid.

3 I use store-bought Ferrero Rochers. I do not make my own!!

4 To fold the mixture, use a rubber spatula or a large spoon and scoop the mixture from the bottom of the bowl to the top. Watch the video for a demonstration (scan the QR code). Don't mix vigorously in circles as you would a cake batter, or you will deflate a lot of the air out of the cream.

5 If your cake has been in the freezer for a few days, you may need to leave it out for a few minutes to soften slightly before cutting. But if it's made within the last 48 hours, you should be able to cut it straight from the freezer.

LEFTOVERS Freezer 3 months.

MY PERFECT ORANGE POPPY SEED LOAF CAKE

With cream cheese frosting!

SERVES: 8–10 | PREP: 15 MINUTES + COOLING | COOK: 50 MINUTES

I've always wanted a really good orange poppy seed cake recipe. One with a moist, tender crumb with lovely orange flavour but not so strong that you can't taste the nutty flavour of the poppy seeds. This cookbook was just the excuse I needed to create one, and I couldn't be happier! I was going to make it in a round cake form (and you absolutely can) but, because I already have a few round cakes in this chapter, I went for a loaf form. You can even make cupcakes! Whatever shape you bake this in, don't skip the cream cheese frosting. The slight tang is the perfect match for this cake, and it couldn't be simpler to make: just mix it up with a wooden spoon. No electric beater required!

---

300 g (2 cups) plain flour

2½ tsp baking powder*[1]

⅛ tsp salt*

2 tbsp poppy seeds

2½ tbsp orange zest (3–4 large oranges)

250 ml (1 cup) orange juice (at room temperature), squeezed from the oranges

185 ml (¾ cup) vegetable oil

3 large eggs*, at room temperature

200 g (1 cup) caster sugar

1 tsp vanilla extract

MY EASY CREAM CHEESE FROSTING

100 g spreadable cream cheese[2] (tub type, not block)

190 g (1½ cups) soft icing sugar*, sifted

¼ tsp vanilla extract

2 tsp orange zest, plus extra for garnish, if desired

Preheat the oven to 180°C (160°C fan). Grease a 24 x 13.8 x 7.1 cm loaf tin[3] with oil or butter, then line with baking paper.

Batter – Put the flour, baking powder, salt and poppy seeds in a large bowl. Whisk to combine. Place the orange zest, juice, oil, eggs, sugar and vanilla in a separate medium bowl. Whisk well to thoroughly combine. Pour the wet mixture into the flour mixture. Whisk until lump-free, but don't whisk for longer than 10 seconds (overmixing can make the cake tough).

Bake – Pour the batter into the loaf tin. Bake for 50–60 minutes or until a skewer comes out clean.[4]

Cool – Cool for 10 minutes in the tin, then transfer the loaf to a wire rack. Cool completely before frosting.

Frosting – Place all the frosting ingredients in a bowl and mix with a wooden spoon until combined. Spread the frosting over the top of the poppy seed loaf cake. Grate over extra orange zest, if desired.

Serve – Cut into thick slices to serve. Make yourself a cup of tea, grab a slice and devour!

NOTES

1 Dead baking powder is a common baking fail – expiry dates on jars are misleading! See Baking powder testing in the Glossary (page 337).

2 Spreadable cream cheese is sold in tubs and is softer than block cream cheese because it is designed for spreading. Perfect to make quick creamy frostings!

3 The measurement of the base of the tin is 22 x 12 x 7.1 cm (it's smaller because the sides slope slightly). Larger loaf tins can also be used but the loaf will not be as high and will bake faster. The cake can also be baked in a 20 cm round cake tin (oven time 30 minutes) or in a muffin tin to make 10 cupcakes (22 minutes).

4 If the loaf gets too brown before it finishes baking, cover loosely with foil.

LEFTOVERS Keeps for 4 days in the pantry in cooler weather, or 5 days in the fridge in warmer weather. Freezer for 3 months. Always serve at room temperature!

HOT BUTTERSCOTCH CAKE WITH BUTTERSCOTCH SAUCE

Classic warm butterscotch pudding, reborn as a cake.

SERVES: 8–12 | PREP: 15 MINUTES | COOK: 45 MINUTES

This is my beloved self-saucing butterscotch pudding in cake form. It still hits all the best things about the pudding – a rich toffee flavour, warm and steamy sponge, and glossy caramel sauce – but the cake format makes it more elegant and far more practical for transporting and serving at gatherings. Oh, and I also upped the butterscotch sauce. A lot. Because frankly, in my world having too much butterscotch is like having too many pairs of shoes – it's a problem that just doesn't exist!

---

260 g (1¾ cups) plain flour

3½ tsp baking powder*[1]

⅛ tsp salt*

150 g unsalted butter, softened

70 g (⅓ tightly packed cup) dark brown sugar[2]

2 large eggs*, at room temperature

100 g (⅓ cup) golden syrup[3]

1 tsp vanilla extract

170 ml (⅔ cup) full-fat milk, at room temperature

BUTTERSCOTCH SAUCE

200 g (1 tightly packed cup) brown sugar (regular, not dark)

375 ml (1½ cups) thick cream*

½ tsp vanilla extract

70 g unsalted butter

TO SERVE

Vanilla ice cream

Preheat the oven to 180°C (160°C fan). Grease a 20 cm springform tin with butter and line with baking paper.

Dry ingredients – Whisk the flour, baking powder and salt in a bowl. Set aside.

Cream butter – In a stand mixer fitted with the paddle attachment, or with hand-held electric beaters, cream the butter and sugar on high speed for 1 minute until smooth. Beat in the eggs, one at a time, until mixed in. Add the golden syrup and vanilla and beat for 30 seconds on high. It might look a little split – that's okay as it will come together in the next steps.

Flour and milk – Add half the flour mixture and milk. Beat on medium speed for 5 seconds (it's okay if you still see flour). Add the remaining flour mixture and milk, then beat for 10 seconds or until you can no longer see flour. Scrape down the side of the bowl, then beat on medium for 10 seconds or until the batter is smooth – but cap the beating time to 20 seconds.[4]

Bake – Spread the batter into the cake tin. Bake for 45 minutes or until a skewer inserted into the centre comes out clean.

Butterscotch sauce – Place all the ingredients in a medium saucepan* over medium heat. Once the butter has melted, reduce the heat to low and simmer for 5 minutes, stirring regularly. Remove from the heat and cover with a lid to keep warm until required.

Soak – As soon as the cake comes out of the oven, pour 125 ml (½ cup) of the warm butterscotch sauce all over the surface, aiming for full coverage. If you have cracks on the surface of your cake, lucky you – the sauce will soak even better into the sponge! Leave the cake in the tin for 20 minutes before releasing the sides.

Serve – Cut into slices and serve warm[5] with a scoop of ice cream and warm butterscotch sauce.

NOTES

1 Dead baking powder is a common baking fail – expiry dates on jars are misleading! See Baking powder testing in the Glossary (page 337).

2 Dark brown sugar gives the cake a slightly darker colour and a hint more caramelly flavour than regular brown sugar, though you can substitute it in a pinch.

3 Golden syrup gives the caramelly flavour. If you can't find it, the best substitute is maple syrup – though the cake will have a maple flavour rather than butterscotch (still beautiful!).

4 She (or he) who overbeats cake batter will end up with tough cake!

5 This cake is designed to be served warm. You will find it a little on the dry side if you serve it cold. Each slice only requires 20 seconds on High in the microwave to warm through.

LEFTOVERS Fridge 5 days, freezer 3 months.

EASY DEEP-DISH CUSTARD TART

Custard, so much custard!!

SERVES: 12 | **PREP: 20 MINUTES + 8 HOURS REFRIGERATING** | **COOK: 45 MINUTES**

Here's one for those who see a tart recipe and instantly shy away, thinking 'too hard'! For this custard tart I've done away with fiddly shortcrust pastry and replaced it with a simple biscuit crumb base. No rolling out dough, no blind baking – if you can press a button to blitz biscuits, you can make this! Meanwhile the vanilla custard in this tart is an absolute dream. It's a cream-enriched version of the beautiful, luxurious French custard, *crème pâtissière*. Perfectly set with just the right amount of wobble, it's sliceable yet melts in the mouth into a river of creamy heaven. It's so good, I wanted more of it in this tart. So I made this deep-dish style!

SWEETS

BUTTERY CRUMB BASE

100 g digestive biscuits[1]

60 g unsalted butter, melted

2 tsp caster sugar

CREAMY CUSTARD

375 ml (1½ cups) full-fat milk

250 ml (1 cup) thick cream*[2]

1 vanilla bean, split in half lengthways and seeds scraped out (keep the bean) or 2 tsp vanilla bean paste[3]

½ tsp vanilla extract[3]

100 g (½ cup) caster sugar

60 g egg yolks* (4–5 eggs)

1 large egg* (55 g)

40 g (⅓ cup) cornflour

TO SERVE (OPTIONAL)

Raspberries

Icing sugar, to dust

Preheat the oven to 180°C (160°C fan). Invert the base of a 20 cm springform tin.[4] Grease it with butter, then cover with a square sheet of baking paper. Clip the sides of the tin in place (with the paper sticking out the sides), then grease and line the sides with baking paper.

Buttery base – Roughly break up the biscuits by hand and place them in a food processor. Blitz on high until they become fine crumbs.[5] Add the butter and sugar and blitz until combined – it should look like wet sand. Pour the biscuit mixture into the prepared tin and press it very firmly into the base. The firmer you press, the crisper the tart base will be! Bake for 15 minutes, then cool for 15 minutes – this will make the base harden before pouring the custard on so it remains crisp.

Reduce the oven to 160°C (140°C fan).

Infuse milk – Place the milk, cream, vanilla bean seeds, used bean and vanilla extract and half the sugar in a medium saucepan*. Heat over medium–high or until hot (do not let it boil), stirring to dissolve the sugar. Turn the stove off and cover the pan with a lid. Leave for 10 minutes to infuse the milk.[6] Remove the bean and squeeze every droplet of milk back into the saucepan before discarding.

Custard – Place the egg yolks, egg, cornflour and remaining sugar in a medium bowl. Whisk to combine using a hand-held whisk (don't use an electric beater). While whisking, slowly pour the hot milk into the eggs in a thin steady stream. Whisk just until combined, then stop whisking. Pour the mixture back into the saucepan. Cook the mixture over medium–low heat for 3 minutes, whisking constantly, or until it thickens into a custard. When you see lazy bubbles appearing (you'll have to pause whisking to see them), cook for another 45 seconds, whisking constantly, then remove from the stove.

Bake – Pour the custard onto the biscuit base and spread it out evenly – no need to smooth the surface perfectly (this will happen in the oven). Bake for 30 minutes or until just set on the edges but still quite jiggly in the middle (use the QR code to watch the video).

Set – Cool on the counter, then refrigerate for at least 8 hours, which will make the custard set.

Serve – Unclip the sides of the cake tin and slide the tart off the base using the overhanging paper. Leave on the counter for 30 minutes to bring the tart to room temperature before cutting into slices to serve. Decorate with raspberries and dust with icing sugar, if desired.

NOTES

1 A plain semi-sweet wheat biscuit originating from the UK. I love the wheaty flavour and hint of salt. Substitute with any plain sweet biscuit, such as Arnott's Marie biscuits.

2 Pure and whipping cream also work but they must be full-fat or the custard may not set.

3 Vanilla bean will give the best pure vanilla flavour and the impressive little black specks. Vanilla bean paste is a good, convenient substitute. Vanilla extract will also work (I like to add a bit to boost the vanilla flavour). I don't recommend using imitation vanilla essence.

4 Inverting the base makes it easy to slide the finished tart off at the end as you don't need to worry about the lip of the base.

5 Or do this in a ziplock bag* with a rolling pin.

6 Don't worry if a skin forms on the surface – it will dissolve when we whisk it later.

LEFTOVERS Fridge 5 days. Not suitable for freezing.

CINNAMON TEA CAKE

A cinnamon roll's cakey cousin!

SERVES: 8–12 | PREP: 20 MINUTES | COOK: 40 MINUTES

This is a great one to have up your sleeve for those times you want to knock out a cake without having to make a trip to the shops first. It's made solely from ingredients you'll have on hand, but still holds its own as a charming treat to serve with tea and coffee. Glazed with vanilla icing and with cinnamon sugar swirled through, it's reminiscent of a classic cinnamon roll, but in cake form! Unlike the pastry, there's no dough to rise here so it's much quicker to put together. A word of warning: this little number is quite sweet! Much like a cinnamon roll, really. And don't we just love that about them?

---

300 g (2 cups) plain flour

4 tsp baking powder*[1]

⅛ tsp salt*

125 g unsalted butter, softened

150 g (¾ cup) caster sugar

2 large eggs*, at room temperature

2 tsp vanilla extract

170 ml (⅔ cup) full-fat milk, at room temperature

CINNAMON BUTTER SWIRL

150 g (¾ tightly packed cup) brown sugar

1 tbsp ground cinnamon

75 g unsalted butter, melted

VANILLA GLAZE

125 g (1 cup) soft icing sugar*, sifted

5–6 tsp full-fat milk

½ tsp vanilla extract

Preheat the oven to 180°C (160°C fan). Grease a 23 cm springform tin[2] with butter, then line with baking paper.

Cinnamon butter swirl – Mix the cinnamon swirl ingredients in a bowl until combined.

Cake batter – Whisk the flour, baking powder and salt in a bowl to combine. Set aside. In a separate bowl, using hand-held electric beaters or in a stand mixer fitted with the paddle attachment, beat the butter and sugar on medium–high speed for 1 minute or until smooth and fluffy. Add the eggs, one at a time, and beat until combined. Add the vanilla, then half the flour mixture and half the milk. Beat on medium speed until the flour is just about mixed in, then stop beating, even if the batter is lumpy. Add the remaining milk and flour mixture, then beat on medium speed until the batter is lump-free – but no matter what, do not beat longer than 15 seconds.[3]

Swirls[4] – Spread half the batter in the tin (it will be a fairly thin layer). Using half the cinnamon butter, create eight dollops across the surface of the cake. Drag a butter knife through the batter in large 'S' shapes, going through each dollop twice. Dollop, then spread the remaining cake batter across the surface. Dot the surface with eight dollops using the remaining cinnamon butter. Swirl through the batter in 'S' shapes, sticking the butter knife only halfway through the batter.

Bake – Bake for 40 minutes or until a skewer inserted into the middle comes out clean and the top is golden with lots of lovely cracks for the glaze to seep into. Serious cinnamon roll vibes! Cool the cake for 10 minutes in the tin, then pour the glaze over (see below for glaze directions). Leave to cool for another 15 minutes or until the surface of the glaze has set. Release the side of the tin and cut the cake into generous slices. It will still be warm. The cake must always be served warm!

Glaze[5] – Whisk the ingredients in a bowl, starting with 5 teaspoons of milk. Add the extra teaspoon only if needed to thin the glaze into a drizzling consistency.

NOTES

1. Dead baking powder is a common baking fail – expiry dates on jars are misleading! See Baking powder testing in the Glossary (page 337).
2. This cake can be made in a 20 cm tin. Increase the baking time by 15 minutes.
3. Cap your final beating time to 15 seconds to ensure your cake doesn't come out dry!
4. Swirling tips: don't aim for perfection. There's no point because it will look completely different once baked! Limit the swirling time to 15 seconds for each layer. Any longer and the cake may not rise as much as it should!
5. Don't leave the glaze lying around in the bowl or the surface will form a crust.

LEFTOVERS Fridge 5 days, freezer 3 months. Always serve warm!

MAKE IT YOUR OWN!

Limes out of season? Want bursting berries in your custard tart? Feel like ice cream sandwiches? Here are some ideas to make the desserts in this chapter your own!

Brownie Ice Cream Sandwich Cookies

1 RASPBERRY CUSTARD TART

See page 304. Use a 23 cm springform tin and add 200 g fresh raspberries[1]. Pour half the custard in, top with half the raspberries. Cover with remaining custard, then place the remaining raspberries on the surface, gently pressing them in so they are half-submerged in the custard. Bake and cool as per recipe.

2 BROWNIE ICE CREAM SANDWICH COOKIES

See page 294. Sandwich the Brownie Cookies together with your favourite ice cream. My favourite to use is peanut butter ice cream! To do this, soften ice cream and press it into a tin. Freeze until firm, then cut out rounds the same size as the Brownie Cookies. Sandwich between two Brownie Cookies and eat immediately!

3 BLUEBERRY CINNAMON TEA CAKE

See page 306. Blueberries and cinnamon are heavenly together! Toss 190 g (1½ cups) of fresh or frozen (not thawed) blueberries with 1 tablespoon of flour, then gently stir them into the batter. Bake as per the recipe.

Raspberry Custard Tart

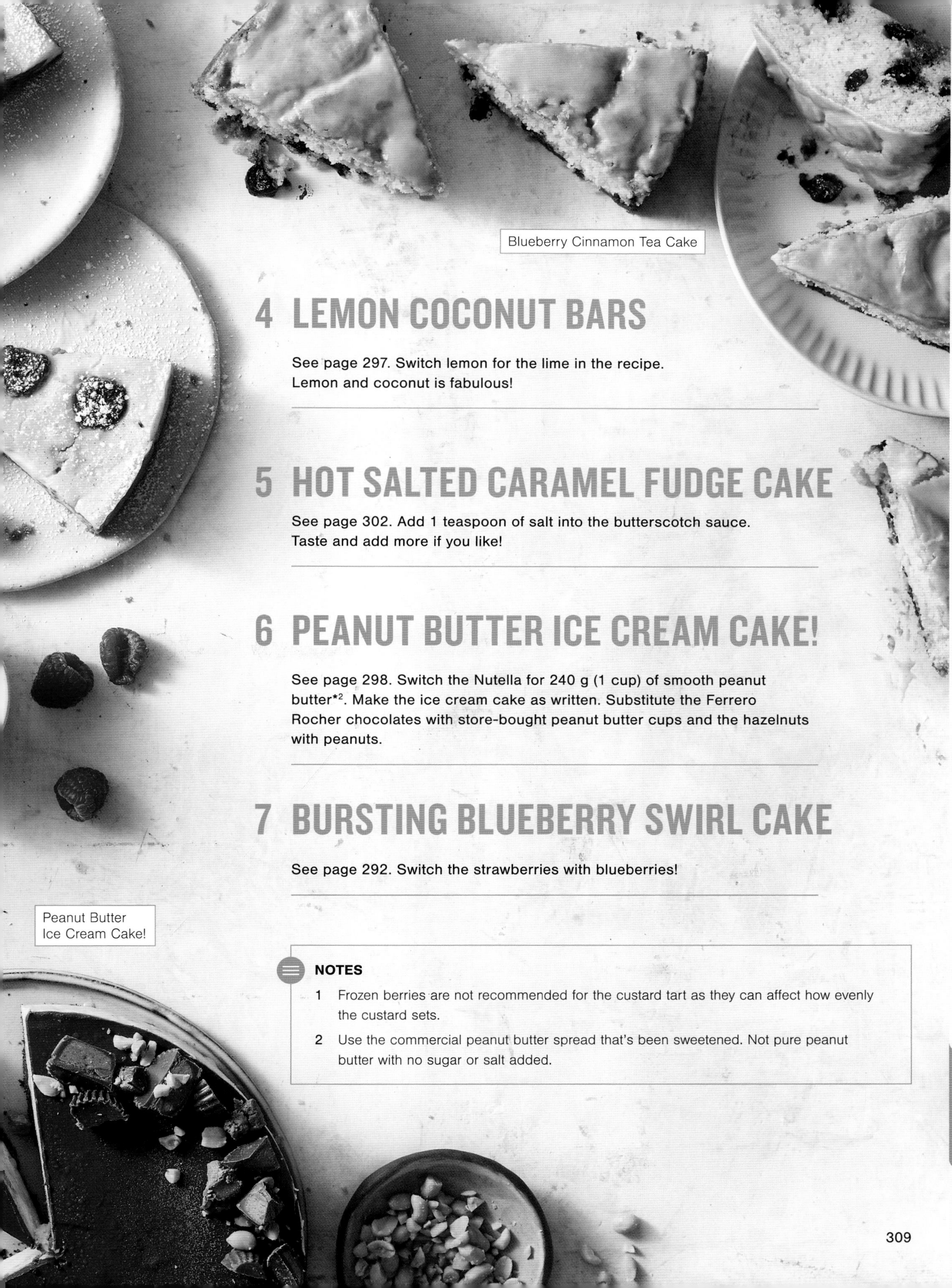

Blueberry Cinnamon Tea Cake

Peanut Butter Ice Cream Cake!

4 LEMON COCONUT BARS

See page 297. Switch lemon for the lime in the recipe. Lemon and coconut is fabulous!

---

5 HOT SALTED CARAMEL FUDGE CAKE

See page 302. Add 1 teaspoon of salt into the butterscotch sauce. Taste and add more if you like!

---

6 PEANUT BUTTER ICE CREAM CAKE!

See page 298. Switch the Nutella for 240 g (1 cup) of smooth peanut butter*[2]. Make the ice cream cake as written. Substitute the Ferrero Rocher chocolates with store-bought peanut butter cups and the hazelnuts with peanuts.

---

7 BURSTING BLUEBERRY SWIRL CAKE

See page 292. Switch the strawberries with blueberries!

NOTES

1. Frozen berries are not recommended for the custard tart as they can affect how evenly the custard sets.
2. Use the commercial peanut butter spread that's been sweetened. Not pure peanut butter with no sugar or salt added.

SIDES

Back-pocket side dishes I reach for 'all the time'!

SALAD DRESSINGS

MAKES ENOUGH DRESSING FOR ...

APPROX. 160–200 G (5 HEAPED CUPS) LEAFY GREENS
400–500 G (4 HEAPED CUPS) CHOPPED VEGETABLES, RAW OR COOKED (SUCH AS CUCUMBERS*, TOMATOES, MANGETOUT)
200–250 G (3 TIGHTLY PACKED CUPS) FINELY SHREDDED CABBAGE AND OTHER VEGETABLES

For the following dressings, simply shake all the ingredients in a jar. Makes enough to dress a side salad for 4–5 servings.

HOUSE SALAD DRESSING (MY MOST USED)

1 tbsp apple cider vinegar
3 tbsp extra-virgin olive oil
1/4 tsp dijon mustard
1/4 tsp finely minced garlic* (optional)
1/4 tsp salt*
1/8 tsp black pepper

LEMON DRESSING

3/4 tsp lemon zest
1 tbsp lemon juice
3 tbsp extra-virgin olive oil
1/4 tsp dijon mustard (optional)
1/4 tsp finely minced garlic*
1/4 tsp salt*
1/8 tsp black pepper

BALSAMIC DRESSING

1 1/2 tbsp balsamic vinegar
3 1/2 tbsp extra-virgin olive oil
1/4 tsp salt*
1/8 tsp black pepper

GINGER DRESSING

1 1/2 tsp finely grated ginger*
1 tbsp light or all-purpose soy sauce*
1 1/2 tbsp sesame oil*
2 tbsp rice vinegar
1/2 tsp caster sugar

FRENCH DRESSING

1 1/2 tbsp white wine vinegar
3 1/2 tbsp extra-virgin olive oil
1/2 tsp dijon mustard
1/4 tsp salt*
Pinch of black pepper

ITALIAN DRESSING

1 tbsp finely grated parmesan*
1 1/2 tbsp red wine vinegar
3 1/2 tbsp extra-virgin olive oil
1/4 tsp caster sugar
1/4 tsp finely minced garlic*
1/4 tsp each dried chilli flakes*, basil, parsley and oregano
1/4 tsp salt*

MEDITERRANEAN DRESSING

1 1/2 tbsp red wine vinegar
3 1/2 tbsp extra-virgin olive oil
3/4 tsp dried oregano
1/2 tsp finely minced garlic*
1/2 tsp cooking salt*
1/8 tsp black pepper

ASIAN SESAME DRESSING

1 tbsp light or all-purpose soy sauce*
1 1/2 tbsp white vinegar
1 1/2 tbsp sesame oil*
2 tsp extra-virgin olive oil
1/2 tsp caster sugar

MIDDLE EASTERN DRESSING

1 1/2 tbsp finely chopped coriander
1 tbsp finely chopped mint leaves
1 tbsp sherry vinegar (or red wine vinegar)
1 tsp lemon zest
1 1/2 tbsp lemon juice
3 tbsp extra-virgin olive oil
1/2 tsp caster sugar
1 garlic clove*, smashed
1/2 tsp salt*
1/4 tsp black pepper

TIP

- It's worth investing in good-quality vinegar and olive oil. It makes all the difference with dressings!

30-second Rocket Salad

(Asian) Broccoli Salad

Cucumber Ribbons

Garden Salad

SIMPLE VEG AND SIDE SALADS

Having a handful of versatile, quick-to-make side salads is essential in my life. Because I focus on the mains, side salads are all too often an afterthought. But nobody needs to know that!

30-SECOND ROCKET SALAD

SERVES: 4–5 | PREP: 30 SECONDS | COOK: NIL

Hands-down, the most made salad in my life. Betting it will become a regular in yours too! PS: Make it once, then you won't need a measuring spoon. Just eyeball it!

---

120 g rocket

2 tsp extra-virgin olive oil

Pinch of salt*

Pinch of black pepper

1 tbsp caramelised balsamic vinegar*, store-bought

10–20 parmesan shavings*, made using a vegetable peeler (optional, but I almost always add this)

2 tbsp pine nuts, toasted* (optional, I add this for company)

Place the rocket in a bowl. Drizzle with the olive oil, then sprinkle with the salt and pepper. Toss. Tumble half into a bowl. Drizzle half the caramelised balsamic vinegar over. Top with the remaining rocket, then drizzle the remaining balsamic vinegar over.

If using the parmesan, shave it straight onto the rocket. (Honestly, this takes 10 seconds and it's worth it.) Sprinkle with toasted pine nuts (again, if using!), then serve!

(ASIAN) BROCCOLI SALAD

SERVES: 5 | PREP: 15 MINUTES + 5 MINUTES STEAM-DRYING | COOK: 2 MINUTES

Broccoli makes such a great salad. I love how the florets act like a sponge for dressing! I've gone in an Asian direction here by using my Asian Sesame Dressing, but you can make this with any dressing on pages 312–13.

---

2 heads broccoli, broken into florets

1 spring onion* stem, finely sliced

1½ batches Asian Sesame Dressing (page 313)

20 g (¼ cup) slivered almonds, toasted*, half roughly chopped, half finely chopped

Bring a large pot* of water to the boil. Add the broccoli, then start the timer immediately and cook for 90 seconds. Drain in a metal colander, then rinse under tap water to stop it cooking further.

Shake the excess water off well, then place the colander over the now-empty pot set on the turned-off stove. Leave to steam-dry for at least 5 minutes. Or, to hurry things up (as is often the case for me) use a salad spinner to remove any excess water.

Place in a bowl. Add half the spring onion and all the dressing. Toss, then transfer half into a serving bowl. Sprinkle with half the almonds. Top with the remaining broccoli, spring onion and almonds. Serve!

CUCUMBER RIBBONS

SERVES: 4–5 | PREP: 10 MINUTES | COOK: NIL

These can be a salad, or lightly pickled using the brine for the Quick Asian Pickles opposite. Or you can just serve the plain cucumber ribbons as a garnish that serves double duty as a side salad. No dressing needed – though, I'm showing them on page 314 with French Dressing. And they're divine!

---

3 cucumbers*, about 17 cm long

1 batch French Dressing (page 313) or any other dressing on pages 312–13

1 tbsp finely chopped red onion (optional)

Use a vegetable peeler and run it down the length of the cucumber to peel 'ribbons'. Keep going and make as many ribbons as you can. You'll end up with a residual piece that's too difficult to use. Chop it up and add it to your garden salad tomorrow!

Pile the ribbons into a serving bowl, arranging them so they drape and curl elegantly. Drizzle with your dressing of choice. Sprinkle with red onion, if using. Serve!

GARDEN SALAD

SERVES: 4–5 | PREP: 15 MINUTES | COOK: NIL

This is my default combination of fridge-staple vegetables that come together to make what I call a Garden Salad only because I don't add in extras like croutons and cheese. So everything in this actually comes from the garden!

SALAD

1 small head iceberg lettuce, cut into quarters, core cut out, then chopped into large bite-sized pieces (6 big handfuls)

150 g (1½ cups) halved cherry tomatoes or 2 tomatoes, each cut into 8 wedges

1 cucumber*, sliced into 5 mm rounds

½ red onion, finely sliced

1 tsp parsley (or chives), very finely chopped (if you're feeling fancy!)

DRESSING

1 batch House Salad Dressing (page 312), or any other dressing of choice (this works with everything!)

Put all the salad ingredients, except the parsley, in a big bowl. Drizzle with the dressing and sprinkle with parsley, then toss well. Transfer to a serving bowl. Serve immediately!

QUICK ASIAN PICKLES

MAKES: 4 CUPS | PREP: 15 MINUTES + 2 HOURS PICKLING | COOK: NIL

These are terrific and commonly found in Vietnamese cuisine alongside plates of marinated grilled meats and stuffed into bánh mi. But the flavour is neutral enough that you can use it with any Asian food (and I do!), which is why I've christened these Quick *Asian* Pickles! Slightly sweet, mostly tart, not too salty. Excellent alongside full-flavoured proteins like Korean BBQ Chicken (page 34) and rich slow-cooked meats like the Vietnamese Coconut Lemongrass Pulled Pork (page 284).

4 tsp salt*

100 g (½ cup) white sugar

375 ml (1½ cups) boiling water

185 ml (¾ cup) rice wine vinegar (substitute apple cider vinegar)

2 carrots[1], peeled and cut into 3 mm batons

½ large daikon[1] (white radish), peeled and cut into 3 mm batons (same quantity as the carrots)

In a large bowl, dissolve the salt and sugar in the hot water. Stir in the vinegar. Add the carrot and daikon – they should just about be covered. Set aside for 2 hours until the vegetables are slightly floppy.

Drain well to use it all in one go. Or store the vegetables in the pickling liquid in airtight glass containers or jars (not plastic). They will keep in the fridge for 2 months.

NOTE

1 A mix of carrot and daikon is commonly used in Vietnamese cuisine and I like them because they retain a great *crunch* when pickled. However, feel free to experiment with other vegetables with a similar texture, or to change the ratios of the carrot and daikon.

RICE

Knowing how to make a steaming mound of hot, fluffy rice is a life essential.

PLAIN RICE RECIPES

WHITE RICE

MAKES: 3 CUPS, SERVES 2–3 | PREP: 1 MINUTE | COOK: 25–35 MINUTES

200 g (1 cup) white rice – long-grain and medium-grain

375 ml (1½ cups) water

Place the rice and water in a medium saucepan* over medium–high heat. Once the water is bubbling all across the surface, place the lid on, reduce the heat to medium–low and cook for 13 minutes (no peeking, no stirring!) or until all the water is absorbed.

Remove the saucepan from the stove and leave to rest for 10 minutes with the lid on.

Using a rice paddle or rubber spatula, turn the rice over and fluff it up. Let it steam-dry for a minute or two (no lid), then serve!

BROWN RICE

MAKES: 2¾ CUPS, SERVES 2–3 | PREP: 1 MINUTE | COOK: 35 MINUTES

Despite what most rice packets say, skip the absorption method for brown rice. The boil-and-drain method works much better. I cooked a LOT of brown rice to confirm this!

---

2 litres water

190 g (1 cup) brown rice – medium-grain, long-grain and basmati

Bring the water to the boil in a medium saucepan* over high heat. Add the rice, then boil until the rice is just cooked. For medium and long-grain brown rice, cook for 30 minutes. For brown basmati, cook for 14 minutes (but check at 12 minutes).

Drain the rice in a colander and thoroughly shake the excess water out of the pan. Return the rice to the pan, cover and place it on the turned-off stove to rest for 10 minutes. Fluff and serve!

JASMINE RICE

200 g (1 cup) jasmine rice

310 ml (1¼ cups) water

Use the same cooking method as for White Rice (above). The only difference is that less water is used for jasmine rice because it is a softer variety.

BASMATI RICE

180 g (1 cup) white basmati rice

375 ml (1½ cups) water

Use the same method as for White Rice (above). Fluff gently so you don't break the long basmati rice grains!

MY TIPS FOR GUARANTEED FLUFFY STOVETOP RICE EVERY SINGLE TIME!

- 1 cup uncooked rice = 3 cups cooked
- Serves 2–3 as a side
- Cooking vessel size: 1–2 cups in a medium saucepan*, 3–4 cups in a large saucepan* or small pot*, 6–8 cups in a large pot*

1. NEVER stir the rice or lift the lid while cooking. That is the path to mushy rice!
2. Never, ever, ever skip resting rice! The rice finishes cooking during this time.
3. No need to rinse rice purchased in packets from grocery stores (except for coconut rice). This doesn't make rice fluffy; the correct water to rice ratio does. But if you do rinse (for cleanliness or if you just can't break the habit), reduce the water by 60 ml (¼ cup) for each cup of rice, to account for water-logging.
4. Cooking vessel size matters! Too much rice in a small saucepan = mushy rice. See left for the right saucepan size.

LEFTOVERS Fridge 3 days, freezer 3 months. Reheat from frozen in the microwave, 1½ minutes on High, covered, per 1 cup cooked rice.

CAULIFLOWER RICE

MAKES: 6–8 CUPS, SERVES 5–6 | PREP: 10 MINUTES | COOK: 15 MINUTES

Baked cauliflower trumps boiled cauliflower every day of the week. And this holds especially true for cauliflower rice!

1 head cauliflower, broken into florets

1 tbsp olive oil

Pinch of finely minced parsley

Push the cauliflower florets through the feeding tube of a food processor fitted with the grating disc, with the motor running on low. The cauliflower will blitz into little rice-shaped bits! Alternative: Cut the cauliflower into quarters, then grate by hand using a box grater.

Preheat the oven to 220°C (200°C fan).

Spread 600–800 g (6–8 cups) of the cauliflower rice on a large baking tray. Drizzle with the olive oil and toss to coat. Bake for 15 minutes, tossing halfway, until still a bit firm. Don't overcook, as it goes watery and soggy!

Serve sprinkled with a pinch of parsley. Use as a substitute for any dish served with rice, such as stir-fries.

LEFTOVERS Fridge 3 days, cooked or raw.

FLUFFY COCONUT RICE

MAKES: 6 CUPS, SERVES 5–6 | PREP: 5 MINUTES + 1 HOUR SOAKING | COOK: 45 MINUTES

The secret to truly excellent coconut rice is to use the oven rather than the stove. Fluffy rice and no scorched pot, every single time!

380 g (2 cups) jasmine rice[1]

400 ml good-quality coconut milk*[2]

250 ml (1 cup) water

5 tsp white sugar

½ tsp salt*

1 pandan leaf*[3], knotted, or 2 makrut lime leaves*[3], crushed (optional)

Rinse the rice by placing it in a large bowl, then filling the bowl with water and swishing it around with your hands for 5 seconds. Drain off the milky water, leaving the rice in the bowl, then repeat three more times. Fill the bowl with water, then leave the rice to soak for 1 hour. Drain in a colander and leave the rice in the colander for 5 minutes to drain well.

Preheat the oven to 200°C (180°C fan).

Place the coconut milk, water, sugar and salt in a small saucepan* over high heat. Bring to the boil, then stir to dissolve the sugar.

Place the rice and pandan leaf or makrut lime leaves in a roughly 20 cm square tin (metal or ceramic)[4]. Pour the hot coconut milk in and give it a quick stir to spread the rice out evenly. Working quickly, cover the tin tightly with a double layer of foil, then bake in the oven for 40 minutes.

Remove the rice from the oven and leave to rest, with the foil on, for 15 minutes. Remove the foil (there will be a layer of reduced coconut milk on the surface), turn out into a bowl and gently fluff with a rice paddle or rubber spatula. Serve!

NOTES

1 This recipe will also work with long-grain and medium-grain white rice and basmati rice.

2 Be sure to use a good-quality coconut milk made with at least 50% coconut extract (check the ingredient label on the can). Cheaper brands use less, which means less coconut flavour.

3 Either a pandan leaf or makrut lime leaves will add a touch of real South-East Asian restaurant flavour to your coconut rice, but it is still absolutely delicious without! Pandan leaves are sold fresh and frozen in Asian grocery stores and some produce stores. To prepare for use, tie the pandan leaf into a knot (like a rope!) to hold it together to fit in the pan and release its flavour. For the makrut lime leaves, crush them in your fist a couple of times to release their flavour.

4 You may get faint tinges of golden colour on the edges or sides of the rice, depending on the pan you use. Once mixed through, though, it's barely noticeable.

BREADS

For slathering, dunking, stuffing and toasting. These are my essential bread recipes that I use most often in my everyday life.

OLD-SCHOOL BUTTER-OOZING GARLIC BREAD

SERVES: 5–6 | PREP: 10 MINUTES | COOK: 15 MINUTES

Old-school garlic bread, done right. If butter doesn't ooze when you squeeze the bread, it's not done right. And if you use a fancy crusty baguette instead of an old-school French stick, it's also not done right!

---

1 French stick/baguette, about 60 cm long[1]

125 g unsalted butter, softened

2 tsp finely minced garlic* (about 3–4 cloves)

½ tsp salt*

½ tsp finely minced parsley (optional)

Preheat the oven to 200°C (180°C fan).

Cut the French stick in half, then cut the bread almost all the way through into 1.8 cm thick slices.

Mix together the butter, garlic, salt and parsley. Taste to see if it's salty/garlicky enough for your taste. If not, add more of either! Smear most of the garlic butter between the slices onto the cut face of each bread slice, being sure to do both sides of each slice. Smear the remaining butter on the top and sides of the bread.

Wrap each bread in foil. Place the two foiled wrapped garlic breads on a baking tray and bake for 15 minutes until the crust is crisp. Unwrap and rip into it! If you're having this alongside the Slow-baked Italian Meatballs on page 259, I want to be you.

NOTE

1 Don't use bread with a thick, crunchy crust or chewy bread like sourdough. For a truly religious garlic bread experience, you want a French stick/baguette with a thin crust and standard soft white crumb, like regular sandwich bread!

CROSTINI

MAKES: 40 PIECES | PREP: 15 MINUTES | COOK: 10 MINUTES

Toasting bread in the oven until crisp might sound simple, but it's got teeth! I'm pretty sure I use crostini more frequently than any other bread recipe. Dunking in stew-y foods like Shakshuka Fish (page 41) and Black Bean Chilli (page 114), as a scooping vehicle for Whipped Ricotta (with Burst Tomatoes) on page 222, with toppings for canapés and for swiping through dips. Plus, it's an excellent way to use up left-over bits of bread. If you've got larger loaves rather than baguettes, just cut the slices into smaller pieces!

---

80 ml (1/3 cup) extra-virgin olive oil[1]

1 crusty baguette, 50 cm long, cut 1 cm thick on a steep diagonal

1/2 tsp salt*

1 garlic clove, skin on, cut in half (optional)

Sea salt flakes, for sprinkling (optional)

Preheat the oven to 180°C (both standard and fan).

Brush the olive oil lightly on the bread. Sprinkle with half the salt. Turn the bread and repeat. Spread the crostini in a single layer on one large baking tray (or two trays, if necessary). Bake for 10 minutes, turning halfway, or until the crostini are fully crispy.

Rub the bread very lightly on one side with the cut face of the garlic (if using) – not too much, or the raw garlic flavour is too sharp. Sprinkle with sea salt, then use immediately! Leftovers will keep for at least a week in an airtight container in the pantry.

NOTE

1 You mightn't use all the olive oil, or you might need a little more depending on how generous you are and what type of brush you use.

EASY FLATBREAD

MAKES: 6 | PREP: 15 MINUTES + 30 MINUTES RESTING | COOK: 15 MINUTES

This has been my go-to flatbread recipe for decades. Use as wraps or for dunking into spiced stews and curries. Consider this a simple way to make naan!

50 g unsalted butter

185 ml (¾ cup) milk

300 g (2 cups) plain flour, plus 2–3 tbsp extra for dusting

½ tsp salt*

Put the butter and milk in a heatproof jug and microwave on High for 1 minute or until the butter is melted. (Or do this in a saucepan on the stove over medium heat.)

Put the flour and salt in a bowl and pour in the milk mixture. Mix with a wooden spoon until it mostly comes together into a shaggy dough.

Sprinkle a work surface with half the extra flour, then turn the dough out. Knead for 3 minutes until it becomes smooth. Add extra flour if it's too sticky (but try to keep the flour to a minimum, otherwise the flatbread will be dry). Shape the dough into a ball, put back in the bowl, cover with plastic wrap and leave on the counter for 30 minutes.

Sprinkle another work surface area with a bit of extra flour. Cut the dough into six pieces and roll each portion into balls. With a rolling pin, roll each ball out into a 20 cm wide circle, about 2–3 mm thick.

Heat a medium non-stick frying pan* over high heat. Cook one flatbread at a time for 1½ minutes on the first side until it puffs up dramatically and the underside has lots of golden splotches. Flip and cook the other side for 45 seconds to 1 minute until the underside has golden spots and it puffs up again.

Transfer to a clean tea towel and loosely wrap the flatbread to keep it warm. This also makes the flatbread soft (rather than crispy), which is what we want. Repeat with the remaining flatbreads.

EASY CRUSTY ARTISAN BREAD

MAKES: 1 LOAF, SERVES 6 | PREP: 5 MINUTES + 3 HOURS RISING | COOK: 45 MINUTES

This is a wildly popular bread based on a simple no-knead method made famous by the *New York Times*. With a thick, crispy crust and a crumb with authentically large irregular holes, it's easy enough for first-timers, yet has artisan-like characteristics that even bread connoisseurs appreciate!

---

450 g (3 cups) bread flour[1], plus 2 tbsp extra for dusting

2 tsp instant/rapid-rise yeast[2]

2 tsp salt*

375 ml (1½ cups) very warm tap water (35–40°C)

Mix the flour, yeast and salt in a bowl, then add the water and stir with the handle of a wooden spoon. The dough should be too sticky to knead. Cover with plastic wrap and rest in a warm (25–30°C) place for 2–3 hours[3] until doubled in volume and the surface is bubbly and jiggles when you shake it.

Preheat a 24–26 cm cast-iron pot,[4] with a lid on, in a 230°C (220°C fan, not 210°C) oven for 30 minutes.

Scrape the dough onto a floured work surface and sprinkle the surface of the dough with the extra flour. Fold the sides in using a scraper[5], then flip the dough upside down onto a sheet of baking paper, so the folded seams are underneath. Shape into a rough round – no need to get too meticulous about a neat shape, this is a rustic loaf!

Lift the paper with the dough on it into the HOT pot. Bake with the lid on for 30 minutes, then with the lid off for 15 minutes, until deep golden. Cool for 10 minutes on a wire rack before cutting.

NOTES

1 Can substitute with plain flour.

2 If using normal active dry yeast (not instant), dissolve the yeast in the water, then add the flour and salt and mix (no need to foam). Proceed with the recipe.

3 If your house is warmer, your dough will rise faster. If cooler, it will take longer. Length of time doesn't matter. Aim for doubled in volume!

4 The cast-iron pot creates a home version of a professional bakery bread steamer oven environment. Don't have one? Bake your bread on a baking tray and place a 20 cm square tin filled with boiling water on the shelf directly underneath.

5 Or large knife, cake cutter or spatula.

SIDES

PARMESAN TOASTIES

MAKES: 4 SLICES | PREP: 2 MINUTES | COOK: 3 MINUTES

What do you mean, you've never pan-fried bread coated with parmesan? You're missing out!! The parmesan melts into a golden crispy sheet creating the ultimate crostini-cross-cheese-toastie that's made for dunking into soups. It's especially great with The Most Amazing Pantry Tomato Soup on page 128!

---

40 g unsalted butter, softened

4 x 1 cm thick slices sourdough, ciabatta or other chewy, crusty bread[1]

25 g (4 tightly packed tbsp) finely grated parmesan* (I use store-bought!)[2]

Set aside about 2 teaspoons (10 g) of the butter for cooking. Spread the remaining butter on both sides of each piece of bread, buttering one side more generously (this will be the cheese side). Sprinkle parmesan across the generously buttered side of the bread and press down to make it stick as best you can (it won't stick completely).

Melt the reserved butter in a large non-stick frying pan* over medium–high heat until foamy. Place the bread in the pan, cheese-side down, and cook – moving the bread around as needed to encourage the surface to colour evenly – until the cheese is melted and is light golden, about 90 seconds. Turn and cook the other side for 1 minute until light golden and crispy. Serve immediately!

NOTES

1 The Easy Crusty Artisan Bread (page 326) is ideal. Sandwich bread will work and is delicious but it doesn't become as crisp. I cut the slices diagonally into triangles.

2 I use the sandy type of store-bought pre-grated parmesan for this. The grains are thicker than finely grating it yourself so you get a better layer of cheese! But you can absolutely grate your own. You might also find you need a little more or less parmesan, depending on the size of your bread.

OTHER STARCHY VEHICLES

To smother with sauce, as a bed for chops or to serve on the side of Sunday roasts.

CREAMY MASHED POTATO

SERVES: 5–6 AS A SIDE | PREP: 10 MINUTES | COOK: 20 MINUTES

1 kg sebago*[1] potatoes, peeled and cut into 2.5 cm cubes

1 tbsp plus ½ tsp salt*

40 g unsalted butter, cut into 1.5 cm cubes (plus extra optional melted butter)

60 ml (¼ cup) milk, preferably full-fat

Finely chopped parsley, to serve (optional)

Place the potatoes in a small pot* with the 1 tablespoon of salt and fill the pot with water until 10 cm above the potatoes. Bring to the boil over high heat, then reduce to medium–high and simmer rapidly for 15 minutes until the potatoes are very soft.

Drain well. Turn off the heat and return the potatoes to the empty pot. Add the butter, milk and the ½ teaspoon of salt. Mash with a potato masher until smooth.

Serve with a drizzle of extra melted butter and a pinch of parsley, if you want to get fancy!

NOTE

1 Or any other all-purpose or floury potatoes.

CREAMY CAULIFLOWER MASH

SERVES: 4–5 AS A SIDE | PREP: 5 MINUTES | COOK: 15 MINUTES

Not just a low-carb alternative to potato, cauliflower puree is a favourite of posh restaurants to serve alongside rich mains like the Roast Chicken for Company on page 249.

1 kg cauliflower florets (from 2 medium heads)

2 garlic cloves, peeled

30 g unsalted butter

25 g (¼ cup) finely grated parmesan*

50 g (¼ cup) sour cream

½ tsp salt*

⅛ tsp black pepper

1–3 tbsp reserved water from cooking the cauliflower

SERVING GARNISHES (OPTIONAL)

10 g (2 tsp) melted butter

Pinch of finely chopped parsley

Boil the cauliflower and garlic in a large pot* of water for 10 minutes until very soft. Reserve 250 ml (1 cup) of cooking water, then drain.

Blitz the cauliflower and garlic in a food processor (or use a stick blender) with the remaining ingredients until smooth. Adjust the thickness with the reserved cooking water – sometimes I like it a little thicker, like mashed potato, other times I want it to be a puree. Transfer to a bowl and make swirls on the surface to capture the melted butter. Drizzle with the butter and sprinkle with parsley.

Serve as a side with anything you'd usually serve mashed potato with!

GARLIC WHITE BEAN MASH

SERVES: 4–5 AS A SIDE | **PREP: 5 MINUTES** | **COOK: 5 MINUTES**

This is such a handy recipe for a quick side made using canned beans. I use it in place of mashed potatoes, and even as a dip for crusty bread, crackers or – if I'm feeling virtuous – vegetable sticks. (Admittedly this is the least common.)

---

1 tbsp extra-virgin olive oil, plus extra for drizzling

1 large garlic clove*, finely minced

2 x 400 g cans cannellini beans, drained

185 ml (3/4 cup) low-salt chicken* or low-salt vegetable stock*

1/8 tsp+ salt*[1]

2 pinches of black pepper

Hot water as needed

OPTIONAL EXTRAS[2]

1/2 tsp finely chopped fresh rosemary leaves

1 1/2 tsp lemon zest

1/2 tbsp lemon juice

Heat the oil in a small saucepan* over medium–high heat. Add the garlic and cook for 15 seconds or until light golden. Add the beans, stock, salt and a pinch of pepper. Stir, bring to a simmer, then lower the heat to medium–low and simmer gently for 3 minutes.

Remove from the stove and use a stick blender to blitz until smooth. Add hot water as needed, to achieve the desired consistency, and extra salt if required.[1] Add the optional extras, if desired, and stir them through.

Divide among bowls or plates for serving. Or transfer into a large bowl, then use the back of a spoon to make swirls on the surface. Drizzle with olive oil and a pinch of pepper, then place on the table and let everyone help themselves.

NOTES

1. The saltiness of beans varies from brand to brand, so it's best to start with less salt and add more if required.
2. I use all for company, and none for midweek!

PEA PUREE

SERVES: 6–8 AS A SIDE | **PREP: 10 MINUTES** | **COOK: 8 MINUTES**

Like the Garlic White Bean Mash opposite, this is a terrific, handy side dish – because don't we all always have a bag of frozen peas in the dark depths of our freezer?

- 125 g unsalted butter
- 2 garlic cloves*, finely minced
- ½ small brown onion, chopped
- 1 kg frozen peas
- 500 ml (2 cups) low-salt vegetable stock*
- ¼ tsp salt*
- ⅛ tsp white pepper (substitute black pepper)

Melt the butter in a large saucepan* or small pot* over medium heat. Add the garlic and onion. Sauté for 3 minutes until the onion is translucent.

Add the frozen peas and stock. Increase the heat to high then, once the stock starts simmering, cover and lower the heat to medium. Simmer for 2 minutes.

Remove 80 ml (⅓ cup) of liquid from the saucepan and set aside. Add the salt and pepper. Use a stick blender to blitz the peas until they are as smooth as you can make them.[1] Add the reserved liquid, a bit at a time, to achieve the desired consistency.

To serve, either dollop/smear onto plates, or serve in share bowls for people to help themselves.

NOTE

1 It won't be completely smooth. If that's what you desire, then use a food processor. For restaurant-level-smooth, press through a mesh colander.

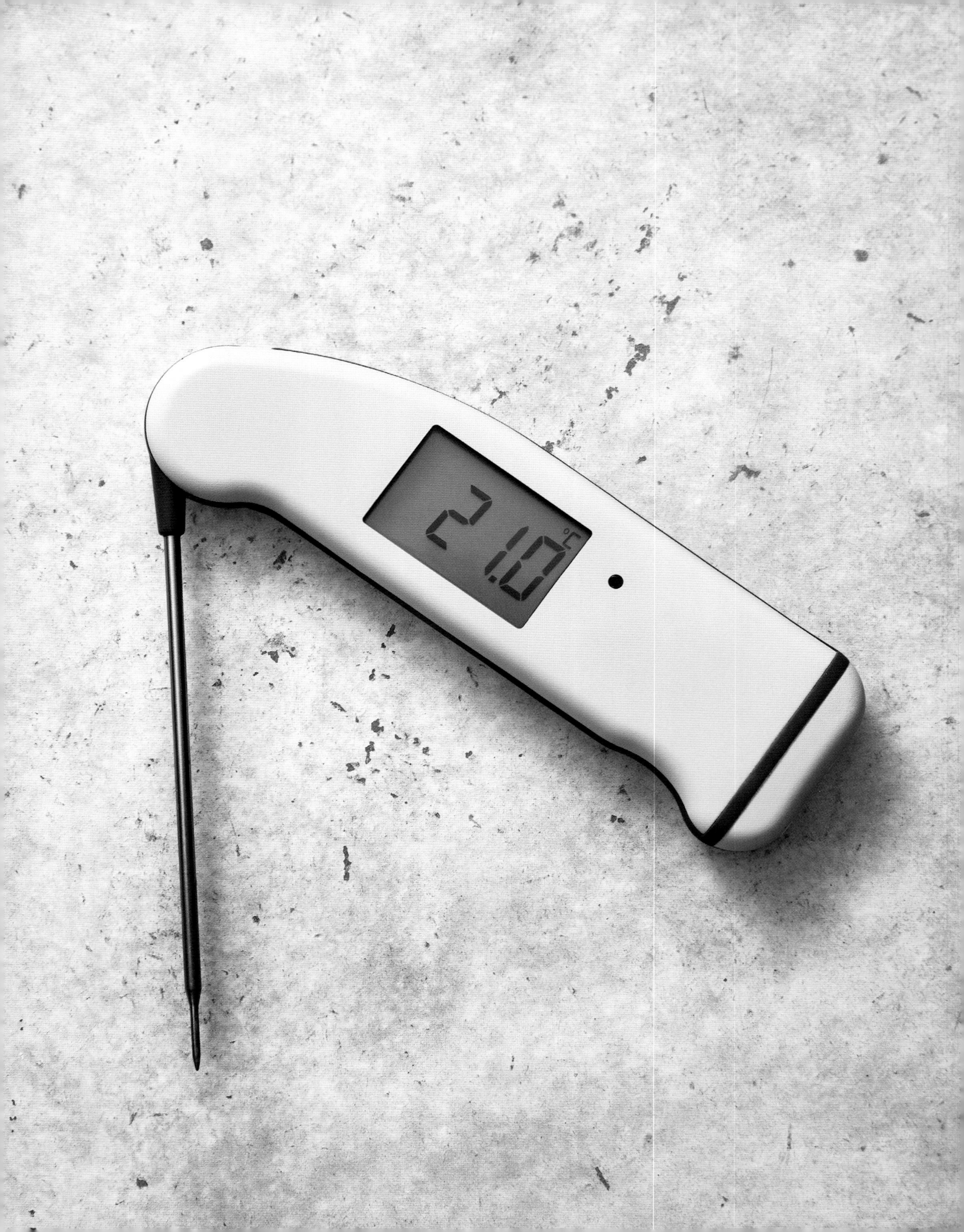
21.0 °C

INTERNAL COOKED TEMPERATURES

The tables below provide the target internal cooked temperatures for varying levels of doneness for proteins used in this cookbook. The PULL TEMPERATURE in the tables below is the target temperature at which the protein should be removed from the heat. The temperature of the protein will continue to rise as it rests (this is called 'carry-over cooking') so the final temperature results in the doneness that you want. This is the RESTED TEMPERATURE in the tables below.

BEEF	RARE		MEDIUM-RARE (recommended)		MEDIUM		MEDIUM-WELL		WELL DONE	
	PULL	RESTED	PULL	RESTED	PULL	RESTED	PULL	RESTED	PULL	RESTED
Steak	48°C	52°C	51°C	56°C	55°C	60°C	60°C	65°C	65°C	70°C

LAMB	MEDIUM-RARE (recommended)		MEDIUM-WELL		WELL DONE	
	PULL	RESTED	PULL	RESTED	PULL	RESTED
Chops	59°C	62°C	62°C	66°C	66°C	70°C
Cutlets	61°C	62°C	64°C	66°C	68°C	70°C

PORK	MEDIUM (recommended)		MEDIUM-WELL		WELL DONE	
	PULL	RESTED	PULL	RESTED	PULL	RESTED
Chops / tenderloin	60°C	63°C	65°C	68°C	68°C	71°C

CHICKEN	COOKED INTERNAL TEMPERATURE	
	PULL	RESTED
Breasts / tenderloin	67°C	71°C
Thigh / wings / drumsticks	72°C	76°C

FISH	MEDIUM (recommended)	
	PULL	RESTED
White fish	55°C	57°C

SALMON	MEDIUM-RARE (recommended)		MEDIUM-WELL	
	PULL	RESTED	PULL	RESTED
Salmon / trout	50°C	53°C	60°C	63°C

It is recommended to cook white fish to medium where it is at the point of just fully cooked with optimum juiciness. White fish is typically not served medium-rare. Salmon, on the other hand, is at its juiciest when cooked to medium-rare.

Some of my favourite kitchen tools -
plus random mint leaves just because!

GLOSSARY

Anchovies
Sold in small jars and cans in oil, anchovies are a well-documented flavour shortcut to add gentle savouriness and depth of flavour. When the right amount is used correctly, there is no hint of fishiness at all. Spoiler: my recipes use it correctly!

Baby corn
Either drained, canned or fresh can be used. Canned is often found in the Asian section of grocery stores.

Baking powder testing
Dead (i.e. inactive) baking powder is a more common cause of baking failures than you'd think! It can be dead even if it's not past the due date. To check if your baking powder is still active, pour 60 ml (¼ cup) boiling water over ½ teaspoon of baking powder. If it bubbles, it's still good. If not, it's no good. Time to get a new one!

Balsamic glaze
This is balsamic vinegar with a bit of sugar added, which has been reduced down into a syrupy glaze. Relatively inexpensive and readily available at large grocery stores these days, an excellent shortcut to add a touch of *je ne sais quoi* with just a little drizzle!

Bay leaves
Fresh leaves are preferable, but can be substituted with dried.

Beef bouillon cubes
Beef stock powder in cube form, sold in the herb and spice aisle of grocery stores. I prefer the cubes to powder as I find the flavour better. However, 1 cube can be substituted with 1 teaspoon of beef stock powder.

Beef stock
For store-bought I always use low-salt, which allows you to control the saltiness of dishes better.

Beurre manié
A softened butter–flour mixture used to thicken sauces by stirring it in towards the end of cooking time. It's a classical French cooking technique, which is sometimes more suitable than other techniques, such as adding flour at the beginning of cooking time. To convert to gluten-free, reduce the flour by 25% and use cornflour instead. Mix with equal parts water (instead of butter), then stir that into the sauce.

Bicarbonate of soda
Also known and labelled as baking soda. Used as a raising agent for cakes and also for tenderising meats in stir-fries – see page 144. I typically prefer to use baking powder for baking, but sometimes bicarbonate of soda works better (either by itself, or combined with baking powder).

Butter, at room temperature
This means at 17°C. The butter is soft enough to indent when pressed with your finger, but will not leave a slick layer of grease on your finger. Butter warmer than 20°C is not recommended to be used in baking recipes where it is beaten until fluffy, as the end result will be adversely affected. For example, cakes may end up greasy or not rise properly.

To bring butter to room temperature quickly, cut into 1.5 cm cubes, then spread on a plate. Microwave a 500 ml (2 cup) jug of tap water for 5 minutes on High. Open the microwave, remove the jug and put the butter in the microwave on the plate. Close the door and leave for 5 minutes, but do not turn the microwave on! The ambient heat will gently soften the butter to (or around) room temperature.

Buttermilk
This is a milk by-product with a slightly creamy consistency, like a thin syrup, which has a slightly tangy flavour. Used in dressings and in baking, find it in the refrigerated dairy section of grocery stores.

Chicken stock
For store-bought I always use low-salt, which allows you to control the saltiness of dishes better.

Chilli (fresh)
The general rule is that the smaller the chilli, the spicier it is.

- *Bird's eye chilli* – A small red chilli used in Asian cooking, which is pretty spicy!
- *Long green/red chilli* – The most common variety in Australia are cayenne peppers. In the UK, serrano chillies are more common. They are available in both red and green. I mostly use red for flavour and also for colour rather than for spiciness.
- *Deseeding chilli* – The spiciness is in the seeds! To deseed, cut the chilli in half lengthways, then scrape out the seeds using a teaspoon. As a precaution, use rubber gloves when handling spicy chillies.
- *Finely mincing chilli* – Deseed the chilli (as above), then finely chop using a sharp knife.

Chilli crisp
A highly addictive Chinese condiment! Red chilli oil packed with crispy bits of chopped chilli and fried garlic, seasoned with salt and sugar. Reasonably accessible these days in the Asian aisle of large grocery stores, or at Asian grocery stores. Lao Gan Ma is my go-to, which is a worldwide brand, though I collect chilli crisp from markets and family-run shops like some people collect cards! My personal favourite is Mrs C's The Apprentice crunchy chilli oil, sold online by a family-run business in Melbourne, Australia.

Chilli flakes
See Dried chilli flakes.

Chilli powder
Ground pure chilli, which is spicy. Substitute with an equal amount of cayenne pepper. Not to be confused with American chilli powder, which is a Tex-Mex spice blend that is not very spicy.

Chinese cooking wine
A type of rice wine for cooking often used in Chinese cuisine. It is widely available these days, sold in the Asian section of grocery stores. It's a secret ingredient that makes recipes truly taste like those you find at Chinese restaurants, adding depth of flavour and complexity with just a small dash. Chinese restaurants use it by the gallon in everything from stir-fry sauces to soup broths, marinades and wontons!

Chinese five spice
Readily available these days, this is a blend of five spices, which is used in Chinese cooking. (Yes that's right, I said FIVE spices. Shock horror!)

Chinese sesame paste
Made from sesame seeds, consider this the Chinese version of tahini*. But the colour is darker and the sesame flavour is more intense. Find it in Asian grocery stores and the Asian aisle of some large grocery stores.

Chipotle in adobo
These are chipotles (dried, smoked jalapeños) in a flavoured red sauce (adobo), which is quite spicy and a common ingredient in Mexican cooking. Fairly readily accessible these days, these can be found (usually canned) in the Mexican section of large supermarkets. Freeze leftovers in small ziplock bags*, flattened, so it's easy to break a bit off to use as needed. *Substitution* – For every 1 tablespoon of chipotle in adobo called for in a recipe, substitute with 1 teaspoon EACH chipotle powder*, smoked paprika* and sriracha*. (YES, really, it's pretty close to adobo sauce!)

Chipotle powder
A staple Mexican spice, this is fried, smoked jalapeños in powder form. It has a terrific smoky, earthy flavour with a bit of a spice kick. Sold at some large grocery stores, Mexican and speciality stores. *Substitution* – For every 1 teaspoon of chipotle powder called for in a recipe, substitute with ½ teaspoon smoked paprika* + ⅛ teaspoon cumin powder + ⅛ teaspoon cayenne pepper (if you want spiciness).

Coconut cream
As with coconut milk*, better brands have a higher percentage of coconut extract in the ingredients and therefore better coconut flavour.

Coconut milk
Not all coconut milk is created equal! Better quality is made with at least 80% coconut and has better coconut flavour than more economical brands, which can be as low as 20%. Choose full-fat for best flavour and mouthfeel. Low-fat is thinner and lacks coconut flavour.

Coconut oil
Readily available these days at grocery stores. While refined coconut oil has had the coconut flavour removed, unrefined still has the coconut flavour (this is what I use for dishes when I want good coconut flavour). Kept in the pantry, it has a texture like butter so it needs to be melted before using for cooking.

Cooking sake
Not to be confused with sake for drinking (save that good stuff!), this rice wine is an essential ingredient in Japanese cooking. Readily available these days in the Asian section of grocery stores and Asian grocery stores.

Cream
The type of cream I use most often is called 'thickened cream' in Australia. This is cream that has been thickened using a thickening agent. It is still pourable in an unwhipped state but pours out in a thicker stream than pure cream. it whips up faster than pure cream and is ideal for making cream-based sauces. In the UK the closest equivalent is thick cream, but double cream is best for cooking.

Crispy fried shallots
Deep-fried slices of eschalot*, which are crunchy and salty. They add great texture and pops of salt into anything you add them to. Readily available in the Asian section of supermarkets these days, but cheaper at Asian grocery stores!

Cucumbers
The variety used for recipes in this cookbook are baby cucumbers, which are typically around 17 cm long. For most recipes, you can substitute two baby cucumbers with one telegraph cucumber, which is about twice as long.

Dried chilli flakes
Dried flakes of chilli that add warm heat into dishes. The flavour is more rounded and earthy than chilli powder.

Dozer
The large mass of golden fur often found lurking in the kitchen waiting for scraps to

'accidentally' fall to the ground. Otherwise known as The Scavenger, the self-appointed RecipeTin Taste Tester spends his days making important contributions to this world, such as eating, sleeping, playing, hoping to eat and hoping to play. Read more about him on page 12.

Eggs

- ***Egg yolks*** – Yolks are easiest to separate from the whites when the eggs are fridge-cold. I crack the eggs, then pass the yolks back and forth between the shells, allowing the whites to slip out. If you are not confident with this method, simply crack the egg into your hand and allow the egg white to slip through your fingers.

- ***Large eggs*** – Eggs that are 55–60 g each (in the shell). The egg cartons should be labelled as 'large eggs', as this is an industry standard.

- ***Room-temperature eggs*** – Eggs that are not fridge-cold so they incorporate better with other ingredients. To de-chill eggs quickly, place them in a bowl of warm tap water for 5 minutes.

- ***Soft-boiled eggs*** – Fill a medium saucepan with 10 cm of water. Bring to the boil over medium–high heat, then carefully lower up to four fridge-cold eggs into the water using a slotted spoon. Set the timer for 6½ minutes. Wait until bubbles reappear on the surface of the water, then lower the heat to medium so there are bubbles rising from the base of the saucepan but not so rapidly that the eggs are bouncing around (shells sometimes crack). Transfer the eggs into a large bowl in the sink. Fill with tap water, then leave the eggs for 5 minutes, changing the water as and when it gets warm, until the eggs are cool enough to handle and peel.

- ***Hard-boiled eggs*** – Follow the directions above for soft-boiled eggs but set the timer for 10 minutes.

Eschalots

Also known as French shallots in the UK, these look like baby onions but have purple-skinned flesh (once the brown skin is removed). Sweeter and finer than brown onions, they are great for dishes where you want delicate onion flavour and/or to avoid big lumps of onion.

Fish

- ***Firm white fish fillets*** – Fish in this category include cod, monkfish, cod, snapper, tilapia, pollock, hake, haddock, John Dory, basa, hoki, perch, sea bass, turbot or flathead.

- ***Oily, strong-tasting fish*** – Mackerel, mullet and sardines.

- ***Fish that dry out easily when cooked*** – Bonito, kingfish, marlin, swordfish, tuna. Unless you're extremely careful, they can become dry inside. I feel these fish are (mostly) better in raw/rare forms, such as in ceviche, poke bowls and tartare.

Garam masala

A spice mix available in most grocery stores these days. Commonly used in Indian cooking, it's like a better version of curry powder!

Garlic

The preparation method matters!

- ***Finely grated garlic*** – Garlic grated using a Microplane* or similar. It will grate garlic into a juicy paste, which works better for some dishes rather than finely mincing it with a knife. You can also use a garlic crusher.

- ***Minced garlic*** – Garlic that is finely chopped using a knife. If a recipe calls for this, do not finely grate it with a Microplane* or garlic crusher, as there is a reason for it. For example, garlic that is pressed with a garlic crusher burns and spits on the stove, instead of turning golden.

- ***Smashed garlic (skin on and off)*** – Place the flat side of a heavy knife blade on a clove of garlic, then smack down on the flat side of the blade with the palm of your hand to make the garlic clove burst open but mostly hold together. The recipe will specify whether the garlic should have the skin on or have the skin peeled off.

- ***Store-bought garlic paste in jars*** – Don't talk to me about that stuff! It bears little resemblance to the real thing.

Ghee

A type of clarified butter used in Indian cooking. It tastes like butter – on steroids!

Ginger

The preparation method matters!

- ***Finely grated ginger*** – Grated using a Microplane* or similar.

- ***Julienned ginger*** – Cut into very fine strands using a knife.

- ***Minced ginger*** – Finely chopped using a knife.

- ***Peeling ginger skin*** – Scrape it off using a teaspoon, or cut a slice approximating the amount you need, then use your knife to cut the skin off.

- ***Store-bought ginger paste*** – Don't do it! Fresh is best.

Gochujang

Spicy, sweet, Korean soybean-based paste. Adds tons of umami (savoury flavour) and a decent amount of spice into anything you add it to! I use spice level 3. Find it in the Asian aisle of most large grocery stores, or Asian grocery stores. Lasts 'forever' in the fridge.

Icing sugar
See Soft icing sugar.

Kale leaves
To easily remove kale leaves from the tough stem, grab the base of the stem with your non-dominant hand, then grasp the stem with your other hand and in one swift motion strip the leaves off the stem away from you. Voila! Kale destemmed in 2 seconds!

Ketchup
I prefer ketchup to tomato sauce. It's just got better flavour! However, tomato sauce can be substituted for ketchup in any recipe.

Kewpie mayonnaise
A popular Japanese mayonnaise easily found these days in the Asian section of grocery stores. Famed for its smooth flavour and gentle rice vinegar tang! Substitute with whole-egg mayonnaise. *See also Mayonnaise.*

Lemongrass
To prepare for use, trim off the woody base and the reedy green top, leaving around 12 cm of the base of the lemongrass stalk. Peel the outer green layers to reveal the softer white and very pale green part that contains the lemongrass flavour – this is the part to use in cooking.

Makrut (kaffir) lime leaves
The leaves of the makrut (kaffir) lime tree, used to add earthy citrus flavours into Asian food. Sold at large grocery stores, independent fresh produce stores and Asian grocery stores. Dried is an okay substitute (same amount), but I really urge you to try to find fresh if you can because it has a better flavour. Freezes 100% perfectly for 6 months, so I always have a stash!

Mandoline
A handy tool to make short work of finely slicing vegetables.

Mayonnaise
For Western dishes, I use whole-egg mayonnaise, which has a smoother, richer flavour than ordinary mayonnaise. *See also Kewpie mayonnaise.*

Measuring spoons
I use 15 ml tablespoons and 5 ml teaspoons. Measuring spoons may vary from one country to another but the difference is not enough to affect the outcome. Baking recipes in this book have been tested with both 15 ml and 20 ml tablespoons.

Microplane
Genuine Microplane graters are (in my opinion) the sharpest and best, most convenient shape for fine grating. I use them for citrus, parmesan, ginger, garlic, making chocolate dust and grating nutmeg.

I particularly love that you can grate garlic and ginger without peeling them – the skin just kind of gets pushed out of the way as you grate and ends up on top, so it's easy to pick off and discard. I'm very passionate and protective about my Microplane – nothing else I've tried comes close to this!

Mirin
A sweet rice wine that is an essential ingredient in Japanese cooking. Easily found these days in the Asian aisle of grocery stores and Asian grocery stores.

Mussels (buying, cleaning and preparation)
These days, cleaned mussels are fairly readily available at seafood stores and even grocery stores. Good mussels should smell like the ocean, and not fishy – even from a vacuum-sealed packet, which is how I usually buy them. Even if the packets say they are cleaned, I still recommend you give them a scrub, just to be sure.

To clean mussels, soak them in a large bowl or sink filled with cold tap water for 5 minutes. They will purge themselves of sand and grit. Use a clean brush to scrub the shells of the mussels to remove any debris, such as seaweed, barnacles, mud or sand. It's okay if you can't remove every speck from the mussel shell, just whatever comes off with a scrub. Remove any 'beards' hanging out from the mussels (the hair-like tufts sticking out of the shell). Just pinch the beard between your thumb and forefinger, then gently pull towards the hinge of the mussel shell (the pointy end) until it comes away. Discard any mussels with large chunks of shell missing. (Minor chips are okay.) If there are any open mussels, press the shells together and, if they stay closed, the mussels are still good. If the shells will not stay closed, then it means the mussels are dead and should be discarded. You can also easily tell if a mussel is off just by smelling it! Place cleaned mussels in an empty bowl until ready to cook. Use any water released by the mussels that collects in the bowl – just add it into whatever you are cooking!

Once the mussels are cooked, prise open any that remain closed using a butter knife (it's a myth that these are off!).

Nuts, toasting
See Toasted nuts.

Oil for deep-frying

- *Temperature testing* – It is best to use an instant-read thermometer* to check the temperature of the oil. Otherwise, test using a small cube of white bread. For 180°C, it should take 15 seconds for it to turn golden and crispy. For 190°C, it should take 10 seconds.
- *Oil reuse* – The number of times oil can be reused depends on what it was used to cook. If it was used for neutral-

flavoured food fried for a short period of time, the oil should be able to be used three times. Less for seafood or heavily flavoured foods. To clean the oil, the easiest way is to strain the oil using a muslin cloth set in a strainer.

Pandan leaves
Pandan leaves are sold fresh and frozen in Asian grocery stores and some fresh produce stores. To prepare for use, tie the pandan leaves into a knot (like a rope!) to hold them together to fit in the pan and release their flavour.

Panko breadcrumbs
A Japanese breadcrumb favoured for the extra-crispy coating it gives crumbed foods. You can buy it at most large grocery stores these days in the Asian food section and also at Asian grocery stores. Substitute with regular breadcrumbs if you can't find it.

Paprika
If a recipe just calls for 'paprika', use regular paprika or sweet paprika. In some recipes I also sometimes call for smoked paprika, which has a lovely smoky flavour.

Parmesan
Different recipes call for varying preparation methods.

- *Finely grated parmesan* – Finely grated using a Microplane* or similar. This is especially important so the parmesan melts effortlessly into creamy sauces and on bubbling bakes.
- *Parmesan shavings* – Use a potato peeler on a block of parmesan to make big, paper-thin shavings.

Peanut butter, natural unsweetened
This is thinner and with a stronger peanut flavour than the commercial, sweetened spread, which makes it ideal for satay sauces. Commercial peanut butter spread can be substituted but sauces/dressings will be thicker, slightly sweeter and the peanut flavour is not quite as strong. I only use smooth peanut butter, though it also comes in chunky.

Pomegranate
To remove the seeds, cut the pomegranate in half. Over a bowl, turn the cut face downwards into the palm of your hand (fingers loosely spread), then use a wooden spoon to (very!) firmly smack the back of the pomegranate. The seeds will fly out through your fingers into the bowl. It's very satisfying!!! Keep smacking all over the skin until all the seeds are out. Pick out any white pith that falls out, then use the seeds as per the recipe. You will probably get some juices pooling in the bowl; add these to the dressing too.

Pomegranate molasses
A syrupy Middle Eastern sauce made of concentrated pomegranate juices. It has a sweet tangy flavour a bit like balsamic glaze*. Fairly readily found in the vinegar aisle of large grocery stores and fresh produce stores. Substitute with balsamic glaze.

Prawns, peeling
To peel prawns, break the head off, then peel the shell off the body. To devein (i.e. to remove the thin black string/digestive tract running through the prawn), make a small incision with a small sharp knife down the back of the prawn to reveal the vein, then lift it out and discard. Alternatively, if you prefer to keep the prawn whole rather than butterfly the back, here's how I do it: enclose the body of the peeled prawn with your fingers so it is held straight. Pinch the end of the black vein from the head-end of the prawn, then carefully pull it out.

Red curry paste
My favourite store-bought red curry paste is the Maesri brand, which comes in small cans. It has the best, most authentic flavour and also happens to be the cheapest. Find it in the Asian section of most large grocery stores or in Asian grocery stores.

Salt
The type of salt you use matters! Use salt made up of medium-sized crystals which includes salt labelled as cooking salt, coarse salt and kosher salt.

The grain size dissolves easily but is large enough to pinch and sprinkle evenly on the surface of food which is virtually impossible to do with table salt because the grains are so fine. Table salt can also penetrate the surface of some foods a little too much.

However, if you only have table salt, reduce the quantity listed in the ingredients by 25%. If you have sea salt flakes, increase the salt quantity by 25%. If you have rock salt, use a grinder to grind coarse grains then measure the quantity per the recipes.

Sambal oelek
An Indonesian chilli paste that is readily available in large grocery stores these days, as well as Asian grocery stores.

Sebago potatoes
The dirty, brushed potatoes that are sold 'everywhere' in Australia. Great all-rounder potatoes suitable for roasting, mashing and boiling, which are a staple in my weekly grocery shop and the most used type of potato in my recipes. The closest floury potato equivalent in the UK would be Maris Piper or King Edward.

Sesame oil
Comes toasted (brown – stronger sesame flavour) and untoasted (clear yellow). I only use toasted, which is most commonly available.

Sesame seeds
To toast white sesame seeds, preheat a small frying pan (no oil) over medium heat. Add the sesame seeds, then toast, shaking the pan regularly, until lightly browned and they smell nutty, about 1½–2 minutes. Remove from the frying pan immediately when ready. Note: I do not toast black sesame seeds.

Shallots
In Australia this is another name for green onions* and in the US, UK and Canada, it is the name for eschalots*. To avoid confusion, you won't see the word 'shallots' in recipes in this cookbook.

Shaoxing wine
See Chinese cooking wine.

Shiitake mushroom
A variety of mushroom native to Asia. It has a more savoury flavour than common mushroom varieties, such as button mushrooms and Swiss brown.

Grated cheese
It is always best to grate your own cheese because it melts better. Store-bought pre-grated cheese contains anti-caking agents, which make sauces grainy. Also, the cheese tends to be grated into larger pieces so it doesn't melt as well.

Sichuan pepper
A Chinese pepper that has a cold numbing spiciness with a faint lemony flavour. Find it in the spice aisle of some large grocery stores, or Asian grocery stores.

Soft icing sugar
A type of icing sugar sold in Australia where a little cornflour is mixed through to make the icing sugar a little softer and less prone to lumping, making it easier to sift. It is the best and easiest to use for creamy frostings, such as buttercream.

Distinguishing between types of icing sugar is not relevant to countries that just sell one type of icing sugar (called confectioners' sugar or powdered sugar in the UK, US and other countries).

Soy sauce
The type of soy sauce you use matters! Here are the different types used in this cookbook:

- *All-purpose soy sauce* – Any soy sauce that is not labelled light soy sauce, dark soy sauce, sweet soy sauce or as another specific type of soy sauce. As the name suggests, it is an all-rounder! Use it as a substitute in recipes calling for light soy sauce.
- *Dark soy sauce* – A more intense flavour than light soy sauce and all-purpose soy sauce, which stains noodles and proteins a deep mahogany colour.
- *Light soy sauce* – Can be substituted with all-purpose soy sauce. Do not substitute with dark soy sauce, which is more intense in flavour and colour.
- *Soy sauce* – If a recipe calls for just 'soy sauce', you can use either light soy sauce or all-purpose soy sauce but not dark soy sauce.

Spring onions
The long, thin, green-stemmed onion, not to be confused with eschalots* or salad onions (green stems with a white bulb attached to the base). Also called 'scallions' in the US. If a recipe calls for '1 spring onion stem', it means the whole spring onion, including the white base (often with roots attached) and the long green stalks, of which there are usually two to three per stem.

Sriracha
A popular chilli sauce that is flavoured with other ingredients including garlic and vinegar. Easily found these days in most grocery stores as well as Asian grocery stores.

Tablespoons
See Measuring spoons.

Tahini
A paste made from pureed sesame seeds, used in Middle Eastern cuisine and now widely used in the rest of the world. Excellent ingredient to make creamy sauces without using mayonnaise* or cream. Easily found these days in the health food or spreads aisle of regular grocery stores.

Teaspoons
See Measuring spoons.

Thai basil
Tastes like normal basil with a more pronounced aniseed flavour. Sold at major supermarkets and Asian grocery stores. As a last resort, substitute with normal basil.

Thermometer
Used to measure the internal temperature of food and cooking oil for deep-frying. I use a Thermapen, which is an instant-read thermometer. It's well designed, folds up neatly, and declares itself the world's best for speed and accuracy – and I believe it, based on my usage! If you like your meat perfectly cooked, this is a worthy investment that I highly recommend.

Toasted nuts
For all nuts, heat a frying pan over medium–high heat without using oil. Add the nuts, then toss or stir regularly until you see golden spots and they smell nutty. This might take 90 seconds for a little amount of small pinenuts, or 4 minutes for a large amount of larger nuts like cashews. Immediately transfer to a small bowl and allow to cool, then use as per the recipe.

Tomatoes
To deseed tomatoes, cut them into quarters, then use the knife to cut out the watery centre. Don't discard the watery seeds – add them to your morning green smoothie, your bolognese sauce or sneak them into a salad (they make a great dressing!).

Tomato passata
Pureed, strained pure tomatoes, readily available in grocery stores nowadays alongside pasta sauces. Passata is excellent for making thick, smooth sauces, rather than slow-cooking chopped or diced tomato until it breaks down into a smooth sauce.

Tortillas
Sold in varying sizes depending on intended purpose. I prefer corn over flour tortillas because they have better flavour. I'd use them for everything from tacos to enchiladas, but large corn tortillas are hard to come by where I live. (Yes I know, your heart bleeds for me!) I use 12–15 cm corn tortillas for tacos, 20 cm flour tortillas for enchiladas, and 25 cm jumbo flour tortillas for burritos.

Vegetable stock
For store-bought I always use low-salt, which allows you to control the saltiness of dishes better.

Wine
Used in cooking to add and enhance flavours. I especially enjoy using wine to make sauces, whether it be quick pan sauces, such as in Crispy Lemon Garlic Butter Chicken (page 26) or slow-cooked dishes like Slow-baked Italian Meatballs (page 259). The two types of wine I always have in stock for cooking are chardonnay (white wine) and pinot noir (red wine) – see below. But in real life, I'm a sauvignon blanc and cab sav gal! *See also Chinese cooking wine.*
Chardonnay – My go-to wine for cooking for the best flavour addition and roundest flavour. Substitute with any dry white wine that is not too woody/oaky, fruity or sweet. No need to use expensive wine.

- ***Pinot noir*** – My most used red wine for cooking, for the smooth, light flavour it adds with richness that is not too heavy or overpowering – meaning it works in just about any dish calling for red wine. It's the traditional wine used in famous dishes like beef bourguignon and the ideal choice for red wine sauce.
- ***Red wine*** – I mostly use pinot noir red wine for cooking. See above. However, you can use other medium-body reds, such as merlot, cabernet sauvignon or even a light shiraz.
- ***White wine*** – Chardonnay is my most used white wine for cooking. See above. However, you can use other moderately dry whites, such as semillon, sauvignon blanc or pinot gris/grigio.
- ***Wine quality*** – It is pretty well documented these days that there's no need to use expensive wine for cooking because, once cooked, you simply can't tell the difference. This is especially the case when something is slow-cooked for hours, and for reducing when deglazing pans. In fact, in some blind-testing scenarios, cheaper wine yielded a better result! I use end-of-bin discounted wine from liquor stores, typically $15–20 wines discounted to $5–7.

Wombok cabbage
A cylindrical-shaped cabbage with a white core and layers of tightly packed, wrinkly green leaves that are softer than standard green cabbage. A great cabbage to use for 'slaw-like' Asian salads.

Ziplock bag
For some recipes, a ziplock bag is the best way to keep meat well surrounded by the marinade. Used bags can be washed in warm soapy water and reused. Alternatively, you can use a glass container that the meat fits in snugly, then toss the meat a few times during marinating time, or increase the marinade by 50% (no need to turn the meat).

POTS AND PANS

Recipes in this book usually specify type and/or size when it comes to cooking vessels. This is because the size of a pot, for example, can affect how long it takes for sauces to thicken to the desired consistency. Below are the types and sizes of pots and pans called for in my cookbook.

Cast-iron frying pan
The best pan to use for high-heat searing, such as steaks and chops, for the best crust. Develops a natural non-stick coating (seasoning) with repeated use. It is also the ideal pan for stove-to-oven cooking. I have a 26 cm Lodge cast-iron skillet. Note: non-stick frying pans are not recommended for high-heat cooking as it will reduce the life of the non-stick coating.

Frying pan sizes (non-stick)
Small 16–18 cm, medium 22 cm, large 28 cm, large deep 30 cm wide and 6.5–7.5 cm deep.

Heavy-based pots and pans
This refers to pots and pans that are made of thicker and heavier materials, so they absorb, distribute and retain heat better than thin, lightweight (cheap!) aluminium pots and pans. A couple of popular examples include cast-iron frying pans (see above) and dutch ovens.

Pot sizes
Small 22 cm, large 24 cm, stockpot 7 litre+ capacity.

Saucepan sizes
Small 16 cm, medium 18 cm, large 20 cm.

THANK YOU

Making a cookbook takes a village ... let me introduce you to mine!

First and foremost, Chef **Tom Sarkis** of Carved Catering, my lead recipe tester who powered through testing over 350 recipes. Thank you for your commitment to the project, for your calmness, your can-do attitude, your ruthless honesty when you were testing my recipes and for bringing entertainment into the kitchen on even the most hectic of days! But mostly, thank you for stepping up and being there when it mattered, and your willingness to help with anything and anybody. That meant more to me than you'll ever really understand.

Theressa Klein, photo chef and recipe tester. I don't know what it is about you but it brings me so much comfort when you're on my shoots! I have such confidence in you, you're so pleasant to work with, you always nail the cook, and I especially love that you're always one step ahead of me. And nobody, nobody can fry pulled pork like you can!

Chef **Jimmy Callaway**, what fun and energy you bring to shoots. Your background as a chef in fine-dining restaurants was invaluable for this project for speed and precision. You are a demon with the knife and a master at the stove!

To **Hunter**, my talented tester of the Sweets chapter, the 12-year-old daughter of one of my dearest childhood friends. You have a natural instinct for baking that can't be taught, and a palate that is beyond your years. You also provided the single most important feedback on a recipe: 'I loved the Nutella ganache on the cake ... but it made me sad there was so little.' So I doubled it!

To my assistant **Elke Malsom**. Herder of Sheep (aka my team!). Dozer Handler. Proofreading Queen. Recipe Tester! Your job description would fill pages. Thank you for juggling the variety of tasks thrown your way with a calmness that brought order to the chaos that can be the RecipeTin world.

Herron Oh, Australia's coolest video editor! I didn't want to mention you, because I secretly fear that someone's going to poach you now that I've revealed the name of the magic sorceress editing my recipe videos ... But it is only right that I thank you publicly for your commitment for all these years you've been part of my team, for being so easy to work with and always willing to help out and do whatever it takes to get the job done.

To **Emma Knowles**, Sydney's foremost food stylist who styled the chapter openers and the 'hard' dishes. There is a reason we call you the Food Whisperer! Thank you for gracing my food with your magic touch to make it look as good as it tastes.

To **Rob Palmer** whom I still introduce as Australia's best food photographer – because I believe it to be true. I hold you in such high regard, for your talent as a photographer, creative mind, ability to think on your feet, willingness to push the boundaries, and how easy you are to work with. Thank you especially for working so hard to make my fingers look less like chipolatas(!), capturing my vision of deliciousness and the most important shots you took – of Dozer and me. This is the last book I will do with Dozer. So I was never going to shoot this book with anyone else.

Rob Palmer, food photographer extraordinaire

Elke Malsom, herder of sheep

Chef Tom Sarkis, chief recipe tester

Hunter, a talented tester of sweets

Herron Oh, Australia's coolest video editor

Theressa Klein, photo chef magician

Emma Knowles, food whisperer (stylist)

To my **RecipeTin team**. My Head Honcho Chef Jean-Baptiste 'JB' Alexandre, my brother Goh Maehashi (IT Guru), Inggrid Gislingham (Human Calculator), Stephen Fixter (RTM Boss Chef), Xiao (Hannah) Huang (RTM Chef) and Daniel Smith (RTM Kitchenhand), plus my mother Yumiko, Elke and Herron.

I once had a dream of starting a food bank, of being able to help provide nourishing meals to people in need. Alone, I could only do so much. Together, it became a reality and it's amazing what we have achieved! We are a mash-up of accents from all around the world, representing eight different countries, with such diverse backgrounds, but together we are a team who gets stuff done – with plenty of laughs along the way!

Thank you for your patience for all those months I went underground (again!) to write another book, keeping me entertained on the hardest of days and most importantly, for keeping the wheels turning and protecting the most precious part of the business: RecipeTin Meals.

To **my family**: my mum, brother, sister and in-laws. Nobody else calls me out like you do, nobody is as ruthlessly honest about everything I do, whether it be my recipes, how I write, photos I take, my triple chin on the cover, the size of my butt! Thanks for keeping me grounded, always making me raise the bar and bringing so much laughter into my life. Nobody cracks me up as much as you guys do!

To the **Pan Macmillan family and their freelance cousins**. Huge thanks to the dedicated team of publishing professionals at Pan Macmillan, led by managing director and chief cheerleader Praveen Naidoo.

On the publishing side of things, publishing director Ingrid Ohlsson, dedicated purchaser of pastries and aspiring motivational coach, captained, while Sally Devenish, production manager, secured paper in far-flung regions and massaged deadlines. Australia's most accomplished editing duo, executive editor Ariane Durkin and freelance editor Ariana Klepac, precision-edited 150+ recipes for three territories in three months with grace, flair, humour and a steely determination to get it right for the home cook. Ariane made sure all the intricately linked parts stayed on their well-oiled tracks, while Ariana joined me for weekend deep-dives into editorial quandaries. Editor and talented baker Rebecca Lay recipe-tested the Sweets chapter and joined Pam Dunne in a two-pronged proofreading mission to ferret out every last typo. The beautiful design is courtesy of Emily O'Neill, whose aesthetic talent is matched by her organisational skill and patience. Creative editor Lucinda Thompson was everyone's right hand: set-decorating, file-wrangling, dummy-mock-up briefing, photo-shopping and problem-solving at the level of a UN official. Thanks also to editor Grace 'never miss a beat' Carter and Vijeta 'queen of cut-and-paste' Prasad for their administrative support. The shoot team was supported by prep chef and all-round team player Sarah Mayoh and make-up artists Gina 'cool as a cucumber' Cartwright and Paulie 'love bomb' Bedggood.

On the promotion and sales side of things, Candice Wyman ran the best pre-campaign campaign in the history of publishing, and is, as I write, nailing media opportunities into the floorboards of an outstanding two months of non-stop touring, as Charlotte Ree, head of marketing, manoeuvres three territories onto the same page for pre-order protocols and turbo-charges promotions across the continent under the watchful eye of Tracey Cheetham, publicity and marketing director. Sales directors Katie Crawford and Maria Fassoulas have led a team that bakes from the book for their accounts and drives excitement (and orders) to stellar levels.

The US and UK teams have joined their Australian counterparts in an exercise in international diplomacy to produce and sign off three editions at once into the respective markets. Special thanks to Ann Treistman, editorial director at Countryman Press (W. W. Norton) and Bluebird publisher Lizzy Gray (Pan Macmillan UK). Agent Laurie Liss from Sterling Lord Literary got me at day one, and I am grateful for her ongoing support.

And lastly, to **Dozer**. What can I say except what everybody already knows – that I love you with all my heart!

– Nagi x

Mum, chief caller-outer

Dozer disrespecting my work, as usual!

TEAM RECIPETIN EXPECTATIONS ...

Clockwise from top left: Xiao (Hannah) Huang, Dozer's assistant (me!), Stephen Fixter, JB Alexandre, Goh Maehashi, Elke Malsom, Mama RecipeTin (Yumiko Maehashi), Herron Oh, our CEO Dozer, Inggrid Gislingham and Daniel Smith

REALITY!

INDEX OF RECIPES

INDEX

First published 2024 in Australia by Pan Macmillan Australia Pty Limited, Level 25, 1 Market Street, Sydney, New South Wales Australia 2000

This edition first published in the UK 2024 by Bluebird, an imprint of Pan Macmillan, The Smithson, 6 Briset Street, London EC1M 5NR

EU representative: Macmillan Publishers Ireland Ltd,
1st Floor, The Liffey Trust Centre,
117–126 Sheriff Street Upper, Dublin 1, D01 YC43
Associated companies throughout the world
www.panmacmillan.com

ISBN 978-1-0350-5186-1

The recipe for Whole Roasted Cauliflower Cheese on page 279 has been reproduced with Andy Hearnden's permission.

Design and typesetting by Emily O'Neill
Edited by Ariana Klepac
Prop and food styling by Nagi Maehashi & Emma Knowles
Food preparation by Jimmy Callaway, Theressa Klein & Sarah Mayoh
Hair and makeup by Paulie Bedggood & Gina Cartwright
Colour + reproduction by Splitting Image Colour Studio
Printed in Italy

MIX
Paper | Supporting responsible forestry
FSC www.fsc.org FSC® C116313

10 9 8 7 6 5 4 3 2 1

A CIP catalogue record for this book is available from the British Library.

Take that, kale!

MUD MAP
4. PANTRY
6. ONE